Dark Age
The Political Odyssey of Emperor Bokassa

Dark Age recounts the turbulent political career of the late Jean-Bedel Bokassa, flamboyant president-for-life and later emperor of the Central African Republic/Empire. Brian Titley examines the myths and legends surrounding the man, probes their origins and veracity, and attempts to provide a more balanced perspective on this controversial and misunderstood figure.

Following a lengthy career in the French army, Bokassa seized power in the Central African Republic in 1966. His excesses soon became legendary: he was accused of cannibalism, feeding enemies to lions and crocodiles, and beating schoolchildren to death. Bokassa's tendency for self-aggrandizement culminated in 1977 when he named himself emperor and orchestrated a coronation based on Napoleon's. He was overthrown by French paratroopers in 1979 and went into exile, but returned to his homeland in 1985 to face a sensational trial.

Titley interprets Bokassa's authoritarian and self-aggrandizing style as an attempt to legitimize his regime in a context devoid of indigenous political structures and explores the troubled relations between France and its former colonies. Combining techniques of historical inquiry and investigative journalism, he has produced a fascinating account of a pivotal chapter in contemporary African history.

BRIAN TITLEY is professor of education, University of Lethbridge.

Dark Age

The Political Odyssey of Emperor Bokassa

BRIAN TITLEY

McGill-Queen's University Press
Montreal & Kingston · London · Buffalo

© McGill-Queen's University Press 1997
ISBN 0-7735-1602-6

Legal deposit second quarter 1997
Bibliothèque nationale du Québec

Printed in Canada on acid-free paper

Published simultaneously in the European Union by
Liverpool University Press

Publication of this book has been made possible by a
grant from the University of Lethbridge.

McGill-Queen's University Press is grateful to the
Canada Council for support of its publishing
program.

Illustrations are published by permission of Agence
France-Presse.

Canadian Cataloguing in Publication Data

Titley, Brian, 1945–
    Dark age : the political odyssey of Emperor Bokassa
    Includes bibliographical references and index.
    ISBN 0-7735-1602-6
    1. Bokassa I, Emperor of the Central African Empire,
    1921–1996. 2. Central African Republic – Politics and
    government – 1966–1979. 3. Dictators – Central
    African Republic – Biography. I. Title.
    DT546.383.B64T58 1997   967'.4105'092   C97-900028-9

Typeset in Palatino 10/12
by Caractéra inc., Quebec City

In memory of my father
Edward Joseph Titley, 1912–1996

Contents

Preface   ix

Illustrations   xiii

Map   xvii

1 Colonial Interlude   3

2 Coup d'état   19

3 Papa Bok   33

4 Extended Family   51

5 The French Connection   65

6 La folie des grandeurs   82

7 Oui, Majesté impériale   99

8 Autumn of the Patriarch   105

9 Barracuda   125

10 Operation Revenge   136

11 The New Republic   152

12 La vérité et l'honneur   166

13 Accounting for His Stewardship   181

Epilogue   204

Conclusion   208

Notes   219

viii   Contents

A Note on Sources   239

Bibliography   243

Index   251

Preface

Dee-Jay: Now you know where we're at. If you're still uncertain, let me tell you that your deejay isn't feeling all that cockshure himself. But there is to be a Coronation. An imperial coronation, first in Africa – at least in the last few decades or so. Emperor Boky, Boky the Cocky, no less – and if you think that's mere boasting, ask him how many daughters presented their credentials when he advertised for his long-lost daughter from Indochina. He confirmed the claims of one and married the others. Man, he's wa-a-a-ay – Out. Also known as Folksy Boksy on account of he likes to meet with the folks. You dig? The common folks, like vagrants, felons and – dig this – school children. Actually rubs feet with them – well, on them sort of – he's gone beyond shaking hands – wow, he's ahead man.   Soyinka, *Opera Wonyosi*[1]

Jean-Bedel Bokassa's appearance as the archetypical African dictator in Wole Soyinka's *Opera Wonyosi* should come as no great surprise. Discovered by the Western media early in his political career, he has been in the headlines ever since. The image is always the same. He is *le roi nègre* – cruel, self-indulgent, extravagant, and sexually obsessed, or he is "The Emperor who ate his People," as one essay about him put it.[2] Werner Herzog's documentary film *Echos d'un sombre empire* is all too typical. Dwelling on the macabre, it shows footage of the imperial walk-in freezer and of lions that allegedly dined on His Majesty's enemies.

In dealing with this controversial figure academics have hardly shown better judgment. Samuel Decalo writes of "documented instances of ritual cannibalism" on Bokassa's part and of his personally bludgeoning schoolchildren to death.[3] The Central African ruler is invariably described as "a brutal and ludicrous tyrant" or something similar.[4] He is in a special category of disdain, along with

Equatorial Guinea's Macias Nguema and Uganda's Idi Amin, men who ruined their respective countries.[5]

The image of Bokassa as a caricature of everything that went wrong in postcolonial African politics stubbornly persists. He is all too readily dismissed as a blood-stained buffoon given to excesses of every description. There is some truth to this characterization, of course, but it is by no means the entire story, and much of what has been said about him is complete nonsense. The major challenge in writing about him, then, is to disentangle fact from fiction, fantasy, folklore, and sheer fabrication. This is the task I set myself in the study that follows. Most of all, I tried to give Bokassa a fair hearing. He deserves it just as much as anyone else.

This is a work of contemporary history, and my major concern is with Bokassa rather than with the Central African Republic or French policy in its former colonies, though both are given necessary attention. The focus is on the man, his views, motivations, and actions. His views are expressed in his own words where it has been possible to capture them, and his actions are sometimes described in blow-by-blow detail. In taking this approach, I was strongly influenced by Lawrence Stone's celebrated article, "The Revival of Narrative." Stone suggests that the new concern with finding out "what it was like to be there" has turned historians towards narrative and even to the "thick description" employed by some anthropologists. This accounts for my use of actual conversation, where it has been recorded, and my attention to the minutiae of some key events, such as the imperial coronation, Opération Barracuda, and the trial. Stone argues persuasively that Le Roy Ladurie's notion of "history without people" had gone out of favour and that people, even single individuals, are once more the historian's concern: "Since man is now our quarry, the narration of a very detailed story of a single incident or personality can make both good reading and good sense."[6] This does not mean that structural considerations have to be abandoned. History will always examine the relationship between structure, events, and human agency. The renewed emphasis on narrative, as Stone points out, is linked to a growing distrust of reductionism and determinism. By giving too much attention to structural and impersonal phenomena, the idiosyncratic actions of individuals are reduced to some predetermined response: men and women no longer influence the course of history; they are mere bystanders.

I take it for granted that a state such as the Central African Republic/ Empire, though officially independent, was constrained by the international environment, political and economic, and in particular by its ties to France, its former colonial master. Within these limitations, however, and those dictated by its own resources, its leader had considerable leeway in his actions. Politics ultimately is about human behaviour, motivation, and action within a given context, which in its own complexity is unique. As Jackson and Rosberg show, many a promising African country has been ruined by its leader while others that were less promising have done well. Human agency is the critical variable.[7]

The study of a complex individual whose career followed many unexpected twists and turns encourages a certain level of modesty. Therefore, the claims I make for the book are necessarily limited. Because the evidence is often fragmentary, anecdotal, and even unreliable, I have resisted the temptation to impose an artificial order and coherence on events and circumstances that have a special vibrancy of their own. A single conceptual framework, as Patrick Chabal admits, just will not work.[8] This does not mean that I have renounced all theoretical considerations, but I have tried to keep them as unobtrusive as possible in order to stay close to the concrete historical process. The following quotation from Stone, I think, puts it well:

No narrative historians, as I have defined them, avoid analysis altogether, but this is not the skeletal framework around which their work is constructed ... They are deeply concerned with the rhetorical aspects of their presentation. Whether successful or not in the attempt, they certainly aspire to stylistic elegance, wit and aphorism. They are not content to throw words down on a page and let them lie there, with the view that, since history is a science, it needs no art to help it along.[9]

Even so, there are a number of concepts borrowed from political science which I have found useful in attempting to explain the Bokassa phenomenon. Neopatrimonialism, with the related notions of clientelism and the search for legitimacy, are the concepts in question. Borrowing from Max Weber, and first applied in the African context by Aristide Zolberg, they allow for a more balanced perspective on much of what happened in the Central African Republic/ Empire.

The problem for the historian, I believe, is not to persuade but to communicate with the reader, who in any case will bring his or her own perception to the text. I am therefore less inclined to "have the last word" on Emperor Bokassa. Instead, I have tried to reconstruct his career as accurately as possible while accounting for the myths and distortions that have grown up around the man.

During the past decade a number of French authors, painting on vast and ambitious canvases, have attempted to explain the complexity of African politics south of the Sahara. Works such as those by Jean-François Bayart and Catherine Coquery-Vidrovitch are only possible when the building blocks of more specialized studies are in place, be they studies of one country, one community, or one individual.[10] This book seeks to serve in the latter capacity.

Colonel Bokassa shows off his military decorations at a press conference following his coup d'état. Bangui, 1 January 1966.

Bokassa is received at the Elysée Palace by President Giscard d'Estaing. Paris, 16 September 1974.

Bokassa and some of his children in exile in France. Château Hardricourt, 20 September 1984.

Bokassa and collaborator Roger Holeindre watch the destruction of the former emperor's autobiography, *Ma vérité*. Paris, 27 May 1985.

Coronation of Emperor Bokassa I. Bangui, 4 December 1977.

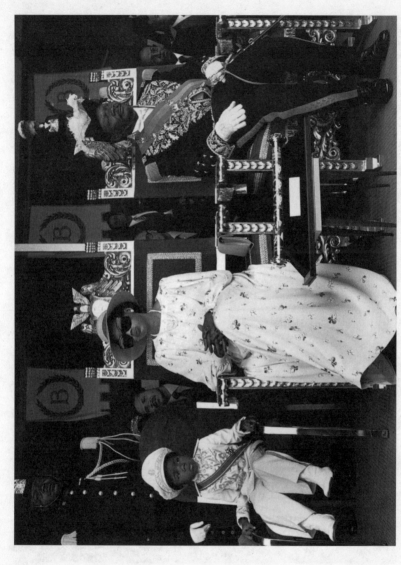

Bokassa, the Empress Catherine, and the crown prince watch a military parade the day after the imperial coronation. Bangui, 5 December 1977.

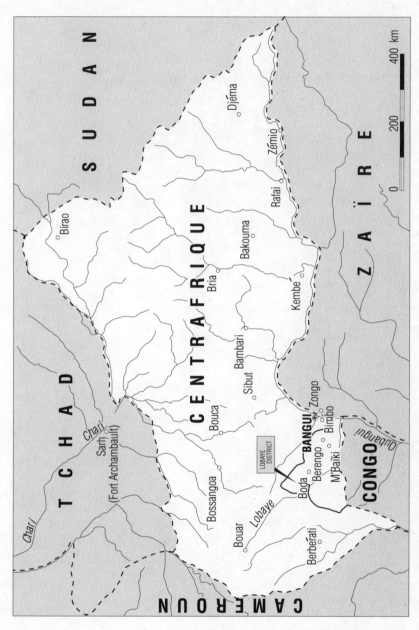

Centrafrique (Dennis Sheppard, 1996)

Dark Age

CHAPTER ONE

Colonial Interlude

A long conversation with two Bakongo village chiefs. But the one who spoke first while alone with us shut up as soon as the other approached. He wouldn't say another word; and nothing was more unsettling than the silence and the fear of compromising himself while we questioned him about the atrocities committed in the Boda prison where he had been incarcerated himself. Later, again alone with us, he told us that he had seen ten men die there in one day following brutal treatment. He still bore the scars of floggings, which he showed us. He confirmed what we had already been told – that the only food given to the prisoners was one fist-sized bowl of manioc a day.

He spoke of the fines customarily imposed by la Compagnie forestière on natives who didn't deliver rubber in sufficient quantity – fines of 40 francs; that is, as much as they could hope to earn in a month. He added that those unable to pay the fine could only avoid jail by borrowing from the better off – if such existed … Terror reigned and the surrounding villages were deserted.[1]

It was 1925 when the French writer André Gide recorded these observations on a visit to Equatorial Africa. Published later in his *Voyage au Congo*, they caused a public outcry. The French were horrified to learn that the atrocities and greed they so readily associated with King Leopold's Belgian Congo were also common practice in their own colonial possessions. It was anything but the romantic image they had come to expect, nothing like the fabled exploits of the Foreign Legion.

France's depredations in Africa began in the seventeenth century with involvement in the slave trade in the vicinity of Senegal. But the first real colony was Algeria, whose conquest was begun in the 1830s. It took many decades to complete the task of subjugation, and even then French rule rested on shaky foundations. Morocco and Tunisia were also unwillingly brought under "protection."[2] The final three decades of the nineteenth century witnessed the "scramble for Africa." This was the era in which European powers carved up the continent among themselves, spurred on by avarice and notions of national prestige. France was quick off the mark in the race for territorial spoils. Its adventurers pushed inland from Senegal in the 1870s, planting the tricolour in the interior. The result of these efforts was a vast domain that was organized as French West Africa in 1895. It comprised the modern states of Mali, Niger, Burkina Faso, Benin, Ivory Coast, Guinea, and Senegal, with Mauritania added a decade later.[3]

Meanwhile, Pierre Savorgnan de Brazza carried France's hopes in the forests of Gabon as he sought a river route to the interior. His great rival was Henry Morton Stanley, who was busily exploring the Congo basin in the 1870s on behalf of his employer King Leopold II of the Belgians. Ivory and rubber were the coveted commodities which the newcomers hoped would bring windfall profits. De Brazza's labours secured for France the right bank of the Congo River above Stanley Pool, and the town of Brazzaville was named in his honour. He and other Frenchmen pushed northward along the Oubangui in the 1880s, signing treaties with the peoples they encountered and placing them under "protection."

As a result, France acquired a large and cumbersome swath of territory stretching from Gabon on the coast to Tchad in the Sahara. Bounded on the west by Germany's Kamerun and hemmed in on the south and east by the Belgian Congo and Sudan, it became known as French Equatorial Africa. Since it was connected in the northwest to French West Africa and hence to Algeria, there was a certain geographical unity to the empire. By the time the imperial powers had agreed on an amicable division of their African plunder (at the Berlin Conference of 1884–85 and the Brussels Conference of 1890), France controlled more than one-quarter of the continent.[4] Much of what it owned was sparsely populated desert, but it looked impressive on the map. These sprawling possessions offered spiritual sustenance to a bruised national ego, which was still smarting from the humiliation of the Franco-Prussian War. France had its revenge on the enemy in the great conflagration of 1914–18, and its triumph was sweetened by the acquisition of the German African colonies of Togo and Kamerun – the latter being henceforth spelled Cameroun. As well as providing prestige and profits, France's empire served as a vast reservoir of military manpower, or cannon fodder. African soldiers helped compensate for France's low birth rate by boosting the size of its armed forces in the wars against Germany. More than 600,000 colonial conscripts served under the tricolour in the First World War, and during the Second World War around 200,000 Africans were in French uniform.[5]

French Equatorial Africa was the most neglected and obscure corner of the empire. When it was formally organized as an administrative federation in 1910, it contained four distinct territories. Gabon and Moyen Congo, opening on the Gulf of Guinea, formed its southernmost flank; Tchad stood at the northern end, the redoubt of desert peoples ever restless under colonial rule; and Oubangui-Chari was the territory in between.[6] On achieving a degree of autonomy in 1958, the latter became the Central African Republic – the land in which this story takes place.

When the French laid claim to Oubangui-Chari in the 1880s, they found a land that straddled the three major climatic zones of the continent. The equatorial forests of the Oubangui basin gave way to a less humid belt of savannah as one moved in a northerly direction – *des vastes prairies*, as André Gide described it. And farther north again, a dry region warned that the Sahara was but a step away. It was a land of pristine beauty blessed with an abundance of fertile soil, numerous rivers, and "big game" animals of an impressive variety.

The territory supported a native population of about one million.[7] The Banda in the east and the Baya in the west were the two major ethnic divisions of Oubangui-Chari, though a minority – the M'Baka, a Bantu people located in the southwestern forested district known as Lobaye – was probably the most important group of all. It was destined to produce the territory's leading native politicians. In spite of the ethnic diversity, a tradition of solidarity existed among the peoples of Oubangui-Chari before the colonial era, but it was the French administrative structure and military presence that ended group conflict, banished the predatory Sudanese slave traders, and ultimately helped forge a new nation. A common trading language, Sango, was useful in this respect, though it was the people's united opposition to the oppressive features of colonial rule that laid the foundations of national consciousness.

In 1889 the French established the town of Bangui on the right bank of the Oubangui River. Initially nothing more than a collection of straw huts, it gradually evolved into a pleasant little settlement with broad tree-lined boulevards fanning outwards from a central administrative district, which contained some interesting buildings in the colonial style. When Oubangui-Chari was given its own governor in 1906, he settled in Bangui, giving it the status of territorial capital. The governor was directly responsible to the governor general of

French Equatorial Africa, who presided over the federation from his residence in Brazzaville.[8]

Around the turn of the century French Equatorial Africa was divided into zones of exploitation, which were granted as exclusive concessions to private companies. The companies had no interest in long-term economic development; they simply sought quick profits without risking much capital. Profits came from ivory, gold, hardwoods, rubber, or anything else of value that could be plundered and carried away. No one bothered investing in roads, railways, or bridges beyond the few rudimentary structures that were needed to haul the booty to the coast.[9] Instead, they turned to the native population as a source of cheap and available labour – *portage à dos d'homme* becoming the principal means of transportation; with private militias backing their authority, they were able to introduce a form of slavery under the old feudal euphemism, *corvée*. One of the most notorious of these consortia was the Compagnie forestière de la Sangha-Oubangui, which was involved in rubber gathering in the Lobaye district of Oubangui-Chari.[10] Forestière officials "recruited" a large local labour force to bring in the wild rubber harvest. Their methods were not gentle. They locked up the women and children of entire villages until the men completed the quotas. They used the lash liberally to keep their "employees" on the move, and they punished insubordination with mutilation or death.

The trade disruptions of the First World War were a setback for the concessionary companies, but with the conflict over they were determined to recoup their losses with the least possible delay. The 1920s were their most rapacious decade. None of these consortia was more determined to wrest a profit from *le travail forcé* than the Forestière. When the wild rubber boom soon collapsed, the cat-o'-nine-tails capitalists simply turned to hardwood exploitation and the establishment of coffee and cotton plantations on the fringes of the equatorial forest. It was Edmond Giscard d'Estaing, a major shareholder in the Forestière, who enunciated the main purpose of these operations: "Produire la plus grosse quantité possible ... de produits coloniaux au plus bas prix possible."[11]

By the mid-1920s the Baya to the north of Lobaye were heeding the call of a prophet named Karnu to resist French rule and forced labour. Karnu claimed to have a magical plant that would turn the colonial invaders into gorillas, and he also supplied his followers with hoehandles that were supposed to protect them from their enemies' bullets. The War of the Hoehandles was the largest peasant insurrection in *Afrique noire* between the two world wars and was put down only with difficulty. During a series of punitive expeditions against the

Baya villages late in 1928, the French cornered Karnu and shot him dead, but resistance continued until the early 1930s.[12] It seemed to residents of metropolitan France that the news from Oubangui-Chari, or indeed from Equatorial Africa in general, was invariably bad. The federation was becoming known as the Cinderella of the Empire – the unsavoury habitat of corrupt officials and predatory capitalists.

In these unfortunate circumstances, two remarkable Oubanguians were born, men who were destined to guide their country's fortunes in the difficult decades ahead. The first was Barthélémy Boganda, who came into the world on 4 April 1910. His birthplace was Bouban-gui, a large M'Baka village at the edge of the equatorial forest, near the town of M'Baïki, which was the administrative centre for the pre-fecture of Lobaye. It is about eighty kilometres from Bangui. When Boganda was young, his mother was beaten to death by officials of the Forestière, and after much hardship he was adopted by Catholic missionaries. The boy showed intellectual promise and a pious demeanour – qualities that encouraged the priests to give him an advanced education. The church's investment paid the desired divi-dend on 17 March 1938 when Boganda was ordained into the priest-hood. He served in a number of missions during the Second World War, and when that conflict ended, changed circumstances enabled him to embark on a new career in politics.[13]

The second man of destiny came from the same ethnic group and village, and was in fact a relative of Boganda. Jean-Bedel Bokassa was born in Boubangui on 22 February 1921.[14] He grew up watching the men of his village leave daily on their *corvées* under the gaze of Forestière enforcers. It was all the more humiliating in that his father, Mindogon Mgboundoulou, as local headman, was forced to organize the rosters of work for his people. Mindogon was no willing collab-orator, and as news of Karnu's revolt spread to Lobaye, he resolved to resist. One day he released from captivity a number of his fellow villagers who were being held hostage by the Forestière as a guaran-tee that their relatives would work. The company considered this an act of rebellion. Its militia seized Mindogon and took him in chains to M'Baïki. There, on 13 November 1927, on the dusty square outside the prefecture office, they beat him to death. His wife, Marie Yokowo, was so shattered by the atrocity that she committed suicide a week later.

The effect of these events on the six-year-old Bokassa can only be imagined. But it would be no exaggeration to say that he learned the art of violence at an early age from some of its most seasoned prac-titioners. A council of his large family, in deliberating his future, decided it would be best if he were to receive a French education, and the Ecole Sainte-Jeanne d'Arc in M'Baïki was prevailed upon to accept him. It was one of the few mission schools in the territory, and Bokassa was one of the few Oubanguians to benefit from the instruction it had to offer. The little orphan sometimes had a tough time at school, where he was taunted by his classmates about his father's execution and his mother's suicide, but although he was short in stature, he was physically strong and soon learned to stand up for himself. His robust constitution, which would serve him well over the years, was already showing its power.

As the young scholar progressed in his studies, he became greatly attached to a grammar book written by a man called Bedel, and this name was given him by his teachers. Hence, Jean-Bedel. Later, he attended the Ecole Saint-Louis, a school run by Father Grüner in Bangui. Grüner, a well-known missionary, was responsible for endowing his pupil with an excellent command of French, and he hoped for a while that he had a priest in the making. But he soon realized that his charge had neither the aptitude for study nor the piety required for that difficult calling, and he advised the lad to try the army instead. "In any case, I don't know if I would have made a good priest" was Bokassa's own frank judgment. He completed his education at Father Compte's school in Brazzaville, where he was able to develop his talents as a cook.

It was 1939, and the graduate, now a young man of eighteen, needed a career. He had always admired soldiers, uniforms, and the exploits of great generals, and the military seemed a logical choice – especially as his grandfather, M'Balanga, had given him much the same advice as Father Grüner. The old patriarch had often said that the man who joined the French army learned as much as if he had lived three lives. With these words echoing in his ears, Bokassa entered the forces as a private on 19 May, just a few months before the world was engulfed once again in the turmoil of total war.[15]

In the springtime of 1940 Europe's "phoney war" came to an abrupt end when Hitler launched his blitzkrieg towards the west. The military might of France crumbled before the panzer assault, and the Third Republic sought a shameful armistice. But as Marshal Pétain's collaborationist regime was put in place at Vichy, one French soldier vowed to fight on. General Charles de Gaulle had fled across the English Channel, and from London, on 18 June, he appealed to his countrymen to continue the struggle against the Germans. France still had its fleet and its colonies, he argued, and with these it could wage war. But the general's call went almost unheeded. The fleet and all the colonies save one stayed loyal to Vichy.

It is undeniably ironic that the much-maligned Cinderella of the Empire, French Equatorial Africa, came to the assistance of the metropolis in its darkest hour. Governors Félix Eboué of Tchad and Pierre de Saint-Mart of Oubangui-Chari quickly declared their support for de Gaulle. A military coup in Brazzaville and a brief civil war in Gabon put the entire federation in the hands of the Free French by the end of August. Equatorial Africa gave de Gaulle not only a base of operations but a claim to legitimacy. It was here that the Free French Army was organized. Marching across the desert, it joined up with the British Eighth Army and played a part in driving the Germans out of North Africa.[16] France was back in the war, though its soldiers were mainly African recruits, including the young Bokassa.

Life in the forces was agreeable to Bokassa. Serving in the Second bataillon de marche under General Delange, he became a corporal in July 1940 and a sergeant in November the following year. In August 1944 he participated in the Allied landing in Provence and subsequently saw action in Germany before the final curtain came down on the Third Reich. With the restoration of peace in Europe, he decided to stay in uniform since the army offered opportunities for training, travel, and advancement that were otherwise unavailable to his countrymen. While stationed at the army camp at Fréjus on the French Riviera, he studied radio transmissions; and after a brief stay in Brazzaville, he went to officer training school in Saint-Louis du Sénégal. Then, on 7 September 1950, he left for Indochina as the transmissions expert with the colonial battalion of Saigon-Cholon.[17]

Thus Bokassa found himself on the losing side in one of the century's most bitter anticolonial wars. He saw action and received injuries, though nothing serious. When his tour of duty ended in March 1953, the French humiliation at Dien Bien Phu was still more than a year away. Bokassa was fortunate to have escaped this confrontation, which left thousands of his comrades dead or maimed. Good luck seemed to follow him, and he came to believe that he was favoured by fortune, that a special destiny was in store for him.

In spite of the hazards of war, Bokassa enjoyed his stay in Southeast Asia. One of the attractions, he readily admitted, was the women, whom he found irresistible. He met one particularly alluring seventeen-year-old named N'guyen-Thi-Hué and married her. Her parents consented to the union, or so he claimed. She bore him a daughter, and three days after the birth he registered the child as a French national. But when Bokassa sailed for Europe, wife and child were left behind. He believed he would be returning to the East on another tour of duty, but it never happened. The family in Saigon was not completely forgotten, however. There was to be a joyful reunion far in the future, when it suited Bokassa. Many years later, in reminiscing on his Indochinese sojourn, Bokassa stated: "Indochina pleased me a lot. There was true camaraderie there. I always liked the army, the French army which was my life. But it was there, in the Far East, that I found it most beautiful and brotherly. Because it was a war, a cruel war, friends were more important than all the gold in the world. But I also liked the Indochinese people, hardworking and intelligent; the women, sometimes violent but loyal nonetheless, shrewd, born business people, capable of a profound attachment to their 'husbands of passage,' which we were."[18]

On his return to Europe, Bokassa was once again stationed in Fréjus, this time teaching African recruits the art of radio transmission. There were further promotions ahead: he became second lieutenant in 1956 and lieutenant in 1958. In December 1958 he was sent to Brazzaville as a military technical assistant, and a year later he was stationed in Bangui. This brought him back to his homeland after a twenty-year absence. (Indeed, during most of the intervening two decades he had not even been in Africa.) Finally, on 1 July 1961, he was promoted to captain – the highest rank he was to achieve in the French forces.

Bokassa was able to advance through the ranks because of his martial qualities, his educational background and the better opportunities for training and promotion available to Africans in the French forces in the 1950s. During the Second World War he had proved to be an able soldier, courageous in combat, and had received the Légion d'honneur, the Médaille militaire, and the Croix de guerre. When peace returned, the army adopted a policy of *promotion africaine*, aimed at increasing the number of African noncommissioned officers and improving their skills. The new military realities demanded fewer soldiers but men who were better educated and were capable of handling more sophisticated weapons and technology. It was in this context that Bokassa, who had already proved himself under fire, was chosen for special training in Fréjus and Saint-Louis. His excellent spoken French and his literate command of the language were other factors in his favour. Without such skills, which were rare enough among the rank and file, advanced technical training would have been impossible. Moreover, because of the *loi-cadre* of 1956 (described below) and the educational opportunities provided by l'Ecole de formation des officiers du régime transitoire des territoires d'outre-mer (EFORTOM) at Fréjus, the promotion of Africans was more pronounced.[19] Consequently, Bokassa was able to advance to second lieutenant, lieutenant, and captain during these auspicious years when France recognized that it would have to concede more responsibility to its colonized peoples.

When Bokassa arrived in Bangui late in 1959, he found that much had changed since his departure twenty years earlier. While he had been away fighting to maintain the empire in distant lands, French rule had been disintegrating in his homeland and in the neighbouring colonies of *Afrique noire*. Indeed, Oubangui-Chari was now the fledgling Central African Republic and was on the eve of independence. Here, a word should be said on how all this came about.

Colonialism had never recovered from the Second World War. The Japanese rout of the European powers (and the Americans) in the Far East in the initial fighting dealt a death blow to the illusion that rule by the white race was a matter of divine providence. This was bitter medicine for the champions of the colonial system, and the French in particular found it hard to swallow. To make matters worse, the collapse of the Third Republic before the German behemoth had reminded francophone Africans of their masters' vulnerability. Finally, the vital role played by the colonial troops in de Gaulle's army meant that the relationship between France and its African subjects could never again be the same.

The contours of a new African policy were outlined at a conference of French colonial administrators that opened in Brazzaville in January 1944. The subject peoples were promised an end to the worst abuses of the system and a voice in designing a constitution for the Fourth Republic at the end of hostilities. De Gaulle, who was present at the conference, proclaimed that his country's mission was "to elevate men step by step toward the peaks of dignity and fraternity." These pronouncements simply meant that France intended to invest in education and economic development until such time as Africans embraced French culture and civilization. Autonomy for the colonies was not envisaged.[20]

These were limited promises, and in some respects they were of dubious value. But constructive reforms did follow. Shortly after the war, the hated practice of forced labour and the *indigénat* were abolished (the latter being a code that had given colonial administrators arbitrary power to fine or imprison Africans for even the most trivial offences). Moreover, administrators were now deprived of their judicial powers, which they had often abused, and a colonial magistracy was put in place so that some semblance of justice might prevail.

There were political adjustments too. The constitution of the Fourth Republic, which was adopted in a referendum in October

1946, allowed for colonial representation in both houses of parliament; 7 per cent of the seats in the National Assembly and 15 per cent of those in the Council of the Republic were given to the colonies. To allow for some devolution of authority, each colony was also given its own local assembly with limited powers. (The assemblies were only at liberty to approve local budget items and many of these they could not refuse.) Furthermore, elections to the overseas and metropolitan assemblies were based on what was known as the double-college system – one college was for French nationals living abroad; the other for indigenous peoples – and the native franchise was limited to a tiny educated minority. Changes in nomenclature completed the process. Colonies were no longer referred to as such but as *territoires d'outre-mer* (overseas territories), and the term "empire" was abandoned for the less offensive "French Union."[21]

By these adjustments France hoped to convince the colonized peoples as well as a sceptical international community that the French Union was based on mutual consent rather than military might. No one was fooled. Even before these structures were put in place, serious flaws were apparent. When the Algerians rioted in May 1945 demanding political reforms, brutal repression followed in which thousands were killed. In December 1946 the bloody and protracted war to drive the French from Indochina began in earnest. And in March 1947 the people of Madagascar were in open revolt. In quelling that rebellion, French troops took the lives of tens of thousands of men and women.[22]

It was the twilight of empire even if France refused to recognize it. In *Afrique noire* there was as yet no call to arms, but the road to independence was being charted slowly and cautiously. The creation of overseas assemblies and overseas representation in Paris fostered the emergence of native African leaders of a different genre. These men took advantage of the new political structures to assail the abuses of colonial rule and ultimately demanded autonomy as a permanent solution to their people's ills. Senegal's Léopold Senghor and the Ivory Coast's Félix Houphouët-Boigny were typical of this new generation of leaders. As members of a small French-educated élite, they fitted comfortably into the National Assembly of the Fourth Republic, and they were destined to rule their respective countries after the disintegration of the empire.

Senghor and Houphouët-Boigny were joined in the National Assembly by another African man of destiny, Oubangui-Chari's Barthélémy Boganda. Father Boganda, who was elected in November 1946, arrived in the French capital attired in his clerical garb and introduced himself as the son of a polygamous cannibal. But his attachment to his chosen calling weakened when he met and fell in love with a young Frenchwoman, Michelle Jourdain, who was employed as a parliamentary secretary. They were married in 1949, and Boganda was expelled from the priesthood as a result. The affair between the black priest and the white secretary caused a minor scandal in Paris, but it did little to impair Boganda's popularity with his people. He continued to be returned to the National Assembly, where he battled, often in vain, against repressive features of the French administration in his homeland. Arbitrary arrest, low wages, compulsory cotton cultivation, and the exclusion of blacks from restaurants and cinemas were among the objects of his invective.[23]

Boganda also turned his attention to organizing Oubanguians at the grass-roots level. In September 1949 he was in Bangui, where he established a political party known as the Mouvement d'évolution sociale d'Afrique noire (MESAN). It quickly came to dominate the local assembly. Boganda's political creed was summed up in the Sango phrase *zo kwe zo*, which means "every human being is a person." In effect, he was looking for equal treatment for blacks within the French Union rather than independence as such, at least for the immediate future. The activities of MESAN drew the ire of the French administration and of companies trading in cotton, coffee, diamonds, and other commodities. The Bangui chamber of commerce was the mouthpiece of these companies. The men who gathered at this club strongly resented the demise of forced labour and the concomitant rise of black nationalism. They hated Boganda in particular, viewing him as a dangerous demagogue and a threat to their "free enterprise," and they resolved to be rid of him.[24]

Meanwhile, the French Union was in serious trouble; 1954 was unquestionably one of its worst years. On 7 May the French forces beseiged at Dien Bien Phu surrendered to the superior might of the Viet Minh. It was a major disaster and paved the way for France's withdrawal from Indochina. A few months later, the Algerians took up arms in what was to be an equally bloody and prolonged struggle to extricate themselves from the unloved union. In view of these developments, it began to dawn on the more astute politicians in Paris that *Afrique noire* might go the way of Indochina and Algeria unless imaginative measures were taken. There was still no thought of independence for either Equatorial or West Africa, but it was clear that something had to be done. Gaston Deferre, who became minister of France d'outre-mer in February 1956, came to the conclusion that fundamental changes were necessary in order to convince black Africans of France's benevolent intentions. Although giving the subject nations an element of self-government might weaken the structure of the French Union, it might also preserve the union indefinitely. This was the reasoning behind Deferre's *loi-cadre*, or framework law, which received approval in June 1956. It gave his government a free hand to reform the colonial structure as it saw fit.[25]

In the spring of 1957 new colonial assemblies were chosen under the liberal aegis of the *loi-cadre*. This time there was universal suffrage and the double-college voting system was abolished. The assemblies were granted real legislative powers and were permitted to choose government councils (cabinets) of up to eight ministers. The councillor receiving the highest vote became vice-president of the council in each territory, though the local French governor held the title of president – and retained substantial powers. Nevertheless, the vice-presidents emerged as influential figures. In July 1958 they became presidents of their respective councils and the governors' role was reduced considerably. In this way, much of the local administration became the responsibility of Africans.[26]

The *loi-cadre* also allowed for the election of "great councils" in the two federations of *Afrique noire*. Houphouët-Boigny became president of the great council of French West Africa and Boganda was chosen for the equivalent position in Equatorial Africa. Boganda interpreted his election as a mandate to lead his federation to independence. He hoped that in due course the four territories of Gabon, Moyen Congo, Oubangui-Chari, and Tchad would emerge from French rule as one united country under the name Central African Republic. Meanwhile, he pressured local French administrators to relax the reins of control and grant Africans the power to make real decisions. "Fewer civil servants and more technicians" was his cry.[27]

It was at this critical juncture that Charles de Gaulle re-entered French politics. He had resigned the premiership back in January 1946, frustrated by his inability to hold together a coalition of diverse parties. But in June 1958 he again formed a government. He was the man of the hour, the man who would enable his country to end the Algerian crisis and heal the wounds it had inflicted on the body politic. One of his first moves was to call for a new constitution – one that concentrated considerable power in the hands of the president of the republic. The general had himself in mind for this important job.

With the Gold Coast casting off the Union Jackboot in 1957, decolonization in Africa had begun. De Gaulle was conscious of this trend, but in spite of the catastrophe in Vietnam and the ongoing Algerian struggle, he was unable to conceive of France bereft of its overseas possessions. He therefore devised a scheme, and built it into his constitutional proposal, whereby the French empire could be preserved as an apparently voluntary entity. The constitution of the Fifth Republic offered the overseas territories immediate independence by simply voting "no" in the referendum. Those that made this choice would lose all further French aid. Those that accepted the constitution could either be fully integrated with the metropolis as *départements* or could become semi-autonomous member states of what was to be called the French Community.

In the constitutional referendum of October 1958 only Guinea, under Sékou Touré, chose immediate independence; and it received the promised retribution. The French left in haste taking everything of value with them. France's other possessions in *Afrique noire*, including Oubangui-Chari, accepted the constitution and membership in the *communauté*. These territories now found themselves in a rather ambiguous situation. They had achieved a strong measure of self-government, but France retained control of such essentials as defence, foreign policy, trade, and currency. Nor were they eligible for membership in the United Nations – an annoying reminder of their subservient status.[28]

As these events unfolded, Boganda's dream of leading French Equatorial Africa to independence, or even semi-independence, as a single country foundered on the rocks of regional jealousy and personal ambition. The leaders of Tchad, Gabon, and Moyen Congo (Congo-Brazzaville) were determined to go their own way, and these territories became republics within the French Community on 28 November 1958. Thus, on 1 December 1958, when Boganda declared the establishment of his Central African Republic ("la République centrafricaine" or "le Centrafrique," in French), it was simply Oubangui-Chari under a different name.

On 6 December the first government of the Central African Republic came into being with Boganda as premier. His actual title was president of the Council of Government. A French governor remained in the country, though he was now called high commissioner – a more appropriate designation in the circumstances. Boganda's cabinet contained two men deserving of note, since they played critical roles in the political drama that was about to unfold. One was Abel Goumba, who was vice-president of the Council of Government and was also in charge of finance. Born in September 1927 in Grimari, he was the son of a well-known writer and interpreter. He had studied medicine in his youth and later practised in Moyen Congo. Intelligent, honest, and strongly nationalistic, he was Boganda's right-hand man. The other person of note was the minister of the interior, twenty-nine-year-old David Dacko. He was a M'Baka, the son of a nightwatchman on a plantation in Lobaye, and he was a distant cousin of Bokassa.

Dacko had studied to be a teacher at the Ecole normale of Mouyoundzi in Moyen Congo, and after working in mission schools for
some time had become head of the major primary school in Bangui.[29]

The new Central African government made its debut by adopting
a law banning nudity and vagabondage. These measures were proposed by Boganda, his missionary education still showing its effects.[30]
The government's main task, however, was to draw up a constitution
for the republic. It succeeded in drafting such a document, modelling
it to some extent on that of France. It was approved by the assembly
on 16 February 1959.

On 29 March Boganda boarded a plane at Berbérati for a flight to
Bangui, but he never arrived there. The aircraft crashed in the district
of Boda, killing all passengers and crew. The infant nation was
shocked at the death of its revered leader, and sabotage was widely
suspected. Indeed, the Paris weekly, L'Express, revealed shortly afterwards that experts had found traces of explosive in the wreckage.
The French high commissioner banned the sale of that edition of the
magazine when it appeared in the Central African Republic. Many
believe that the expatriate businessmen of the Bangui chamber of
commerce, perhaps with a little help from the French secret service,
had a hand in the tragedy. Michelle Jourdain was also implicated. By
1959 relations between Boganda and his French wife had soured, and
he had been thinking of leaving her and returning to the priesthood.
She had a large insurance policy on his life, a precaution taken just
days before the accident. There are good reasons for suspecting her
motives and for connecting her to the secret service.[31]

To Oubanguians/Central Africans, Boganda was more than just a
charismatic political leader. He was considered the "black Christ," a
great religious figure endowed with extraordinary powers. A few
months before his death, large crowds had gathered on the banks of
the Oubangui River in response to a rumour that he was to walk
across its waters. Now that he was dead, his mystique was even
greater. He was a national martyr, and miracles were regularly attributed to his name. Those who were related to him even tenuously,
such as Bokassa, were able to capture some of that aura and use it
to advantage.

With Boganda dead, Abel Goumba emerged as his logical successor, but he was considered too nationalistic and the expatriates con-
spired to outmanoeuvre him. France's high commissioner, Colonel
Roger Barberot, with the support of the chamber of commerce and
Michelle Jourdain, turned to David Dacko as the man most likely to
lead a regime deferential to foreign interests, and Dacko accordingly
took control of the government in May. In July, as yet uncertain of

his grip on power, he dismissed Goumba from his post as minister of finance.

Dacko felt a little more secure with his main rival out of the cabinet, but a major threat appeared in October, when his government faced a motion of censure sponsored by Pierre Maleombho, president of the National Assembly. Fearing that the motion might succeed, Dacko moved to thwart it. With money generously donated by the European community, he lavished bribes on the deputies and, as an added measure of security, surrounded the assembly with his fellow M'Bakas in a show of force. The combination of carrot and stick proved irresistible and the government survived the censure motion. In the aftermath, Maleombho lost his position to Michel Adama-Tamboux, a close friend of Dacko. Nevertheless, Goumba and Maleombho did not give up. In May 1960 they abandoned MESAN and organized an opposition party, the Mouvement d'évolution démocratique de l'Afrique centrale (MEDAC). They hoped to play a role in the continuing political development of their country towards complete independence. They were to be disappointed.[32]

Meanwhile, de Gaulle's French Community was proving unequal to the task of stemming the rising tide of African nationalism. The member states, including Centrafrique, were increasingly dissatisfied with their truncated autonomy. They sought genuine statehood and the international recognition that went with it. Moreover, they watched enviously as the British and Belgian colonies prepared for the day when their European masters would depart. Sékou Touré's Guinea, which had spurned the Fifth Republic's constitution in 1958, had survived the severance of French aid by turning to the Soviets. De Gaulle derived little satisfaction from this example; it had resulted in the eclipse of French influence in Guinea, and it seemed to demonstrate to other francophone territories that real independence was indeed viable. Consequently, when the *communauté* states began to demand full political freedom without loss of French aid, the general agreed. He reasoned that peaceful disengagement would restore French prestige while retaining economic and cultural influence in the former colonies.[33] During the month of August 1960, France officially granted independence to the four states that had comprised the federation of French Equatorial Africa. Centrafrique's turn came on the thirteenth of the month. At ceremonies marking the event in Bangui, André Malraux, representing Paris, declared, "France bequeaths you her administration because there can be no state without management."[34]

The late transfer of democratic institutions to Africa by the departing colonial power was an attempt to leave a European political legacy to the new states, to define the rules of the political game, and to ensure that only those socialized into European patterns of behaviour could participate.[35] But France's support for real democracy in its former colonies was half-hearted at best. Pressure from metropolitan leftist parties as well as a desire to withdraw with dignity lay behind these decisions rather than a firm commitment to the idea of the popular will. The difficulty with democratic processes was that they did not ensure continuing metropolitan economic domination. France was therefore willing to intervene in the process to ensure that compliant leaders came to power. The elimination of Boganda and his succession by Dacko are strongly suggestive of such intervention. France would continue to play a key role in the political and economic evolution of Centrafrique.

CHAPTER TWO

Coup d'état

Although the tricolour came down over Africa, France never really relinquished control of its possessions. De Gaulle was determined to maintain his country's influence in its former colonies for strategic, economic, and prestige reasons. This called for continual handouts as well as constant meddling in the internal affairs of the newly independent countries in order to keep governments friendly to Paris in power. The key figure in these machinations was Jacques Foccart, the president's "secretary-general for African and Malagasy affairs." Foccart had the powers of a superminister. He had senior civil servants in several ministeries – Cooperation, Defence, External Affairs – at his beck and call; he took a hand in the selection of ambassadors and secret service agents for Africa; and he cultivated close personal ties with many African leaders. Everything was held together by the "Foccart network" – a discreet system of agents placed in key commercial and government roles in the former colonies who provided vital information to the Elysée Palace through Foccart.[1]

The secret service requires a few words of explanation. At the end of the Second World War, France created two secret agencies: the Direction de la sûreté du territoire (DST) and the Service de documentation extérieure et de contre-espionnage (SDECE). The DST is responsible for internal security and approximates Britain's MI5. Its headquarters are in Paris on the rue des Saussaies, just around the corner from the Elysée Palace. The SDECE (which has since been reorganized as the DGSE) looks after counterespionage and France's interests abroad. It is similar to MI6 and the CIA. Because of its headquarters on boulevard Mortier, near Piscine des Tournelles, it is popularly known as La Piscine ("The Swimming Pool").[2] It is best remembered in the anglophone world for its exploit of July 1985 when its agents sank the Greenpeace vessel *Rainbow Warrior* as it lay moored in Auckland harbour. Needless to say, SDECE agents, or *bar-bouzes* (to use the colourful French word), were keeping a close eye on things as the Central African Republic came into existence.

On the day following independence, the Central African National Assembly confirmed David Dacko as acting head of state. Soon after-wards, with a little prompting from his supporters, Dacko came to realize that democracy could have its dangerous side. The lesson was brought home on 20 September when MEDAC won substantial sup-port in a number of by-elections. With the popular will in such an unpredictable state, there was no guarantee that Dacko would be leading the country after a general election. Thus, expediency required that the opposition be eliminated before he sought the approbation of the people. Dacko therefore demanded, and received from the National Assembly, extraordinary powers with which to deal with his opponents. In December MEDAC was dissolved and Goumba arrested. His crime: fomenting disorder by questioning Dacko's assumption of power. Before the month was out, the rest of Goumba's followers in the assembly had been detained. In his New Year's Eve radio broadcast, Roger Barberot, presumably on instruc-tions from Paris, called on all French citizens in the country to support the Dacko regime. France evidently had approved of the elimination of political opposition. The collusion of the former colo-nial power was also evident in a related incident. On 22 February 1962 the Supreme Court sentenced Goumba and two of his closest collaborators to life imprisonment for their crime of dissent; the court was made up entirely of French magistrates.[3]

With the opposition banished or gagged, political life took on an aspect that was all too familiar in newly independent African states. In July 1962, at a major congress of the ruling party, Dacko announced that MESAN would henceforth be the sole political movement in the country. All citizens were required to take out membership and pay dues; in this way they would have a voice in government. Within two years, they were able to exercise the franchise when the long-awaited election was called under the new constitution. In January 1964 MESAN put Dacko forward as the sole candidate for president. As the sole candidate of the sole political party, he garnered 100 per cent of the ballots cast and found himself firmly entrenched for a seven-year term of office. The electorate was also unanimous in acclaiming Dacko's sixty hand-picked MESAN candidates for the assembly. The people had spoken. The new president was in a virtually unassailable position, and he thanked the citizens for granting him the "magical confidence" they had once reserved for Boganda.[4]

The inheritors of the new state were a distinct group characterized by their French education and their participation in some capacity in the former colonial regime. Preponderantly conservative and élitist in outlook, they had benefited from their collaboration with the French and wished to retain their privileges in the future. Various terms have been coined to describe such groups; "state bourgeoisie" is a popular choice.[5] The extension of the franchise before independence in Oubangui-Chari and other French colonies had sparked the mobilization of political party systems to rally the people around the educated élite. But once support had been consolidated, elections tended to be either abolished or transformed into less than meaningful rituals.[6] The vote of January 1964 in Centrafrique was a plebiscitary rather than a competitive election and could serve only as a symbolic ratification of government policy. Even so, it did allow the leadership to communicate with the masses, and in this way it fostered legitimacy for the regime.[7]

Enthusiasm for the political party that had achieved independence declined in many states once the changeover of power took place. High expectations could not be met, and tactics such as mass rallies, which had been appropriate in opposing colonial rule, were ineffective for governing. Parties such as MESAN were little more than loose alliances of office seekers, unbound by ideological commitment, and they began to break into factions after independence. The leadership, fearing threats to its privileges, sought to maintain unity by eliminating opposition. But the use of force for such ends created an unfortunate precedent. If force was a legitimate instrument for retaining power, it could also be used by those either excluded from the system or confined to the periphery.[8]

The Central African Republic was stillborn. It achieved independence in name only. The French chose the new head of state and helped consolidate his power in order to pursue their own interests. French nationals remained in the country in large numbers and continued to play critical roles in various managerial and technical areas. They staffed a substantial number of senior positions in the civil service and in business, often out of necessity. There were simply not enough Central Africans trained to do these jobs.[9] While the Dacko regime took some important initiatives to promote education and agriculture, it was incapable of running the country in an honest and efficient manner. Creating government jobs was its principal activity. Not only did the number of public servants of one sort or another multiply, but they received enormous salary increases and extraordinary benefits such as free lodging and interest-free loans.[10]

The friends and relations of the president and his entourage were doing well for themselves in the patronage system.[11]

Senior government officials, who but shortly before had been lowly underlings in the colonial administration, now found themselves in dizzying positions of privilege with open access to the public purse. The temptation was irresistible, and they began to behave in the manner of their former masters, spending money on villas, luxury cars, mistresses, and junkets abroad. Some cabinet ministers enriched themselves by running bars and taxi services. Others built apartment blocks with public funds and rented them out for further gain. Even Dacko, who initially had urged his supporters not to feel ashamed of wealth, was shocked at the avarice. On a tour of the countryside in 1961, he was alarmed to hear peasants denounce his officials and demand the return of the French. He felt obliged to lecture the members of the assembly, admonishing them for excessive drinking, laziness, and graft.[12]

Yet President Dacko himself was no model politician and was not above using his position to advantage in developing profitable interests in coffee plantations and other business ventures. But although his regime was venal and authoritarian, it was never tyrannical. Lacking Boganda's charisma, he used a mixture of devious and tough measures to outwit potential opponents and hang on to power. He never won popular support and was considered a *munzo vucko* – a black man who thinks like whites. He was known locally as *la vache qui rit* because of his unfortunate resemblance to the cow on the popular brand of cheese.[13]

If political culture under Dacko was never a model of propriety, it would be wrong, as some have done, to dismiss it as a cesspool of corruption, graft, and nepotism without making allowances for the context. Those employed by the state in newly independent countries, including Centrafrique, came under enormous pressure from friends and relatives for jobs and favours. They found it impossible to shed the reciprocal kinship expectations for the impersonal ethos of the modern bureaucracy. Salaried employment was a result of formal education, which had usually been acquired through the support and sacrifice of family and community. The official who refused to repay this debt was condemned rather than admired. Abstract codes of public conduct were poorly established and could not compete with older value systems.[14]

In 1961 the Central African finance minister admitted that his government's revenues could barely cover three-fifths of its expenditure. France was providing the balance. As the government spent more and more, France continued to hand out budget supplements, though not always on time or with great enthusiasm. Yet Paris had little choice but to keep its client regime afloat if it wished its multinational companies to continue unmolested in their control of the economy. There was a lot at stake.

Economic dependency on France was underlined by the fact that the Central African Republic remained within the franc monetary zone after 1960. The official currency was the CFA franc, which had been developed by the French government for its African colonies at the end of the Second World War. The CFA franc was (and remained until recently) fully convertible to French francs at a fixed rate of fifty to one, and the African banks issuing this money were French controlled. While there were several clear advantages to this arrangement for the countries in the zone, French domination was the real issue. The treaties of cooperation which France signed with its former colonies at independence – and which allowed for a continuing military presence, the training of officers for new national armies, and so forth – all reinforced this domination.[15]

It was this world of machiavellian politics that greeted Jean-Bedel Bokassa on his return to his homeland. In some important respects, little had changed except that now many of the spoils of office were open to Africans. He was not slow to recognize this. Because of the nature of his employment in the French forces, Bokassa had played no role in the political manoeuvrings that accompanied the birth of the nation. But the new country would need its own defence forces, and it was here that he found a part to play. A fledgling Central African army was slowly taking shape under the direction of the local French commander, General Marcel Bigeard. While this was happening, Captain Bokassa was seconded to Dacko as a member of his military cabinet. This was a committee that advised the president (who was also minister of defence) on military matters. On 1 January 1962 Bokassa resigned his commission in the French army and was integrated into the Central African forces with the rank of battalion commandant. A little over a year later, on 1 February 1963, he became commander-in-chief of the Central African army – an assemblage of five hundred poorly trained and poorly equipped soldiers. On 1 December 1964 he became the army's first and only colonel.[16]

Bokassa owed his sudden rise to prominence to his lengthy military career and the fact that he was the only officer of Oubanguian origin at the dawn of independence. The fact that he was a M'Baka and was related to both Boganda and Dacko also helped. Moreover, he was convinced that he was a man of destiny and that greatness lay before him. Although his education was limited, he had travelled widely and was wise in the ways of the world. He was a shrewd observer of men and of opportunities, and was possessed of an over-weaning ambition that would not be denied. He could be charming and humorous and had that indefinable quality of charisma that appealed to ordinary people.

Perhaps the critical flaw in Bokassa's character was his vanity. Elements of pompous self-importance were already evident in these early days, though few could have guessed at the extremes of grandiose delusion that would eventually appear. Some clues, however, were not hard to find. Bokassa wanted recognition, especially on state occasions, and he rarely appeared in public without his military medals arrayed on his chest. His insistence on being next to or right behind President Dacko at public ceremonies led to bitter arguments with the chief of protocol, Jean-Paul Douate. Douate was frequently obliged to point out that after the president came the president of the assembly, followed by the ministers of state; Bokassa, as a senior civil servant, could then come next in line. In spite of these admonitions, Bokassa was always angling to sit at the presidential table, to walk beside the president, or to drive his car in presidential cortèges. The rebuffs Douate was obliged to give in order to uphold the rules of protocol ultimately cost him his life.

At first, Dacko found the pretensions of his cousin amusing. He certainly underestimated him, dismissing him as an inveterate drunkard, a womanizer and braggart. Early in 1965 he humiliated Bokassa at an official dinner in the presence of foreign diplomats. "Colonel Bokassa only wants to collect medals," he jeered, "and he is too stupid to pull off a coup d'état."[17] The slight was not easily forgotten. The president soon came to realize that his army chief's ambition posed a serious threat to the regime. The minister of the interior, Jean-Arthur Bandio, suggested that Bokassa be brought into the cabinet. This would at once satisfy his desire for recognition and sever him from command of the army, a potentially dangerous power base. But Bokassa was wary of navigating the shoals of politics without his soldiers behind him – he had seen many a promising political career cut short by sudden arrest and imprisonment.

Dacko could see other African civilian regimes tumbling to military coups, and he hoped to avoid a similar fate by balancing the army with an armed police force of five hundred men, the gendarmerie. The police chief, Jean Izamo, was a man he trusted. As an added precaution, he created a brigade of presidential security guards under the command of Prosper Mounoumbaye. These men, 120 in all, were feared as an incipient secret police. Mostly, however, they stood on guard around the Palais de la Renaissance, the futuristic presidential palace in the centre of Bangui.[18]

Dacko sent Bokassa to Paris in the summer of 1965 as part of an annual delegation to the 14 July celebrations. Bokassa took some of his family with him, including his sixth wife, whom he had recently married; they stayed at the Cercle des officiers, in place Saint-Augustin. Along with a number of African politicians, Bokassa had also been invited to a ceremony marking the closure of EFORTOM, the school for training officers for overseas territories. He attended this event at Fréjus on 23 July. Then, as he prepared to leave for home, he was told that it would not be possible – President Dacko had forbidden it. Bokassa was furious, believing he had been tricked into an unwilling exile by his increasingly nervous cousin. Months went by as he sought the support of friends in the French and Central African armed forces. As a result of his efforts, pressure was brought to bear, and in October Dacko backed down and allowed Bokassa back to Bangui. According to Bokassa's rather fanciful account, it was the personal intervention of General de Gaulle that made the difference. The general allegedly said, "Bokassa must be immediately returned to his post. I cannot tolerate the mistreatment of my companion-in-arms."[19]

Bokassa was one of a multitude of problems facing the regime in 1965. In September of the previous year the Central African Republic had established diplomatic relations with the People's Republic of China. Dacko had taken this step under pressure from radical elements in MESAN but also in order to seek alternatives to French aid. Beijing welcomed the chance to gain a foothold in the country and sent a special envoy, Meng Yieng, to cultivate the relationship. Other Chinese agents began to tour the country showing propaganda films in the villages. An economic and cultural agreement followed, sweetened by an interest-free loan of one billion CFA francs. The French watched in dismay as the communist message made headway in their former colony. They were coming to the conclusion that Dacko was no longer their obedient servant. In truth, the president was rapidly losing control of the situation. Chinese aid failed to banish the spectre of financial collapse. Not only was the economy stagnant and the bureaucracy an inefficient shambles, but the very security of the state was threatened. Rebel Lumumbists from the former Belgian Congo had infiltrated the southern frontier, while irregulars from the Sudan had come in from the east. The republic's poorly paid, poorly trained, and poorly equipped army was incapable of defending its citizenry from these marauders.

The army headquarters were at Camp de Roux, a barracks carved out of La Colline, a forested hill that dominates Bangui. It was only a few blocks from the presidential palace, and ever since Bokassa's return from France, Dacko had been keeping an anxious eye on troop movements in the neighbourhood. The two men had a stormy encounter in November during which the president threatened the army chief with demotion. Tensions between the rivals continued to mount. In mid-December Dacko approved a budget increase for the gendarmerie while rejecting the budget that Bokassa put forward for the army.[20] Bokassa was enraged and made no attempt to conceal his feelings. "I am properly annoyed," he was heard to say to his friends. "They refused me the credits I asked for. I'm going for a coup d'état."[21]

Dacko was counting on surviving by strengthening the police and weakening the army. He was planning to make the gendarmerie chief, Izamo, his personal military adviser in place of Bokassa; and he was hoping to promote army officers whom he considered loyal while getting rid of Bokassa and some of his close military associates. Dacko was indiscreet enough to hint at these plans to elders in Boubangui village, who in turn tipped off Bokassa. The army chief now knew that he had to act or risk losing everything. But he hesitated on the brink of rebellion. He lacked confidence in his rag-tag army – he was not certain that the troops would follow him – and even if he overcame the gendarmerie and the presidential guard, there was always the danger of French intervention. This had happened, as he knew, after the coup d'état of 23 February 1964 against Gabonese President Léon M'Ba. M'Ba had succeeded in evading capture, and his vice-president had appealed to Paris for help. French paratroopers were on the spot within hours and M'Ba was restored. However, Bokassa found the courage to act when aided and abetted by a capable subordinate, Captain Alexandre Banza. Banza was the commander of Camp Kassaï, a military base on the northeastern fringes of Bangui. Born in 1932, he had served the French army in Gabon, Morocco, Tunisia, and a number of other colonial locations. Intelligent, ambitious, and unscrupulous, he played a decisive role in Bokassa's bid for power.[22]

By the end of December a strange atmosphere gripped Bangui. Rumours of coups and countercoups were circulating ominously. Several of Dacko's advisers warned him that Bokassa showed signs of mental instability and urged that the army chief be arrested before he could precipitate a crisis.[23] But the president refused to act. On the fateful evening of 31 December 1965, he calmly left the Palais de la Renaissance and went to visit the plantation of Clément Hassen, one of his ministers, southwest of Bangui. He also planned to call on Simon Samba, an Aka Pygmy leader, for a year-end ritual. His departure from the capital took him from the scene of the first blows of the coup.

At 10:30 that same evening Banza gave his officers the orders that set things in motion. Captain Mandaba was to neutralize the security guard at the presidential palace and arrest Dacko. Captain M'Bongo was to occupy a hill overlooking the police camp to discourage opposition from that quarter. And Lieutenant Malendoma was to seize Radio-Bangui and prevent further transmission. Bokassa felt it advisable, however, to deal with Izamo before sending the troops into action. Around 10:30 he phoned the police chief at his headquarters insisting that he come to Camp de Roux to sign some documents that needed attention before the year expired. Izamo, who was in the midst of a celebration with his friends, protested at this inconvenience. But Bokassa stressed the urgency of the matter and promised that it would not take long. The policeman fell for the ruse, jumped in his wife's car, and set out for his rendezvous with destiny. On arriving at the camp he was confronted by Bokassa and Banza, who informed him of the coup in progress and asked if he would support it. He refused. It was a fatal decision. He was immediately overpowered and locked in a cellar.[24]

By midnight the major obstacle between Bokassa and power had been overturned. The plotters now assembled their troops and told them of their true intentions. They said that Dacko had resigned and had given the presidency to Izamo, and since the gendarmerie would now take precedence over the army, they had to strike in order to maintain their position. Most of the men present supported the proposed course of action and those who refused were locked up. The coup could now proceed as planned.[25] At 12:30 the various military units left Camp de Roux to take up their positions around the city. Bokassa and Banza led the entourage in a white Peugeot 404. They met only token resistance and in no time at all the capital was theirs. As soon as the security guards at the Palais de la Renaissance had thrown down their arms, Bokassa and Banza rushed inside to arrest Dacko, only to find that their quarry had eluded them. This unexpected complication brought an already edgy Bokassa to the verge of panic. Had the president been forewarned of the coup? Had he contacted the French, who might at that very moment be sending in paratroopers to prop up the collapsing regime? Soldiers were ordered to scour the countryside until the president was found. There could be no rest until he was detained and had offered his resignation.

Meanwhile, Dacko was following his itinerary as planned, oblivious of the events that were reshaping the course of history all round him. He left the Hassen plantation close to midnight and carried on to Simon Samba's house at Kilomètre 17. There he lingered but an hour, for merrymakers returning from the capital apprised him of the coup and of his alleged death. He decided to return to Bangui, where he hoped to lead resistance with the help of loyal officers and the French. But at the Pétévo Junction, on the city's western edge, he encountered a patrol of soldiers who placed him under arrest. From there he was taken back to the palace, where the architects of his downfall eagerly awaited him. Bokassa embraced the president (he was fond of displays of affection) saying, "I tried to warn you – but now it's too late."

Dacko was then led by his captors to Ngaragba Prison in Bangui's east end, arriving around 2:15 AM. Bokassa immediately ordered the release of all the prisoners – a gesture he believed would enhance his popularity. Otto Sacher, the prison director, at first demurred, arguing that such a rash act would endanger public order. But then he saw Dacko in one of the cars that had brought the visitors. A gun was being pointed at the president's head, and Sacher quickly surmised that Bokassa was the new master of the country. Besides, Banza was now menacing him with a pistol. So the prison doors were flung open and the prisoners poured forth singing the praises of the liberator, Bokassa. It was the first of a series of unexpected and spontaneous acts of clemency that were to characterize the new regime.

From there, Dacko was taken to Camp Kassaï, just up the hill, and at 3:20 AM, with a little prodding from Banza, he signed his resignation as president. He was in a state of shock, weeping uncontrollably and begging that his life be spared. Banza wanted to kill him there and then, but Bokassa would not allow it. There was no question of releasing the former head of state, however, since there was still much to be done in crushing potential sources of opposition. Shortly afterwards, Radio-Bangui announced the fall of the government and the assumption of power by Bokassa and the army. Later in the morning the new leader addressed the nation on the airwaves: "Central Africans! Central Africans! This is Colonel Bokassa speaking to you. Since 3:00 AM this morning your army has taken control of the country. The Dacko government has resigned. The hour of justice is at hand. The bourgeoisie is abolished. A new era of equality among all has begun. Central Africans, wherever you may be, be assured that the army will defend you and your property … Long live the Central African Republic!"[26]

The military remained active throughout what was left of the night, rounding up Dacko's supporters and friends. Ngaragba Prison, which had been conveniently emptied but a few hours before, soon began to fill again. The arrests continued for weeks afterwards. Among those who lost their freedom were sixty-four members of the presidential security guard. Many of them were never to emerge from behind the prison walls. Simon Samba and Jean-Paul Douate, both of whom have made brief appearances on these pages, were on the list of detainees.

There were two individuals whom Bokassa considered particularly dangerous, and he did not rest until they were eliminated: Prosper Mounoumbaye and Jean Izamo. Mounoumbaye, director of the presidential security service, managed to flee the country. But after a few weeks on the other side of the Oubangui River, the Congolese detained him, handing him back on 23 January. At Camp Kassaï, in the presence of Banza, Bokassa, and Dacko, he was beaten and tortured to death. It will be recalled that Izamo, the commander of the gendarmerie, was the first to be arrested on the night of Saint-Sylvestre. Held initially at Camp de Roux, he was transferred to Ngaragba around 10 January. By the end of the month he was dead from brutal mistreatment.[27] Nevertheless, it was a remarkably bloodless coup by some standards. Gunfire between soldiers and policemen on the night of Saint-Sylvestre caused only eight deaths officially, including that of a night watchman at the radio station who defied the army with his bow and arrows.

Dacko himself survived the bloodshed. The fact that he was related to Bokassa was probably in his favour. But it was French intervention on his behalf that likely tipped the scales against his execution. The coup had taken the de Gaulle regime by surprise, but Paris hastened to warn that French aid would be jeopardized should Dacko's life be lost. Consequently, Bokassa, who was anxious to have his government recognized abroad, ensured that his predecessor was kept alive. Throughout January, Dacko was detained in a barrack-room at Camp Kassaï, and for most of the month he was denied visitors and all communication with the outside world. He was also subjected to a harsh diet, which reduced his portly figure. Then, on 1 February, he was taken to Camp de Roux, where he remained isolated except for occasional visits by those whom Bokassa wished to assure that the former president was still alive.[28]

One of the regime's most pressing problems was securing international recognition. A suspicious aloofness is the usual diplomatic response to military officers who grab the reins of power, and Bokassa was not spared this icy treatment. In his early weeks at the helm, he went to great pains in explaining and justifying the coup. His principal argument was that Izamo and his "pro-Chinese accomplices" had been plotting to seize power and that only his timely intervention had saved the country from the red menace. Furthermore, he alleged that the Chinese had been arming a popular revolutionary force, which had been training on land provided by the Pygmies. In support of this claim, he produced a motley collection of weapons supposedly belonging to the insurgents. The evidence was so unconvincing that it merely provoked laughter. Nevertheless, Bokassa clung to his story, and less than a week after the coup – on 6 January 1966 – he expelled the Chinese and broke diplomatic relations with Beijing. His other rationale for the coup was the utter corruption and profligacy of the government he had overthrown.

The first break in the diplomatic ostracism came in March when President François Tombalbaye of neighbouring Tchad came to visit the Central African Republic and met Bokassa at Bouca. Bokassa reciprocated on 2 April when he went to Fort Archambault. These meetings not only resulted in Tchad's recognition of the government in Bangui; as well, the two presidents evidently agreed to assist one another if either became the victim of a coup. "We are no longer alone and we shall never be alone again," exulted *Terre africaine*, the official government newspaper.[29]

Before long, other neighbouring countries followed Tchad's lead in coming to terms with Bokassa's regime. But France, whose approval was critical, remained aloof. Banza was in Paris in May and made some progress in convincing French officials that the coup had been necessary. Thus, the way was paved for Bokassa to pay a private visit to France, and on 7 July he met Prime Minister Georges Pompidou. He took the occasion to describe his government's achievements since coming to power, but although the French were receptive to his overtures, they remained noncommittal and continued to seek assurances for Dacko's safety. Months went by, and Bokassa began to speak of withdrawing from the franc monetary zone. Then, at last, de Gaulle relented and offered an official visit. Thus, on 17 November, Bokassa was received at the Elysée Palace by the man he worshipped. The visit marked complete acceptance. In his joy at this long-awaited moment, Bokassa entertained the press with banter about his love of France and of de Gaulle, "our only hope after God, and for me a father." He returned to his homeland in a state of exhilaration; his regime was legitimate.[30]

Although postcolonial Africa's first coup – in January 1963 in Togo – had provoked international outrage and condemnation, military takeovers had become commonplace by the time Bokassa seized power. Indeed, the events of Saint-Sylvestre came in the midst of a flurry of coups: November 1965, Congo-Kinshasa (Zaïre); December 1965, Dahomey (Benin); January 1966, Upper Volta (Burkina Faso) and Nigeria; February 1966, Ghana. In such a context, Bokassa's admission to the fellowship of legitimate leaders was the only realistic response. But what caused this proliferation of military interventions and the Bokassa coup in particular? Much of the literature on the subject emphasizes the weaknesses in the structure and traditions of political and military life. Yet these same weaknesses existed in the many African states that retained civilian rule. Structural explanations, therefore, are of limited utility and account only for the conditions in which a coup might take place. On the other hand, writers such as Decalo have stressed the peculiar circumstances of each coup and the personal motivation of the various actors.[31] These considerations add an important dimension to our understanding and also provide insight into the unique features of the various military regimes.

In the Central African Republic the structural conditions conducive to a military takeover were certainly present a few years after independence. The death of Boganda had robbed the country of a charismatic leader who might have achieved the status of a Houphouët-Boigny or a Senghor and whose prestige alone might have sufficed to retain civilian rule. Dacko had no hope of filling the national martyr's shoes, and his regime lacked broad support from the outset. His unpopularity grew as the high expectations of independence went unfulfilled and as it became clear that the only beneficiaries of the system were members of the presidential entourage and their kinfolk. The transformation of MESAN into an exploitative arm of the government and the elimination of legitimate opposition groups brought further disillusionment and a decline in political participation.

There were problems on the military side too. The Central African army was poorly trained and poorly disciplined and lacked the professional ethos that might have kept it out of politics. Having played no role in the struggle for independence, its status in the new state was ambiguous at best. The government's undisguised preference for the gendarmerie and the presidential guard only enhanced this ambiguity. In many ways, the army was little more than a series of armed camps owing allegiance only to their leaders – though it had competent and ambitious leaders, especially Banza and Bokassa, and this was ultimately the decisive factor.

Being army chief was never enough to satisfy Bokassa's vanity or his desire for recognition. Garrison duty at Camp de Roux was anything but exciting and afforded few opportunities for personal enrichment. To others went the best villas, the mistresses, and the junkets abroad. Bokassa's only overseas trip proved to be an attempt to get rid of him, and after that he knew he would have to act. The coup of Saint-Sylvestre was therefore a straightforward grab for power, instigated by vanity and ambition on the one hand and by fear of elimination on the other. The political and economic woes of the Dacko regime became the justification for acting and in some respects ensured that the new order would have popular support.

CHAPTER THREE

Papa Bok

At the time he seized power, Colonel Bokassa was relatively unknown in the country except around Bangui and in his home district of Lobaye, but his talent for self-promotion soon made his presence felt in every walk of life. Early on the morning of the coup, Bokassa had himself photographed in his battle fatigues, striking aggressive poses and issuing orders to his men.[1] Later in the day, he met the press at his Camp de Roux office, where his military medals were displayed on the wall. Drawing attention to the decorations, he went on at length about his service record in the French forces. The image making had begun and in a direction that was unmistakable. Here was a man with experience of the world, who had fought in France's wars, earned legitimate honours, and had risen through the ranks to command even Frenchmen. Physical strength, virility, willpower, fearlessness – these were what he was made of.

Fortunately for Bokassa, his predecessor was perceived in very different terms. Dacko was shifty, vacillating, and a lacky of the French, and it was all the easier for the new president to emphasize the contrast and put himself forward as the alternative. The country needed discipline and a strong hand, it was said. It needed Bokassa. In fact, Dacko and Bokassa became identified in the popular mind with two mythical creatures, Tere and Ngakola. Tere was weak but crafty, and Dacko was his reincarnation. Ngakola was strong and cruel, which fitted Bokassa's image.[2]

During the evening of 2 January, President Bokassa formed a new government, which he called the Revolutionary Council. He then abolished the National Assembly, disparaging it as "a lifeless organ no longer representing the people." There would be elections later, he assured the country, and a new assembly would be formed. He also threw out the constitution but promised that another would be drawn up and submitted to the people. Meanwhile, the president would rule by decree.[3] As he dismantled the existing apparatus of state, Bokassa was shrewd enough to allow MESAN, the only political party, to remain untouched. He was unsparing, however, in his attack on its leading officials, whom he described as "a band of thieves and swindlers." These officials were fired, and compulsory membership dues were ended. MESAN's exactions from the public had long been resented, but the party was still revered as part of Boganda's legacy. It was now made to serve the new head of state, and no other political organizations were permitted.

All the while, the public was reassured by frequent pronouncements that the drift towards rule by one man was purely temporary. Bokassa readily declared his intention of relinquishing power as soon as corruption had been rooted out, the Chinese threat removed, and the economy put back on its feet. He confessed that he had little inclination for the political life, preferring that of a soldier, and he spurned the opulence of the Palais de la Renaissance, choosing to live in the spartan accommodation of Camp de Roux. Elections were coming, he promised, and he would have no objection to Dacko entering the lists and resuming the presidency should the people so decide.

There were other favourable omens. Alexandre Banza, as minister of finance, devoted his considerable energy and ability to the formidable task of lifting the country out of bankruptcy. Some other cabinet appointments also were obvious improvements on what had been before. Ange Patassé and Antoine Kezza, both educated in France, were responsible between them for development, public offices, and labour, and progress was made in these areas in the months following the coup. Meanwhile, the campaign against corruption was enjoined with vigour. Bokassa was particularly critical of the civil service, accusing senior officials not only of graft and inertia but of using their offices for rendezvous with their mistresses. Fornication, he alleged, was the major activity in public buildings. A decree in January banned government ministers and senior civil servants from places of "public pleasure" such as dance halls and bars. Attendance at cinemas was permitted, but only in the line of duty. This "wake-up" crusade against "dopey officials" was not all fanciful rhetoric; the mayor of Bangui and his secretary general were banished to the countryside when they failed to live up to the new expectations.

The apparently vigorous pace of reform was often paraded before the world as justification for the seizure of power. Bokassa claimed that the old regime had been about to plunge the country "into a

bottomless abyss." His coup, he said, had saved it from the threatened calamity; it had been nothing less than "a miracle" achieved in
the memory of Boganda. (Invoking the name of the national hero
was always a clever move and Bokassa never hesitated to use this
ploy.) Having rescued his people, he now proposed to set them to
work. A decree of the Revolutionary Council ordered all men and
women between the ages of eighteen to fifty-five to provide proof
that they were working for a living. Idleness would henceforth be
punished by fines or imprisonment.

A flurry of decrees sought to regulate the people's lives in ways
never dreamed of before. Bokassa seemed most concerned to project
a modern image of his country to foreigners, and he therefore
attempted to restrict scenes of poverty and nudity, which he felt fostered a primitive stereotype. Begging was banned, tom-tom playing
was allowed only at night and on weekends, and a morality brigade
was formed in Bangui to keep a vigilant eye on bars and dance halls.[4]
There were moves to advance the status of women which drew the
support of the powerful Union des femmes centrafricaines. A decree
abolishing polygamy, for instance, was loudly applauded by Madame
Franck, president of the union. Considering Bokassa's adventure-
some relations with women, there was an undeniable irony in this
particular law. Another decree provided punishment for parents who
interfered with the educational opportunities of their daughters.
Dowries were outlawed and so was female circumcision.[5]

The list of positive achievements goes on. Bangui was one of the
few African capitals without a system of public transport; Bokassa
moved to remedy this embarrassment to national pride by ordering
a fleet of buses from France. The president counted music among his
many enthusiasms, and he subsidized the establishment of two
national orchestras – Centrafricain Jazz and Vibro-Succès; a load of
instruments for the ensembles was imported from Paris.[6] In order to
cultivate the support of the Catholic missions, whose influence in the
country was considerable, the new leader made frequent appearances
in church, sometimes demonstrating an ostentatious piousness in his
prayers before the Virgin Mary's statue. Indeed, dramatic gestures
became an enduring characteristic of the presidential style. One of his
earliest official visits was to Bangui Hospital, where he announced
that he was donating his first month's salary to its operations.

To all appearances, a regime had come into being that was driven
by reforming zeal. Morality, austerity, honesty, and hard work were
the new values of public life. The disappointments of independence
would now be overturned and Boganda's dream for his people realized. But little came of all the posturing. Hopes of a better tomorrow

quickly foundered as the true nature of the "revolutionary" government revealed itself. Bokassa's attacks on privilege and on the "bourgeoisie" turned out to be slogans of convenience. The president was
fully aware that he would need the support of powerful interests to
maintain his position and pursue his ambition. He was ready to
chastise the public service and perhaps purge it of hostile elements,
but he was not prepared to alienate it completely. Consequently, a
10 per cent salary cut which Dacko had introduced before his downfall was restored. Meanwhile, the army had to be rewarded for its
role in toppling the *ancien régime*. There were salary increases, promotions, and decorations all round. Bokassa became a general and
Banza rose from captain to lieutenant-colonel. The austerity program
began to lose some of its momentum.

Although the president's zeal for reform was quickly spent, it continued to manifest itself in unpredictable outbursts until the very end
of his days in power. His enthusiasm for democracy, on the other
hand, died an early death and, once buried, never reappeared. In the
days following the coup there was much talk of elections and con-
stitutions, but this was heard less and less as the weeks went by.
Bokassa had at long last the one thing he had always wanted –
power, and the prestige and recognition that went with it. He
enjoyed it immensely and believed it was the fulfilment of his destiny. He had little inclination either to lose it or to share it with
others.

Addressing a large crowd at Boganda Stadium early in February,
Bokassa announced that he would stay at the helm a while longer
"for better or worse" in response to numerous messages of support
from around the country. His early speeches were often in Sango and
were well attended. Women were particularly captivated by his
words, and many came forward to wipe the sweat from his brow
with their dresses. In October he admitted his intention of remaining
indefinitely as the "nation's guide" and made the following pro-
nouncement: "I am everywhere and nowhere. I see nothing yet I see
all. I listen to nothing and hear everything. Such is the role of a head
of state." Soon his image began to appear on office walls, billboards,
т-shirts, and the covers of school exercise books. Public buildings
and streets were renamed in his honour.[7] Perhaps there was some
truth to his assertion that he was everywhere.

Bokassa was developing a style of his own. After the initial period
of austerity, his receptions became lavish affairs at which champagne flowed and bands pounded out lively African rhythms. Traditional chiefs were invited and mingled with diplomats and cabinet
ministers – something that had rarely happened in Dacko's day.[8] The

president was a generous host and urged his guests to eat and drink as much as he did himself. His consumption of food and alcohol was enormous, and it served to cultivate the legend that he could indulge all the human appetites to excess without apparent ill effect.

The cult of personality and the blandishments against corruption initially shielded the true heart of the new order from the outside world. Growing numbers of citizens, however, were receiving a first-hand acquaintance with its unsavoury side and nowhere more so than within the grim walls of Ngaragba Prison. This place of confinement was to emerge as one of the most sinister instruments of the Bokassa regime. Its very name came to be whispered in hushed tones; it was synonymous with death. Known locally as *le trou du diable* ("the devil's hole"), the prison has a sombre appearance even from the outside. Imposing concrete walls surround a central courtyard 100 metres square containing the various cell blocks and offices. In Bokassa's day, common criminals as well as political prisoners were held there, the former on the east side, the latter on the west. A women's block, Porte Rouge, was in the southeast corner. Political detainees were kept in three buildings. The first of these, Birao, named after the remote northern town notorious for its heat, featured fourteen "disciplinary" cells opposite one another. The second, l'Isolement, had the same number of cells but was for those condemned to death. Before execution, prisoners often spent some time in the third building, Safari. Death row, as it was known, had but two small adjacent cells measuring 2.5 by 3.0 metres each. Tomblike concrete structures, they were designed to hold one person each but usually accommodated three or four. Safari was named after the nearby luxury hotel.

Prison life has little to commend it, but it can be made considerably better or worse by the degree of compassion shown by those in charge. Ngaragba was unfortunate in its choice of such men, for neither its guards nor administrators were conspicuous for their humanity, though there were some exceptions in the case of the guards. There were two directors of the prison during the years of Bokassa's rule: Otto Sacher and Edouard Ngbongo. Sacher was a native of Prague. An adventurer and soldier of fortune, he had served in the French Foreign Legion during the Second World War, and in 1947 he settled in Oubangui-Chari, becoming a planter in the Lobaye district. Later, in 1960, he was appointed director of Ngaragba, and he is said to have trained the guards in torture techniques. He remained in charge until December 1971, when he was suddenly arrested following the escape of a condemned man. He was replaced by Ngbongo, a M'Baka and a loyal supporter of the president. Then in 1972, on 14 July, the French national festival, Bokassa, in one of his unpredictable acts of clemency, liberated Sacher and made him a technical adviser to Ngbongo. One more name must be mentioned in association with Ngaragba, that of Mokoa. In July 1976 Bokassa created a special security force, the Third Company, to protect the jail's administrative building and to move prisoners about on work gangs. This force, recruited mainly in Lobaye, was headed by Joseph Mokoa, a M'Baka from the village of Boubangui who exhibited the appropriate ruthlessness and cruelty for the job.

Before detainees were sent to Ngaragba, they were usually held in police commissariats for questioning. If they were from wealthy families, this "interrogation" might go on for weeks. Meanwhile, officials preyed on the prisoner's relatives, relieving them of money and goods. Sometimes these *cadeaux* secured the prisoner's release; often they did not. On arrival in Ngaragba, prisoners had their heads shaved, the first of several humiliations. Then they were stripped of all their possessions, including their clothes, which were divided among the guards, and they were issued with prison garb – striped shorts and shirt. All prisoners were not treated equally. Much depended on one's social standing, ethnic affiliation, and the nature of one's crime. Beatings were common, but someone of high status who was guilty of a minor offence might get off lightly, for the guards knew that such a person, on release, would be in a position to avenge mistreatment. Besides, a wealthy prisoner's family could be taken advantage of while their relative was in prison.

In so far as one can generalize, common criminals were treated better than their political counterparts. They were often released from their cells for light work, such as cleaning Bokassa's villas, and they did odd jobs around the prison yard – even, on occasion guarding the political prisoners, who were never allowed out of their chains. Even so, much depended on the offence that had landed them there in the first place. The murder of women was considered particularly odious in Centrafrique, and those guilty of such a crime were likely to rot in their cells. Or they might suffer swift retribution. On 6 June (Mothers' Day) 1971, Bokassa suddenly ordered the execution of all those guilty of raping or killing women. At the same time all female prisoners were released.[9]

It was the political prisoners, especially those accused of threatening the president in some way, who bore the brunt of the cruelty that was Ngaragba. They were the ones marked out for the beatings, tortures, starvation diets, and firing squads. The daily existence for these prisoners alternated between terror and relief. Tension rose in the afternoon as the prison truck arrived in the courtyard, sometimes disgorging new detainees for their rendezvous with *justice à la Bokassa*. Observers of the chilling scene knew that when the truck left late at night, it might well be carrying corpses for burial on the outside – perhaps their own. The firing squad usually performed its duty around 8 PM, so the minutes preceding that hour were those of greatest nervousness. With every movement of the guards a ripple of unease spread through the cells. Whose turn would it be this time? By 10 PM the worst danger was past and the inmates settled down for another night as best they could in the dreary squalor of their cells.

The executioner's bullet was but one of many menaces facing those trapped behind the prison walls. Malnutrition was equally hazardous. In normal circumstances, if indeed such a term can be used, miserable meals were served at noon and at 5 PM – a mouthful of water, a helping of manioc, and a morsel of banana. Meat was rarely served, and when it was it was often rotten. The paltry portions were never adequate and sometimes were drastically reduced or even suspended entirely. Many perished from starvation or succumbed to the ravages of diseases brought on by dietary deficiency. Then there were the ever-present mosquitoes and rats – and little protection from the annoyances of either.

Escapes were rare – the guards saw to that. They knew that their jobs, indeed their very lives, depended on it. There were grim reminders of what could happen if they failed in this regard. The fate of Fidèle Mzafio is a case in point. In February 1975 a prisoner whom Mzafio was escorting to the Palais de la Renaissance managed to get away in the marketplace. Bokassa was incensed to find the guard arriving empty-handed and beat him so ferociously that he was barely alive when he was returned to the prison. He died shortly afterwards. With examples like this to inspire them, it is no wonder that the guards were merciless to prisoners caught in the act of escaping. Typical was the fate of Guillaume Kondotene, who in December 1976 slipped away from a work brigade labouring outside the prison. When he was recaptured a little later, the guards turned on him, pounding him savagely, especially in the genitals. He was cast into his cell in the throes of agony, only to be hauled out later by Mokoa for another beating. This time he did not survive.

Prisoners were without rights, and they knew it. Their lives hung by a fragile thread, controlled not only by the head of state but also by his prison guards. Survival was possible, but it depended on meekly submitting to the rules of the institution – and, most of all, on good luck. The inmates passed the time marking the days on crude calendars which they scrawled on the walls with pieces of charcoal. Conversation helped, as did the sending of messages from cell to cell, and sometimes there was news from the outside as new prisoners came in. While morale was difficult to sustain in such inhuman conditions, there was one glimmer of hope to prevent total despair: it was always possible to benefit from one of Bokassa's unpredictable outbursts of magnanimity. This is what happened on 24 June 1972 when the president, exultant over a successful trip to Paris, issued a general amnesty. Ngaragba's gates were flung open, and the haggard, dazed figures limped to freedom, incredulous at their good fortune.[10]

It has been necesssary to dwell at some length on the harsh realities of Ngaragba, since the prison played such a vital role in Bokassa's political machinations. Within hours of seizing power he was harnessing it to his service, and it remained the scourge of his enemies until the moment of his downfall. But what of the prisoners taken during the coup of Saint-Sylvestre? For how long did they languish in jail merely because of their association with the previous government? It was not until 13 October 1969 – almost four years later – that some of them were released. Simon Samba, who was seriously ill, was among those liberated at that time. Others were given their freedom on 1 January 1970 and were brought to see the president. This group included Michel Adama-Tamboux, former president of the National Assembly, whom Bokassa barely recognized with his wild dishevelled hair and withered skeletal body.

Although Dacko was in many ways more fortunate than his associates, he too had his spell in purgatory. He remained in detention at Camp de Roux, where his diet was often inadequate. In August 1967 he went on hunger strike (an odd thing to do in the circumstances) to protest his treatment. The French government and some African heads of state expressed concern for his welfare, and he was visited by the French military attaché, to whom he complained of having had nothing to read for the best part of two years – a great deprivation for a former teacher. He was allowed some books as a result, but apart from this there was little improvement. The months of dreary isolation dragged on. A year passed and then another. Then, in June 1969, Dacko took a step that almost cost him his life: he wrote to the Chinese ambassador in Brazzaville requesting financial assistance for his family. By some quirk of misfortune, the message was intercepted and fell into Bokassa's hands. The president was elated. Here was the pretext he had long sought to rid himself of a man who might still become a rallying point for opposition to his regime. Was this not proof of the Chinese intrigue with which he had justified his coup?

Dacko was charged with threatening state security and was transferred to Ngaragba. He was by now a worried man, believing that
Bokassa had a plausible excuse to dispose of him; and with de Gaulle
out of power in France, he could no longer count on protection from
that quarter. It looked hopeless for the former president – but only
temporarily. Judge Albert Kouda managed to persuade Bokassa that
the charges were based on spurious evidence and would never lead
to conviction in a fair trial. On the other hand, arbitrary execution
would probably cause an international outcry. On 14 July (the French
national holiday often brought surprises) Bokassa dropped the
charges. Dacko, by now weak and thin, was taken from Ngaragba
and brought to stay at the Palais de la Renaissance until his physical
condition improved. Once in better health, he was sent to live "in
retirement" in Mokinda, Lobaye, where he was kept under close
surveillance by a contingent of police and military personnel.[11]

Those who seize power from behind the barrel of a gun must be
ever vigilant lest they lose it in like manner. There can be no peace,
for there is always the fear of sudden arrest or the assassin's bullet.
Above all, potential rivals must be identified and eliminated. Dacko
and his supporters represented a clear threat to the "revolutionary"
regime following the coup, and it was for this reason that they were
either killed or locked away. Yet Bokassa soon realized that the greatest danger came not from the Dacko clique but from within his own
entourage. The man he feared most, and with good reason, was Lieutenant Alexandre Banza, the driving force behind the Saint-Sylvestre
coup.

It will be recalled that Banza had been appointed minister of
finance in the new government and had put his intelligence and
organizational skills to good use. On a visit to Europe, where the
coup had been badly received, he made a good impression on journalists and politicians. The young minister seemed resolute and
determined and had the appearance of a natural leader. Many
believed that he would not consent for long to play second fiddle to
a man he considered a bit of a buffoon. This proved to be true.
Relations between Bokassa and Banza began to deteriorate openly
during 1967. The budget was a major source of contention. The
finance minister was firmly opposed to government extravagance,
while the president was beginning to reveal his inclination for luxury
and indulgence. Sensing his rival's yearning for power, Bokassa took
the precaution of running the country from the comparative safety
of Camp de Roux. There he felt secure, surrounded by his soldiers
and with a pistol at the ready whenever Banza came to visit. A
violent showdown never materialized at these meetings, but the two

men continued to jockey for position, awaiting the right moment to strike.

Banza tried to develop a wide base of support in the army, spending as much time as possible in the company of soldiers. Bokassa could see what was happening and sent the military units most friendly to his rival far from Bangui in small detachments on the pretext of frontier duty. He kept soldiers he could rely on in the capital and ensured that weapons and ammunition were issued only to the most loyal troops. As an additional precaution, he made a special trip to Paris in September 1967 where he begged for protection by French troops. On 10 November a contingent of eighty paratroopers arrived discreetly in Bangui. Their ostensible role was to protect Sudanese Zande refugees who had crossed the border in the east.[12]

On 13 April 1968 Bokassa announced another of his frequent cabinet shuffles. Banza found himself demoted to the Health portfolio but was allowed to retain his standing as minister of state. He knew that he was slowly being pried away from the centre of power. Nonetheless, he continued to make his views known in the Council of Ministers. He alone had the courage to disagree with the president. Early in 1969 he made a number of critical remarks about the management of the economy and about Bokassa personally, and it became clear to all that the long-awaited confrontation could not be far off. Bokassa reacted a few weeks later, abolishing the rank of minister of state. This was in effect another demotion for Banza, who now began to avoid the Council of Ministers and became all the more determined to launch a coup. At the beginning of April, Banza confided his plans to Lieutenant Jean-Claude Mandaba, the officer commanding Camp Kassaï, whom he believed would offer support. Mandaba appeared to agree, but his loyalties lay elsewhere. When Banza telephoned his fellow conspirators on 9 April to say that they would move the next day at nightfall, Mandaba tipped off Bokassa. Precautions were taken and the president waited for his rival to fall into the trap.

The following afternoon Banza arrived at Camp Kassaï with plans for the coup in his pocket. With the camp commander and his men behind him, he hoped to occupy the usual strategic points in the capital – the airport, radio, palace, and so forth. But as he stepped from his car, Mandaba and a couple of soldiers grabbed him. So fiercely did he struggle to escape that the soldiers had to break one of his arms before overpowering him. The ambushers then tied him up, stuffed him in the trunk of a Mercedes, and took him to meet the man he had sought to depose. At the time, Bokassa was staying at Berengo, eighty kilometres southwest of Bangui. He had built a house there, not far from his native village of Boubangui, and was beginning to farm a stretch of land that had once been worked by his grandfather. He was jubilant at the sight of his former companion-in-arms being brought to him in chains. Banza was in poor shape after the journey to Berengo, but his torments were only beginning. Bokassa launched the interrogation by beating the prisoner almost senseless with his ever-present walking stick.

Bokassa wanted to kill Banza there and then and dispose of the body unceremoniously, but Mandaba advised a trial, if only for the sake of appearances, and his counsel prevailed. The military tribunal began its deliberations at Camp de Roux on 12 April. Banza, weak and exhausted from beatings and torture, presented his case with as much dignity as he could muster. He did not deny his intention of overthrowing the government but argued that he had not intended to kill the president. Had he succeeded, he would simply have sent Bokassa to some unspecified destination. This was confirmed by the plans found in his pocket, but it mattered little. Banza was a dead man, and he knew it. The inevitable death sentence was pronounced, and he was led to a field behind Camp Kassaï where a firing squad awaited him. There are many conflicting accounts of his last moments, but one thing is certain: he faced death bravely. He was buried in an unmarked grave on the spot where he fell.

On the evening of the execution, Banza's mistress, Julienne Kombo, entered the Palais de la Renaissance crying and lamenting, her breasts bare in mourning. She was hoping to avenge her lover's death. Instead, she was arrested and was jailed until the general amnesty of 24 June 1972. Banza's wife and nine children were sent to live in Birao, a remote northern spot, where they were kept under close surveillance. They were not permitted to return to Bangui until 6 June 1971. While in the north, the children were denied an education. Banza's father was thrown in jail, where he died of hunger and exhaustion on 24 April 1970. Banza had two younger brothers, Beouane and Goboulo, who also came to a sorry end. They were dismissed from the gendarmerie in July and, after a spell in Birao, were imprisoned in Ngaragba. In August 1971 they were driven away from the prison and were never seen again.[13] The Banza affair showed that Bokassa was prepared not only to eliminate dangerous rivals but also to deal ruthlessly with their families and friends. Casting a wide net of terror made revenge less probable and served as a warning to would-be conspirators and assassins.

Long before Banza was eliminated, Bokassa had been busily concentrating power in his own hands. Holding down numerous ministerial portfolios was one of his strategies. Right from the start, he held those of National Defence, Justice, and the Interior. In 1968 he added Information; in 1970, Agriculture, Health, and Population; in 1971, Civil and Military Aviation; and in 1973, Public Service and Social Security. The pattern of accumulation continued until the empire came into being. Most governments function by dividing up responsibilities, but not Bokassa's. He trusted few people beyond those of his immediate family and *ethnie*. But trying to keep an eye on everything meant that he often wasted time dealing with trivial matters while major issues were neglected. Things were especially bad when he was abroad, an increasingly frequent occurrence in the 1970s. Decisions could not be made, and the entire government ground to a halt.

Things were better when the president was in town, but not noticeably so. His rule became more and more arbitrary and unpredictable, especially after the fall of Banza. An ordinance of 24 April 1970 gave Bokassa complete control over promotion and demotion in the army. It was suddenly a free-for-all. Second Lieutenant François Bozize, for example, instantly became a general after he hit a Frenchman who was showing disrespect for the president. Merit now counted for nothing. All that mattered was unswerving loyalty to the ruler. In such a system morale, discipline, and *esprit de corps* were rapidly undermined. It was the same in civilian life. Visiting a large business one evening, Bokassa found that only the janitor was on duty. He immediately appointed him director of the firm. In another case, Bokassa was so pleased with the services of a nurse that he promoted her to doctor.

The absence of an assembly and rule by presidential decree created a general climate of uncertainty. Nobody knew what was permitted and what was not. Edicts were announced on the radio, and news of them spread among the populace through the network of rumour and gossip. The reliance on hearsay meant that fantastic stories were always circulating – and widely believed. There could be no concept of law or human rights in these circumstances. Everything depended on the will or impulse of the ruler, whose views were so fickle that almost anything might be prohibited or allowed.[14]

With Banza out of the way, the coast was clear for Bokassa not only to exercise complete power but to enjoy its accoutrements to the full. No more did he have to endure the penny-pinching admonitions of his erstwhile rival; no more did he have to direct his government from a military camp. He could now surround himself with sycophants, who were all too willing to nurture his growing delusions of grandeur. And he could spend money with abandon on whatever he wished, pillaging the national coffers as the need arose.

He revelled in new titles too. On 4 March 1972 the MESAN congress voted to declare Bokassa, who was already a two-star general, "President for Life of the Republic." On 15 May 1974 he became "Marshal of the Republic," a title that had ominous echoes of the Napoleonic era. With the new status came a new uniform – a blue military outfit adorned with generous trimmings of gold braid. It was modelled on that of Marshal Ney, one of Bonaparte's officers. A ceremonial baton encrusted with diamonds costing 500,000 francs went with the uniform.[15]

In his monologues of self-praise, Marshal Bokassa referred to himself as "the most decorated black soldier in the French army." It was no secret that he loved decorations as much as titles. Much has been made of this, but it should be remembered that at least some of his medals were acquired legitimately in combat with the French forces. The following were all awarded before his accession to power: the Légion d'honneur, Médaille militaire, Croix de guerre, Médaille des combattants de la résistance, and Médaille des engagés volontaires, as well as the Star of Benin (for service in the colonial army) and commemorative medals for the Second World War and Indochina. In addition, after assuming the presidency, a deluge of Central African awards had come his way: Grand maître of the Ordre national du Mérite centrafricain and of the Ordre de l'Opération Bokassa; and Commandeur of Palmes académiques, Mérite agricole, Mérite postal, Mérite industriel et artisanal, travail, and Mérite militaire. On visits abroad he was decorated by at least twenty-five countries, including France, Japan, and the Soviet Union.[16] To add to his collection, he often went shopping at Maison Arthus Bertrand at place Saint-Germain-des-Prés in Paris, an establishment specializing in military laurels and expensive jewellery.

In fairness to Bokassa, he probably acquired his fondness for medals from the French, who tend to hand them out for reasons that people elsewhere might find curious. For example, long-serving French firemen earn the Médaille d'honneur des sapeurs pompiers, while productive fishermen and farmers are eligible, respectively, for the Ordre du Mérite maritime and the Ordre du Mérite agricole. However, it was not so much Bokassa's penchant for accumulating medals that attracted attention as his habit of wearing the entire collection spread over the front of his jacket on every possible public occasion. Ordinary jackets would have sagged under the weight, so Bokassa had his reinforced to support all the brass.

The Bokassa style was unquestionably unique, even though comparisons might be made with others who wielded personal power. The marshal preferred to think of himself as father of the nation rather than head of state in the conventional sense.[17] As a father, he could be severe or lenient, even indulgent, as his mood dictated. He encouraged his ministers to address him as Papa, and they did. In his penchant for rule according to arbitrary whim and impulse, Papa Bok had much in common with his Haïtian contemporary, Papa Doc Duvalier.

The president-for-life, marshal, and papa was fond of carrying an ebony walking stick topped with an ivory knob. It helped disguise the limp that appeared during his occasional bouts of gout, but he claimed that it represented justice – the stern justice of a father towards his children. This was the infamous *canne de justice* with which he had assaulted Banza on the night of the abortive coup. It was not only his enemies, real or perceived, who found themselves at its receiving end. Anyone who displeased him was at risk. Presidential servants and chauffeurs were in an especially vulnerable position, being within ready striking distance of the cane. Paulin Yomboda, Bokassa's valet between 1972 and 1976, recalled frequent floggings in the course of his duties. In 1973, for instance, he was soundly beaten for not ironing a dress belonging to "the Lebanese," one of the president's wives.

The cane, Ngaragba, and the firing squad were the three principal instruments of retribution awaiting those who stepped out of line. Any combination of the three was possible. It was rare to experience imprisonment without physical abuse. When the terrors of his "justice" system failed to compel law-abiding and subservient behaviour, Bokassa proved adept at thinking up innovative deterrents. For example, in July 1972 he introduced a punishment that provoked international condemnation. Three men had been caught stealing tires from the parking lot of the Palais de la Renaissance, and the president (who until then had shown little interest in Islam) remembered that the Koran prescribed the amputation of thieves' hands. He liked the idea but decided to implement his own unique variation on the theme; he ordered his security guards to cut off the criminals' ears using scissors and knives.

Pleased with this novel form of penance, Bokassa decided to give it statutory sanction. This did not take long in a country without a national assembly and in which laws were simply decrees signed by the president as he saw fit. Ordinance 72.058 of 29 July 1972 set out the following punishments for those caught in the act of theft:

1 One ear amputated for a first offence
2 The other ear cut off for a second offence
3 Loss of the right hand for a third

Surgeons were supposed to carry out the "operations" within twenty-four hours of sentencing. Moreover, robbers unable to plead extenuating circumstances were to receive an additional five-year prison term.

Two days after these echoes of Islamic law entered the statute books, Bokassa, accompanied by some of his ministers, turned up at Ngaragba. The prison held forty-six thieves who already had had their ears sheared in accordance with the recent edict. These unfortunates were now dragged from their cells and assembled in the courtyard, where Papa Bok rebuked them severely for their crimes. He then commanded the prison guards to beat the thieves to death with their nightsticks. One cabinet minister was so repulsed by the bloody spectacle that he sought refuge in his car. When Bokassa called a halt after five minutes, three of the prisoners were already dead. The next morning he ordered the survivors to be displayed on a platform at place de la République, and the public was invited to promenade past on a tour of inspection. The same grisly scene was repeated at Kilomètre 5.[18] On learning of the atrocity, Kurt Waldheim, secretary general of the United Nations, protested strongly, but Bokassa dismissed him as "a pimp, a colonialist and an imperialist." A few days later a dozen more thieves had their ears removed under the president's watchful gaze. This time the international outcry was so virulent that the practice was abandoned. The world was at last beginning to take notice of the obscure little country and its capricious ruler.[19]

In the *kodros*, the popular residential districts that surround Bangui's modern core, a criminal element known as *godobé* preyed on the better off and the unwary. Bokassa's harsh measures – spontaneous, sporadic, and unpredictable – failed to purge them of their criminal inclinations. Survival in the *kodros* simply became a little more uncertain than usual. For many, it was indeed uncertain. Those with the security of a government job could afford to live within the boundaries of the ill-defined legal system, but the very nature of their employment brought its own hazards. The closer one was to the president, the greater the perils as well as the privileges. It did not pay to become prominent, popular, or successful, for it was not just Bokassa's fickle temperament that gave grounds for alarm; there was also his growing paranoia – his morbid fear of being overthrown. He had informers everywhere, keeping an eye on those who might aspire to replace him, and he encouraged his associates to betray their colleagues if they had word of a conspiracy. A chance remark here, a suspicious move there, brought many a promising career to an abrupt end. The favourite of yesterday, showered with honours and fêted lavishly, could suddenly become the pariah of today and the corpse, horribly mutilated, of tomorrow.

Serving in the frequently shuffled Council of Ministers was a risky occupation. The lucky ones fled the country when a fall from grace seemed imminent; the foolhardy waited until it was too late. Only two ministers managed to stay in office for the duration of the regime – Louis Alazoula and André Magalé – though in Magalé's case there were interruptions while he filled other posts. Ange Patassé also had a lengthy ministerial career – from the Saint-Sylvestre coup until 29 March 1978 when he went to France for medical treatment. Most other appointments were brief, and many ended in tragedy. Lamine Marcelin, for example, lasted only a few months as minister of external trade. When the price of beer rose –which irritated Bokassa – Marcelin was fired and placed under house arrest.[20]

Finding a ministerial career that ended in tragedy is not difficult, but the fall of Auguste M'Bongo is a good example because it was recalled many years later to Bokassa's great discomfort. In 1973 M'Bongo was minister of public works and a powerful member of the cabinet. He was a M'Baka and had once been close to the president, but with the passing of time they had grown apart. M'Bongo's arrogance and his tendency to flaunt his privileges apparently annoyed Bokassa, who felt that such behaviour was his own exclusive prerogative. Ultimately, however, M'Bongo had one fatally dangerous habit: he liked to speak his mind and none too discreetly. After a couple of insulting remarks about the man at the top, his days were numbered. He was arrested on 12 April 1973 and imprisoned in M'Baïki. Deprived of adequate nourishment, his health deteriorated as the months went by. Later he was transferred to Ngaragba, where the ill-treatment continued. He died in February 1974.[21]

Ambitious officers in the army and gendarmerie were also playing a dangerous game. After all, it was from these quarters that a coup was most likely to come. Plotting undoubtedly took place among the officer corps, but probably not with the frequency that Bokassa suspected. The president-for-life was taking no chances, however, and he kept the officers off guard by means of frequent promotions, demotions, and reassignments of duty. It would be tedious to recount all the details of these conspiracies, real or imagined, but the case of Martin Lingoupou deserves to be told if only by way of illustration. Lingoupou was appointed commander of the gendarmerie in 1966, on completing his military training in France. He acquitted himself well on the job, transforming the police into a disciplined and effective force. Bokassa at first admired his competence but later began to resent his popularity and came to perceive him as a dangerous rival.

Following his usual tactics, he relieved Lingoupou of his command at the end of August 1974 – a humiliating disgrace for the officer. This done, the president-for-life left for a lengthy visit to Europe. A little later, Lingoupou heard that a coup was being planned by a cabal of high-placed officers and ministers and that he, as well as Bokassa, were its intended victims. He gave some consideration to launching a pre-emptive coup of his own and was incautious enough to share his thoughts with associates. Neither coup in fact took place, and when Bokassa returned on 9 November he conducted an inquiry into the affairs. Lingoupou was named the principal conspirator, in spite of his protests of innocence, and was sentenced to ten years imprisonment. A few weeks of Ngaragba's grim hospitality followed and then, probably on the 27 December, he was taken away to join the swelling ranks of the disappeared.

Lingoupou's family, as was the custom, did not escape unscathed. His wife, a French national, was deported to her homeland, along with their five children – after a brief sojourn as guests of the state. His mother and pregnant mistress found themselves sharing a cell in Ngaragba's l'Isolement block. The mistress, Lucienne Sokpawo, gave birth to a daughter while in prison and was released two years later during the imperial amnesty. The mother, Monique Imalé, was not so fortunate. She was known as "the monkey woman" and had a formidable reputation as a sorceress. It was widely believed that she had four breasts – the alleged source of her magical powers. Although Bokassa had not personally verified her anatomical anomaly, he feared her prowess in the black arts and dared not release her lest she avenge the death of her son. She was murdered on 7 January 1977.[22]

Monique Imalé's multiple breasts raise the interesting question of sorcery in this part of Africa. Among the M'Baka and other Bantu peoples along the Oubangui River there are secret societies of women who practise magical rituals from which men are excluded. It is said that if, by chance, men discover the secrets of these rites, they fall ill, victims of an evil spirit that possesses them and gnaws away at their insides. This belief in the magic powers of women keeps men from being too abusive to their wives. Catherine M'Balanga, Bokassa's sister, was regarded as one of the most powerful practitioners of sorcery in Centrafrique. She was a trusted confidante of her brother, connecting him to the women's occult network, and was widely feared throughout the land.[23]

Bokassa himself, despite his missionary education and the formative decades spent abroad, seemed to believe in the occult. More important, he believed that he could use it for his own advantage.

He encouraged the notion that he was a formidable sorcerer in his own right, that the women's societies were behind him, and that secret rituals, perhaps involving cannibalism, had given him extraordinary powers. It was believed that he could be in several places at once, a notion that caused understandable unease. The ability to read people's minds was another of his alleged powers. It sometimes happened that underlings who had engaged in mischief fell spontaneously on their knees in his presence confessing their crimes; they thought he could read their minds. Most valuable of all, perhaps, was the belief that he was invulnerable to gunfire. It was said that a bullet aimed at Bokassa's head would turn in mid-air and kill the would-be assassin.[24]

Within a few years of his coup, Bokassa had vanquished his main rivals and had concentrated power in his own hands. He did not have to seek re-election, and there were no constitutional restraints on his authority. With loyal kinsmen in key security positions and an established network of espionage and terror, opposition was subdued and appeared to be futile. Politics took on the form of personal rule. The medals, titles, ubiquitous images, and claims to occult powers fostered a cult of personality and semi-divine identification between state and ruler. Bokassa was the stern yet benevolent father of the nation whose will had to be obeyed. He was Papa Bok.

CHAPTER FOUR

Extended Family

I also liked women and I had many of them. There is an Iranian proverb (before Khomeini), to which I subscribe completely, which says, "If God didn't like beautiful women, he would not have created them."

Jean-Bedel Bokassa[1]

Bokassa loved women, loved to show off his latest conquest, and made no secret of his successes. The women provided sensual pleasure, but they also served to enhance his image. They symbolized his power and domination. His adventures with the opposite sex began in his French army days. In accordance with military custom, most of his relationships were short-lived hit-and-run affairs. The soldiery considered women to be part of the spoils of war, and Bokassa was not one to flout the tradition. But while such philandering was all very fine in coping with the excesses of youthful vigour, a man with dynastic ambitions needed something more stable – he needed a wife and an heir. Bokassa was taking no chances. During his careers as soldier and head of state he had seventeen wives in all. Some of these marriages were brief tempestuous affairs that ended in divorce, but after the Saint-Sylvestre coup there were at least a half-dozen wives who were kept in luxury in various villas awaiting their master's attention.

Bokassa's first wife was a Belgian, whom he married in the euphoria of victory following the Second World War. They were divorced after a short period. In the late 1940s, while stationed briefly in Brazzaville, he married Marguerite Green, a woman of mixed English and Angolan background. She had just given birth to their son when he left for France en route to Indochina. In 1959 she died in an accident. In Saigon, as noted earlier, Bokassa married N'guyen-Thi-Hué in a traditional Vietnamese ceremony, and a daughter was born of the union. He abandoned them when he sailed for Europe. Nonetheless, he was greatly enamoured of Vietnamese women and when stationed in Brazzaville once more in the late 1950s, he met and married another of that nationality, Jacqueline Nguyen-Thin-Than. The marriage ended in divorce in 1961. After the break-up the ex-wife remarried and was reported to be living in Montpellier in the early 1980s. In March 1962, now stationed in Bangui, Bokassa married seventeen-year-old Astrid Elizabeth Van Erpe, who came of a Franco-Belgian family that was involved in Centrafrique's unsavoury ivory trade. That, too, ended in a quick divorce.[2]

By the early 1960s Bokassa was already in his forties and had decided to make a permanent home and career in his native Centrafrique. It was time to look for a wife who would give him a stable family life and would help him create the dynasty of which he already dreamed. One day in 1962, as he was cruising the streets of Bangui in his car, he spotted the perfect candidate. She was a student at Lycée Pie XII and was walking home from school. Although she was only thirteen, she was already tall and stunningly beautiful. The gallant soldier was determined to make her aquaintance. He loitered around the school for a few days until he managed to strike up a conversation. Her name was Catherine Denguiade, and she was flattered by the attentions of the middle-aged suitor in the smart military uniform. An introduction to her parents followed, and Bokassa discovered that she was a M'Baka and a distant cousin. Her mother came from Tchad and Catherine herself had been born in that country, in Fort Archambault (Sarh today) in 1949. In spite of the distant family connection, the girl's father would not hear of the marriage. Her mother, on the other hand, was not opposed to it. Bokassa was not yet in a position to have his way regardless of parental views, but he did not give up. He continued to woo, flatter, and cajole until the father gave in, and in June 1965 the happy couple tied the knot. Catherine was a mere sixteen. Her husband was forty-four.[3]

When Bokassa went to France in July he took his bride with him, and she remained at his side during the months of exile and political crisis that followed. It was not long before Catherine found herself transported onto the world stage as wife of the president of the republic. There were glittering receptions and official trips abroad. The teenager who but recently had slipped into a school uniform for another day in the classroom was now adorned in the latest Paris fashions and dined with popes and princes. Maman Cathy, as Central Africans called her, came to love the attention, the clothes, and the jewellery, and she was able to develop her one remarkable attribute, a talent for shopping. She became an avid collector and acquired an enormous hoard of dolls and stuffed animals.[4] Bokassa also liked to collect things, but his taste turned to cameras, musical instruments, and shoes.

During the 1970s, Anne-Aymone, wife of French President Giscard d'Estaing, was often obliged to entertain Catherine while their husbands discussed matters of state, and she evidently found the experience a test of endurance. Madame Bokassa's conversation rarely transcended such profundities as the weather and the prices in Paris boutiques. The prices were forever a sore point, since Bokassa's generosity to himself did not extend to his wife, especially after his early years of infatuation. Bokassa was a jealous and possessive lover. He would not tolerate anyone gazing at Catherine. Those appearing before her were obliged to keep their eyes down and remain silent unless spoken to. In July 1973 he found out that his wife had visited a friend's house without authorization. To make matters worse, her chauffeur, who was supposed to report on all her comings and goings, had failed to do so. Bokassa summoned the young man before him and beat him so savagely that he died on the spot.[5]

Catherine found that she had to share her husband's life with his mistresses and eventually with other wives. This she resented, but she managed for the most part to retain her number-one position among Bokassa's potpourri of bedfellows, as well as her claim to the privilege of accompanying him on official visits abroad. For the first few years of her marriage there was no rival wife, but Bokassa was back at the altar in 1973 – and again in 1974, when he married Alda, the daughter of Adrien Geddaï, a Lebanese casino owner and diamond dealer with investments in Centrafrique. The twenty-year-old Alda, who was reported to be fluent in six languages, was established in a luxury apartment on avenue Henri-Martin in Paris, from where she made occasional sorties to Bangui in order to protect her father's standing among her husband's business partners. She was known to Central Africans simply as the Lebanese.[6] In fact, all Bokassa's wives, with the exception of Maman Cathy, were referred to by their nationality. Thus, there were the Camerounian, the Chinese, the German, the Gabonese, the Romanian, the Swede, the Vietnamese, the Zaïroise, and so forth.

Some of these wives were acquired in a casual manner, like the Gabonese. It was the end of an official visit to Gabon, and everyone of importance in Libreville had gathered at the airport to bid the Central African president farewell. While making his way through the departure lounge, Bokassa spied a beautiful young woman. He stopped in his tracks, approached her, and whispered in her ear, "Don't leave the airport. I shall return right away." He then embraced his host, President Omar Bongo, boarded his plane and took off. A quarter of an hour later, he ordered the pilot to return to Libreville. Bongo, en route to his palace, was notified by the control tower of the change in flight plans and hurried back to the airport. Bokassa met him there and explained, "I was here on an official visit. I now come back on a private visit to marry one of your citizens." And it was done. The woman's name was Joëlle.[7]

Some wives were unwilling partners but succumbed to Bokassa's will, fearing for their lives and the safety of their families. This was the case with Marie-Reine Hassen. She was of a well-to-do Bangui clan, and her father had once served in Dacko's cabinet. In 1974 she was still a schoolgirl and was working for the summer in a downtown bank. She was slim and good-looking, and Bokassa came to hear of her beauty. One day towards the end of July, an official arrived at the bank and told her that Papa wished to see her. At first she was puzzled, but when the man explained who Papa was, she realized what was happening. A car was waiting outside to take her straight to the Palais de la Renaissance, just a short distance away. Knowing something of the marshal-president's reputation, she was understandably terrified.

Inside the palace, Marie-Reine was introduced to Bokassa, whose presence overawed her. He took her trembling hand and led her into his private quarters, where a large bed lay in readiness. She was a virgin but not so innocent as to be unaware of what was expected. He moved towards her, and in spite of his gentle words of encouragement, she became hysterical and began to cry uncontrollably. To her surprise he hesitated, did not push his advantage, and indicated that he understood how she felt. Then he called on his underlings to take her home. There, Marie-Reine regained her composure and told her mother of her close encounter. Her mother weighed the situation and made a quick decision: they had better get out of Centrafrique. She gathered her children and took off on the long road to Cameroun in the family car. But at Bouar, a few short hours from the frontier and freedom, they were detained by the police. What happened next was only to be expected – return to Bangui under heavy guard and accommodation in Ngaragba. Marie-Reine's three brothers were put among the political prisoners, while she and her mother were placed in the women's block.

Almost two years of unrelieved misery went by. Then one night in March 1976 two armed soldiers entered Marie-Reine's cell and ordered her to accompany them. The hour was suspiciously late, the soldiers uncommunicative, and she was convinced that she was about to join the ranks of the disappeared. It was with some relief that she realized she was being taken once again to the Palais de la Renaissance. As before, Bokassa was waiting to greet her. He took her by the hand, speaking words of kindness, addressing her as his daughter, and acting as if nothing had happened. In his private quarters he prepared a bubble bath and helped her out of her clothes and into the tub. She was so weak and thin from the prison diet that she was neither able to resist nor do those things for herself.

Marie-Reine now knew that Bokassa wanted her as much as ever and that she would have to give in if she hoped to gain her freedom and that of her family. She had not seen her brothers, the youngest of whom was only fourteen, for the two years of their imprisonment, and she had no idea how they were faring. When Bokassa helped her from the bathtub, she faced the inevitable and gave herself to him. After three days of the same ritual, she felt confident enough to inquire about her family. Bokassa agreed to have them released immediately. Marie-Reine was subsequently installed in one of his villas, and until the fall of the regime she was available whenever he needed her.[8]

Bokassa tried to be even-handed and divide his time fairly among his women, but it was inevitable that some would be favoured over others, at least temporarily. One of them, the Romanian, held special status for a while and came close to toppling Catherine from her premier position. Bokassa had befriended Romania in 1970 and in return had received promises of technical and financial assistance. These ties allowed him to make a number of official visits to Bucharest, where he showered gifts of diamonds on President Ceauşescu, the country's sado-marxist strongman. On a visit in 1973, Bokassa was entertained by a folkdance troupe and was smitten by one of the dancers, an attractive blonde. After the performance he secured an introduction to the young woman, whose name was Gabriella Drimba. The formalities over, he invited her to his bed. But she was already married and refused his proposition. Undaunted, he made his wishes known to the Romanian authorities and left for home.

A few weeks later, to everyone's surprise, Gabriella stepped off a plane in Bangui. It is not clear why she changed her mind. In all likelihood, she was sent unwillingly by the Ceauşescu regime as a token of friendship for its African ally. Some believe that she was a spy, but that is improbable; there was nothing to spy on. It did not really matter either way; another Bokassa fantasy had been fulfilled. The president-for-life was thrilled with the new addition to his growing entourage of wives. His flattery and attention overcame Gabriella's initial reticence, and he built a palatial home for her, complete with swimming pool, at Kilomètre 12 – the famous Villa Kolongo.

Gabriella became pregnant and subsequently gave birth to a baby girl in a long and difficult delivery. Bokassa brought in top obstetricians to ensure that all went well, and during the labour at Dr Chouaib's clinic, a military band played some of the proud father's favourite tunes – "Sambre et Meuse" and "Marche de la Légion." Mother and child survived, and the newborn was named Anne of Berengo.

The Romanian was happy for a while. Bokassa took her on hunting trips, and she was photographed smiling proudly as her marksman husband posed in triumph, his foot on a fallen beast. He loved to show off his blonde and insisted that she accompany him to public events in Centrafrique. When he went to Beijing in November 1976, he brought her along as his escort, Catherine being pregnant at the time.[9] But although Gabriella's star was ascendant, even she had to endure slights from her wayward husband on occasion. After the trip to Beijing, the couple went to Taiwan, where Bokassa met Chiang Kai-shek. Here an opportunity arose for him to revive his fascination with oriental women and, in fact, acquire a new wife, the Chinese. As Bokassa described it: "One day I attended a majorette parade; a hundred magnificent girls waving the Chinese Nationalist and Central African flags. One of the girls was so beautiful that I asked for her in marriage. Two months later she arrived in Bangui escorted by a princess. We were married in the presence of the official representatives of her country. Later she gave me two beautiful children ... Protocol is sometimes good."[10]

The variety of wives, mistresses, and *filles de joie* was impressive. From the women's point of view, however, it could be dangerous, as Brigette Miroux discovered too late. Miroux was a native of Douai in northern France who left for Centrafrique in 1973 to become a "hostess" in Bokassa's Caravelle aircraft. All went well for a while, and she sent her parents glowing accounts of her new life. But the fairy tale ended in tragedy when her strangled body was found in a Safari Hotel bedroom in April 1974. Her murderer was never found. The incident caused a furore in the French press and exacerbated the already tense relations between Paris and Bangui. Bokassa rejected all responsibility for the calamity and issued a communiqué denying that the young woman had ever been in his service. He also ordered an inquiry, which found nothing.[11]

Visits abroad presented Bokassa with further opportunities for amorous adventures, especially if his hosts were genial and considerate. This was evidently the case when he arrived in Mauritius for an official visit in 1975. The government, aware of his inclinations, arranged to have a welcoming party of some of the island's most beautiful women awaiting him at the airport. He could hardly believe his good fortune. Pacing back and forth, he made his choice, pointing at the young woman with his finger: "Celle-là! Celle-là!" ("That one! That one!") That evening, during an official banquet, he announced the opening of a Central African embassy in Mauritius.[12]

Bokassa's numerous liaisons brought forth many progeny. His children numbered in the hundreds, though only about thirty were recognized officially. He had four with his Vietnamese wives: Jean-Charles, Saint-Cyr, Jean-Claude (who died in his youth), and Nicole. When Jacqueline Nguyen-Thin-Than left for France in 1961 she left her children, Jean-Charles and Saint-Cyr, in their father's care. Catherine showed them some maternal affection when she appeared on the scene, but later, when they went to France for their studies, she began to turn her back on them. As in all polygamous situations, the wives were constantly jostling for position, not only for their husband's favour but for their children's future as well. Bokassa claimed that Catherine was jealous of his other children and wanted to ensure that only hers were recognized in the succession. Catherine presented Bokassa with six children in all, beginning with a daughter, Reine, in 1966. Then came Saint-Sylvestre, who was named after the coup of 1966. Dieu-Béni, Marguerite, and Jean-Bedel followed, and finally there was Saint-Jean who was born in March 1977 to a tumultous fanfare as preparations for the imperial coronation were underway.

There were numerous other offspring from the assortment of spouses. Anne of Berengo, the Romanian's daughter, has already been mentioned. Seven daughters bore the name Marie to bring them under the protection of their grandmother, Marie Yokowo: Marie-Anne, Marie-Béatrice, Marie-Claire, Marie-Eléonore, Marie-France, Marie-Jeanne, and Marie-Laure. In addition to those already mentioned, there were four sons called Jean: Jean-Bertrand, Jean-Legrand, Jean-Serge, and Jean-Yves. According to Bokassa, this name was chosen both to honour the apostle and to strengthen the boys' ties to their illustrious father. Then there was Charlemagne (the inspiration for this name is easy to figure out), as well as Gaboula, Georges, Nestor, and Nicaise.

Bokassa was a proud father and liked to be photographed surrounded by a large number of his children. He took an interest in their upbringing and insisted that they learn Sango, the lingua franca used throughout Centrafrique. And when he had the occasion to spend time with them, he loved to regale them with the history and legends of his own M'Baka people.[13] Yet Bokassa was not a permissive father. Although he gave his children opportunities, he demanded a lot in

return. Most of all, he demanded obedience. At the Villa Kolongo
there were several little rooms in which he locked the youngsters
when they displeased him. Nor did he hesitate to throw them in Ngaragba if he deemed it necessary. Georges was in that dreary prison
between 29 September and 25 November 1972. His crime? He had
defied his father's wish that he study engineering or computer science. Nestor was in Ngaragba between 23 and 29 June 1975 for insubordination. Jean-Charles and Saint-Cyr spent eight days there in April
1976. Nicaise endured the longest spell of all: from 7 July 1977 until
22 February 1978.[14]

Bokassa also took a fatherly interest in the children born of his
brief liaisons. One of these liaisons led to a strange episode in his
family's complex evolution, and it almost cost him his life. Bokassa
often reminisced about his military junket in Indochina and of the
young Vietnamese who had borne him a child. On coming to power
he began to press the French authorities to aid in the search for his
daughter. The French consul general in South Vietnam made some
inquiries, and by the autumn of 1970 there were results. A girl claiming the heritage had been found. Her name was Martine Nguyen-
Thi-Ba'i and she had grown up in a Saigon slum in a shack made of
flattened beer cans. She was making a living hawking cigarettes to
American servicemen on the street. Her dark complexion betrayed
her mixed parentage, and her mother affirmed that the father had
been a noncommissioned officer of Oubanguian origin. Bokassa was
delighted at the news and sent the girl a one-way air ticket to Bangui. En route she stopped off in Paris and at her father's request the
French government gave her 2,500 francs in pocket money. She went
straight out and bought a Cartier watch. She seemed to have the
Bokassa blood all right.

Martine arrived in Bangui on 26 November at 3 AM. Bokassa was
at the airport to greet her with a special guard of honour. The radio,
normally closed at that hour, broadcast a message of welcome. Later,
at the Palais de la Renaissance, Martine received tributes from traditional chiefs and a song was sung in her praise. It was all rather
perplexing for her since she spoke only Vietnamese, but Bokassa,
who still had some words in that language, did his best to explain
everything. The proud father was overjoyed at the reunion, and celebrations marking the event went on for several days. Bands played,
dancers danced, and between banquets and balls Martine was presented to everyone of importance – ministers, public servants, and
members of the diplomatic corps. A fairy tale had come true for the
poor little cigarette girl of Saigon. But fairy tales have a way of turning sour. A month later, *Trang den*, a Saigon daily newspaper,

revealed that its own investigation showed the girl to be an imposter. The French government had set the whole thing up, it claimed, just to embarrass the African leader.

Meanwhile, in South Vietnam, aspirants to the presidential family were coming forward by the dozen. Back in 1953 the French movie actress Martine Carole had been all the rage, and soldiers in the Indochina war had been inclined to name their daughters with local women after her. Consequently, there was no shortage of seventeen-year-old half-Vietnamese Martines.[15] Would the real Cinderella be found? A compelling case was made by a certain Mme N'guyen-Thi-Hué, who was able to show the authorities photographs of herself in the company of the young Bokassa and to produce the birth certificate of their daughter Martine, who had been born in Saigon on 30 January 1953. Bokassa was now convinced that this second Martine, who worked in a cement factory, was the authentic claimant, and he invited mother and daughter to join him in Bangui. They arrived on 10 January 1971. On this occasion the reunion was a little more subdued.

Bokassa was furious at being duped by the false Martine and blamed the French government, which he felt was behind it all. The international press gloated at his misadventure, and this infuriated him even more. He made no attempt to conceal his anger when foreign journalists questioned him about the number of his women and children. The false Martine was obviously now in a difficult position, and so was the French ambassador to the Central African Republic, Albert de Schonen. One day Bokassa summoned the ambassador in order to discuss the matter. Standing next to the real Martine, he raised her dress and the legs of his pants and declared, "See, she has my legs." De Schonen could only nod an embarrassed agreement.

Late one evening the ambassador learned that Bokassa was convoking a meeting of his government and the diplomatic corps for the following morning, at which he planned to hand over the false Martine to the custody of the French embassy. Since this would have made France look ridiculous, de Schonen immediately sought a meeting with the president to put a stop to it. The interview was long and difficult, but in the end de Schonen prevailed, arguing that it would be a traumatic experience for the girl who, after all, had been an innocent pawn in the whole affair.[16] Papa Bok then came up with a better idea, which would allow him to pose as a grand *pater familias* and at the same time turn the joke on his detractors. On 22 February 1971, the occasion of his fiftieth birthday, he announced that he was adopting the false Martine. Then, with his customary flair, he invited all Central African men to seek the hands of his half-Vietnamese daughters.

Volunteers were not hard to find. Dr Jean-Bruno Dédéavodé, a physician at Bangui General Hospital, won the heart of the real Martine. Captain Fidèle Obrou, commander of the cadet school at Camp Kassaï, successfully courted the imposter. On 30 January 1973 the two Martines were married to their chosen ones in a joint ceremony at the Palais de la Renaissance. They wore identical white dresses and received identical presents. It was a lavish, festive occasion, attended by numerous dignitaries, including President Omar Bongo of Gabon.[17]

Did they all live happily after? Hardly. Obrou was under suspicion from the start. He was of the Banda, a people distrusted by Bokassa. Indeed, the president feared that the young man had only married his adopted daughter in order to get close to the centre of power – perhaps with an eye to seizing it for himself one day. Obrou had the ideal personality for a conspirator. He was reserved and secretive, and spoke little. Yet he smiled a lot, could be charming, and had a close network of friends. He had expensive tastes and dabbled in business to sustain them. This was not unusual among members of the presidential family, and in fact Papa Bok gave him the money to get started. Eventually Obrou came to own two cinema houses in Bangui – the Apollo in Kilomètre 5 and the Comet in the Fouh district. With the revenues provided by these enterprises, he was able to indulge in his passion for fast cars, fancy clothes, and women.

Those who knew Obrou well claim that he had always detested Bokassa. He soon gathered around himself a coterie of like-minded young officers – men who shared his ambitions and his hatred for Papa Bok. His right-hand man was his inseparable twin brother, Martin Meya, a civil servant in the Ministry of Tourism. He also had the support of Pierre Maleombho, who had been president of the National Assembly at the time of independence. The plotters, more than a dozen in all, resolved to assassinate Bokassa and take power into their own hands. After a number of aborted efforts, their opportunity came. On 3 February 1976, Bokassa was scheduled to fly north to Awakaba National Park for some hunting and relaxation. At 9:30 that morning he arrived at Bangui-M'Poko Airport and entered the VIP lounge. Obrou was all set. He had divided his collaborators into two groups. Adjudant Zoukongo, an expert marksman trained in France and the Soviet Union, positioned himself inside the terminal. He was to throw a grenade at the president as he left the building. Three others stood nearby, ready to move in and neutralize the security guards after the explosion. Another three waited outside. Their task was to cover the flight of the assassins should their bid fail.

At 10 o'clock Bokassa emerged from the lounge and made his way towards the terminal exit, surrounded by security guards, some of his ministers, and others. As he approached the doorway, Zoukongo's grenade whizzed by his head and landed among some plants. Realizing what was happening, his security guards shouted a warning and pushed him out of the door. Others in the presidential entourage hit the ground, while the guard of honour and musicians lining the exit fled in panic. And then – silence. There was no explosion. The grenade was a dud. Stunned by this unexpected development, the plotters lost the nerve to pursue the rest of their plan. In the confusion that followed, they managed to slip away – all, that is, except the one who had had the courage to act. Zoukongo took off on foot with security forces in hot pursuit. He barricaded himself in the offices of Air Afrique and held off his attackers with an automatic pistol. After an hour, realizing that further resistance was futile, he turned his weapon on himself.

Bokassa was badly shaken by the attempt to slay him (although later he would quote the incident as proof of his invulnerability). Recovering his composure, he left the airport under heavy guard, uncertain of his assailants' identities or of the extent of their support. On arriving at the Palais de la Renaissance, he issued a command that all his principal officers were to assemble before him. Obrou, of course, failed to appear, and someone recalled having seen him that morning in the company of Zoukongo. His complicity was confirmed when Gandjia, one of the plotters arrested at a roadblock, was brought to the palace and made a complete confession. The hunt then began in earnest for the other conspirators.

Meanwhile, Obrou, Meya, and Zatao (another participant in the plot) had slipped across the Oubangui to Zaïre. Realizing that Central African agents were on their trail, they surrendered to the Zaïrean authorities. It was a fatal blunder – and a stupid one, since they were aware of the bonds of friendship that united Presidents Bokassa and Mobutu. Soon they were manacled together and hustled aboard a plane to Bangui, where they were taken directly to the palace. There Bokassa, his wife Catherine, other family members, and an assemblage of ministers and diplomats awaited them. The false Martine was sent for, though she was already nine months pregnant and due to give birth any day. She sat next to Catherine, who berated her, saying, "You see – your husband is no good – he wanted to kill Papa." Meanwhile, the chained Obrou expressed regret at his betrayal, though it did him no good.

This confrontation was followed by a more serious interrogation by the military tribunal. Here Obrou insisted that the grenade thrown at the airport had been designed to stun, not kill, Bokassa.

The security personnel who had examined the weapon disagreed. They believed that if it had exploded, the president and several of his entourage would have perished. Obrou denied that he had planned to form a government after overthrowing his father-in-law, but Zatao was more forthright, confessing that Obrou was to have become head of a provisional government that would have included Meya and Maleombho.

While details of the conspiracy were thus being divulged, others implicated in the affair, however tenuously, were being rounded up. Maleombho was among the first to be arrested. Initially, he protested his innocence, but by 9 February, after a little "persuasion," he broke down and admitted his complicity. On 12 February the accused, sixteen in all, were taken to the Omnisports Stadium. Barefoot, barechested, and handcuffed, they were to face the military tribunal once more, this time with the public present. The hearings were broadcast on the radio to reach an even larger audience. Nothing new was revealed during the day-long deliberations, and many felt that the open trial was simply a charade – another of those spectacles with which to terrorize the populace. By 7 PM the tribunal had reached its verdict. Obrou, Meya, Gandjia, Maleombho, Zatao, and three others were condemned to death. Two accomplices were given twenty-year prison sentences with forced labour. Three received ten-year sentences for not disclosing the plot. One was acquitted and another held for further questioning. The last among them, a French business associate of Obrou, was found guilty of criminal evasion and sentenced to three years in prison and a fine of 3 million francs.

With the tribunal over, the plotters were taken by truck to the palace, where Bokassa awaited them. "Get those murderers down here before me," he yelled at the armed soldiers, who were everywhere. It was done, and in the usual rough manner. Bokassa then ordered that the plotters be divided into two groups – those condemned to death and those receiving prison sentences.

"You are lucky," he said to the latter. Turning to the condemned, he addressed them menacingly: "You wanted to kill me, then here I am, go ahead now. What is someone like Obrou able to do in my place?" His greatest venom was reserved for Obrou: "You married my daughter. I spent money on you and you dared to turn against me. And then you insulted me saying that I was a pygmy."

Obrou's twin brother tried to speak – "Papa ..." – but was quickly cut off by Bokassa's angry retort, "Shut up. I am not your father."[18]

At 4:30 AM the condemned men were bundled into an army truck and driven away. Their destination was a firing range above Camp Kassaï. There, in the glare of the truck's headlights, they met their end in a hail of bullets. The bodies were buried not far from the unmarked grave of Banza who, seven years earlier, had fallen in the same cause. Later in the morning, the surviving plotters were taken away to Ngaragba.

As was customary, the friends and relatives of the conspirators were duly punished. Bokassa sent his police among the Banda, Obrou's people, intimidating and interrogating at will. Many were arrested on flimsy pretexts and several were executed in the usual arbitrary manner. Tragedy also awaited Obrou's hapless widow, the fake Martine. A few hours after her husband's death she entered Dr Chouaib's clinic in the throes of labour, and early next morning she gave birth to a healthy boy. She left the clinic on 23 February expecting to go to the Villa Nasser, but she was taken instead to a special pavilion of the General Hospital, which was under the direction of Dr Dédéavodé, the real Martine's husband. The doctor took charge of the baby and, Martine's protests notwithstanding, injected him with several drug doses. The baby went into a coma and then turned blue. Martine was terrified, suspecting that Bokassa wanted the boy dead lest he grow up and avenge the death of his father. She appealed to other doctors to help, but there was nothing they could do at that stage. The baby died and was buried secretly at the Ndrès Cemetery.

The grief-stricken Martine returned to the Villa Nasser, and she continued to live in the bosom of the presidential family for over a year. She then vanished. In accounting for her disappearance, Bokassa claimed that she had returned to her homeland, but that is improbable.[19] He would never have let her go for fear she might implicate him in the death of her baby. However unsavoury his international reputation, he had no wish to don the mantle of King Herod. It is likely that the fake Martine was either strangled or shot in some lonely spot by the presidential guard – a fate shared by so many who appeared to threaten Papa Bok.[20]

Grand *pater familias* and lover of many women are enduring elements in the Bokassa legend. In the latter respect at least, he was not fundamentally different from some contemporary or near-contemporary national leaders. U.S. President John F. Kennedy and the Shah of Iran immediately come to mind.[21] Bokassa invited attention, however, by flaunting his sexual successes before an increasingly curious world. Moreover, the international composition of his wives and mistresses intensified media interest, especially in an age when interracial liaisons were not universally approved.

The extended family had its greatest impact at home. The possession of women from every continent enhanced Bokassa's stature among his people. The women were trophies from his travels, proof that he was accepted as an equal in all corners of the globe, and the numerous offspring were testimony to his virility, itself highly symbolic of power. The family had a practical importance as well. In Africa, kinship ties are paramount and are responsible for a deep sense of belonging and identity. The kinship group may include several hundred people – *cousins* or *parents* in French. Sanctions, traditions, and obligations reinforce group ties and bonds, and cannot be avoided.[22] Bokassa looked after his family by appointing them to key positions and by involving them in business ventures. His eldest son, Georges, became minister of defence, while his sister, Catherine M'Balanga, became mayor of Bimbo. His son-in-law, Fidèle Obrou, had been given money to get started in business – though, as we have seen, he turned against his benefactor. In most cases, however, giving preference to the kinship group and extending it as far as possible built important networks of support throughout the country and kept the family fortune growing.

CHAPTER FIVE

The French Connection

The strong ties that bound the Central African Republic to France in the early years of independence continued under Bokassa. France remained the major player in its former colony's economy and provided considerable subsidies in terms of technical assistance and budget supplements. Centrafrique's principal exports were diamonds, cotton, coffee, and hardwoods, with lesser quantities of tobacco, ivory, leather, pepper, rubber, peanuts, and medicinal plants. Between 1970 and 1975 France annually purchased an average of 48 per cent of these commodities. During the same period Centrafrique was annually taking an average of 58 per cent of its imports from France, manufactured goods in most cases.

France viewed its former colonies as a market for its industrial products and a source of relatively cheap tropical crops and strategic minerals. It was therefore prepared to provide technical and financial assistance to these countries in order to foster political stability and the development of the modern economic sector. Most aid was provided by the Ministry of Cooperation. The following figures (in French francs) show the amounts channelled to Bangui during a typical four-year period:

1973	Fr 49,888,000
1974	67,444,000
1975	71,454,000
1976	83,179,000[1]

Bokassa was fully aware of his dependence on French aid. It was keeping his government from bankruptcy, as well as giving him and his collaborators in the state bourgeoisie numerous opportunities for profit in the modern sector. He felt, however, that the subsidies from

Paris were never adequate, and he was eager to seek alternative sources of support wherever they might be found. The Eastern Bloc was one possibility, and he openly courted such countries as the Soviet Union, Romania, and Yugoslavia. He saw no contradiction in befriending both Taiwan and the People's Republic of China, and he was equally prepared to embrace Israel and Libya as the occasion warranted. Even South Africa did not escape his overtures.[2]

If Bokassa's foreign policy lacked ideological consistency, it did follow a certain logic. He was looking for money and did not seem to care much about the political stripe or motivation of its donors. It is unclear whether he hoped in the long term to break his country's dependence on France. Some of his diplomatic manœuvres seemed principally designed to play on French fears and thus secure a greater flow of aid from Paris.[3] France, then, remained the key player in Bokassa's foreign policy. Relations between Paris and Bangui were sometimes warm, sometimes strained. Much depended on who was in power in France and on Bokassa's latest whim.

The de Gaulle years were amicable enough, largely because of Bokassa's obsessive admiration for the general whom he considered as a father. At the end of May 1968, when France was in the throes of the student revolt, de Gaulle fled Paris, his regime on the verge of collapse. The news shocked Bokassa, and in a call broadcast repeatedly over Radio-Bangui, he appealed to "the man of 1940, the man of 1958, liberator of France, liberator of Africa," to stay in power.[4]

De Gaulle was not amused by Bokassa. Nor did he reciprocate the adulation. In truth he despised the African leader, referring to him as le soudard (literally "the old soldier" but in a pejorative sense; the word has a rough, brutal connotation). Shortly after the Saint-Sylvestre coup, the general turned angrily on his Council of Ministers demanding, "Quel est le con que nous avons a Bangui?" ("Who is the idiot that we have in Bangui?"). He gradually came to accept le soudard as a necessary nuisance, but no more.[5] De Gaulle is credited with dubbing the Central African president Papa Bok, which has a derogative ring to French ears. (Un bock is a small glass of beer.) At the Quai d'Orsay and other government offices, civil servants often referred to Bokassa as Ubu Roi, an allusion to the Alfred Jarry play of the same name that had caused Parisians to riot in 1896. The play recorded the exploits of Pa Ubu, a murdering usurper king of Poland who served excrement to his dinner guests.[6]

On 11 November 1970 shocking news reached Bangui. General de Gaulle had died the evening before during a game of solitaire at his country home in Colombey-les-deux-Eglises. Bokassa left immediately for Paris, the first of the flood of world leaders who arrived for the funeral ceremonies. De Gaulle had requested a simple burial in the little graveyard at Columbey with only his family and the villagers present. It was done according to his wishes on the twelfth. The dignitaries had to content themselves with a mass at Notre-Dame Cathedral.

When it was over, they were invited to a reception at the Elysée Palace, where Bokassa irritated his hosts by turning up in the uniform of a French parachutist. Foreign Minister Maurice Schumann was concerned that, with de Gaulle gone, the Central African president might break totally with France and embrace the Soviets – a direction in which he was already moving – so he asked Finance Minister Valéry Giscard d'Estaing to take Bokassa in hand. On approaching Bokassa, Giscard was treated to a grief-stricken monologue on the loss of *mon père*: "I lost my natural father when I was a child and now it's the turn of my true father, General de Gaulle ... All Central Africans today feel like orphans." Despite this outpouring, Giscard was impressed with the man's presence, his magnetism, his physical vigour, and a subtle cunning that betrayed a hint of cruelty.[7] It was the beginning of a long association.

The next day the foreign visitors were invited to visit the cemetery, and Bokassa was among those who made the pilgrimage to the little village in the forested hills of Champagne. There he was able to rub shoulders with Their Imperial Majesties the Shah of Iran and Haile Selassie of Ethiopia. After a few solemn moments at the graveside, the dignitaries were received by Madame de Gaulle and her son Philippe at their residence, La Boisserie. Throughout the visit, Bokassa was in a state of obvious emotional distress, and his distraught weeping was a source of widespread embarrassment. "I lost my Papa," he was heard to sob repeatedly. Madame de Gaulle was particularly exasperated by his performance.[8]

De Gaulle did not die in office; he had resigned after the defeat of his senate reform proposals in the referendum of April 1969. His successor was Georges Pompidou, a portly ex-banker. Pompidou had no special relationship with Bokassa, and during his presidency, which lasted until 1974, matters between the two countries reached a low ebb. It was during these years that Bokassa decided to launch the first of his several attempts to seek alternatives to French aid. With Banza out of the way, he gathered around him a group of young men who had just finished their studies in Europe. Some of them espoused marxist ideas, which were fashionable among intellectuals at the time, and they encouraged Bokassa to draw closer to the communist bloc and reduce French influence. In July 1970 he signed a cooperative agreement with the Soviet Union and began his long friendship with Romania.

Throughout the summer Bokassa made threatening noises against the French, accusing them of exploiting the country and keeping it underdeveloped. In one of his radio speeches he announced that he would adopt the ideology of the country that would build a railway connecting Bangui to the sea. He apparently expected some gesture from Paris, if only to counteract the red menace, but he received no response. Bokassa then went ahead touting "scientific socialism" as the only path to rapid economic progress. This was all the more curious in view of the virulent anticommunist pronouncements he had made in the wake of seizing power. But consistency was never one of his strong points. In September 1970 he expelled several dozen French agricultural advisers from the country. This rash act was followed by the inauguration of a plan of agricultural reform, which aimed to establish large, state-owned collective farms dedicated to the production of cash crops, using the most modern machinery, fertilizer, and so forth. Government revenues would be increased, it was reasoned, by growing more cotton and coffee for export. Linked with these changes was the creation in August 1970 of the Office national de commercialisation des produits agricoles (ONCPA), which was given a monopoly in all trade in agricultural products. ONCPA's purpose soon became obvious – to commandeer the best agricultural equipment for use on the farms and plantations of Bokassa and his cronies. It was an attempt by the ruling élite to claim a share of the cash crop profits, which were still largely in the hands of the old concessionary companies. ONCPA was referred to by the peasants as "on ne sait pas."9

The agricultural reform was part of a grand plan of national economic development known as Opération Bokassa. This plan aimed at the modernization of society and economic self-sufficiency. A book on the subject published in 1973, *Philosophie de l'Opération Bokassa*, emphasized its humanistic purpose: "Man is at the centre of this ideology. His views are always considered for his own happiness and for his own future ... Opération Bokassa teaches every Central African ... to take charge of his own destiny."10 The book, in fact, was an exercise in public relations – an attempt to convince the world that Bokassa was an enlightened and progressive ruler. It was filled with photographs showing the president-for-life in the company of other great men – de Gaulle, Nasser, Haile Selassie, Tito, and so forth.

Peasant suspicion along with incompetence and poor management ensured that the agricultural reforms of Opération Bokassa were in trouble from the start. Cotton and coffee cultivation was still associated in the popular mind with the forced labour system of old, and the peasants never took to these cash crops with any enthusiasm. The absence of the French experts was unfortunate, for the officials charged with implementing the plan simply did not know what to do. By 1975 cotton production, which was supposed to increase three-fold, had fallen by 19 per cent. The coffee crop was down by 10 per cent.[11] The peasants were worse off than they had ever been. The only places that were doing well were the private farms of the president and his close associates. But they had every imaginable advantage.

Bokassa soon realized that he could not do without the French. His relationship with them remained troubled, but there were occasional good days. Late in 1970 the Pompidou government gave him a private airplane – a Caravelle – in an attempt at reconciliation. This helped, but the business of the two Martines created further difficulties, especially when Bokassa accused Paris of sending the fake Martine to Bangui in revenge for the expulsion of the French agriculturalists.

The Central African Republic was in severe financial difficulties in the early 1970s. The state farms were absorbing huge quantities of cash while giving little in return. Government revenues were simply not large enough to keep the country going. Yet none of this deterred Bokassa from launching ambitious schemes. In 1970 he built a university in Bangui which was named after himself. In the same year he opened a television station with Israeli technical assistance and long-term financial credits. (From then on, some Bangui residents could tune in nightly to crackling footage of his speeches and activities.) In 1971 he established a national airline, Air Centrafrique, and bought a DC8 as its only carrier. He then embarked on the construction of two new luxury hotels. At this stage, the banks said Enough – they refused to offer any more credit either to him or to his government. Annoyed at this rebuff, he closed down the Bangui branch of the Banque nationale de Paris on 31 October 1971 and began to talk about leaving the franc zone and printing his own currency.

Relations between Bangui and Paris were not helped during these years by the increasingly critical stories about Bokassa that were appearing in the French press. This source of friction reached a climax in April 1974 when Brigette Miroux's body was discovered in a Bangui hotel room. The French media claimed that she had been Bokassa's bedmate and implicated him in her murder. Angered at these reports, the president-for-life promptly nationalized the Imprimerie centrale d'Afrique and the Librairie Hachette, French-owned concerns that printed and distributed books and magazines. He also banned the importation of French newspapers and took over the property of Agence France-Presse. The nationalizations extended to the oil business, with Total, Shell, Purfina, Mobil, Texaco, and Agip losing their facilities to the state. Henceforth, CentraHydro, a state body, monopolized the distribution of petroleum products.[12]

Just when relations between the African state and its former colonial overlord had reached a new low, President Pompidou died. His successor, chosen in May 1974, was Valéry Giscard d'Estaing, a man whose personality and inclinations presaged well for a renewal of friendly ties with Centrafrique. Giscard came from a wealthy family that had done well in the world of banking and finance. His father, Edmond, had added the aristocratic designation "d'Estaing" to the family name in 1923, the claim being based on descent from a female cousin of an Admiral d'Estaing who had been guillotined during the French Revolution. His mother, May Bardoux, claimed an illegitimate daughter of Louis XV among her ancestors, allowing Giscard to boast that he was descended from the Bourbons. Although his pedigree was far from impeccable, he was comfortable in the aristocratic role and lived a life of château weekends and dinner parties with the rich and titled.[13]

Here was a man with whom Bokassa, who had regal ambitions of his own, could readily identify. The two leaders had got on well ever since their first meeting at de Gaulle's funeral ceremonies, and Giscard's special interest in Africa continued to bind them together. The French president, in spite of his snobbery, was a philistine at heart. He had none of the love of literature and history that his successor, François Mitterrand, was to display. Indeed, his favourite hobby was the slaughter of wild beasts. The Central African Republic, with its abundance of big game, became one of his regular vacation spots. He was never happier than when foraging across the savannah, rifle in hand, on the trail of another four-legged victim. And Bokassa was always delighted to play host to such a distinguished visitor.

Giscard first went to Centrafrique in December 1970 to hunt for antelope in the Koumbola Reserve in the northern part of the country. He enjoyed himself so much that he came back for more in March 1971. He returned once again in April 1973 on official business and took advantage of the occasion to go on another safari. Bokassa threw a dinner party in his honour at the appropriately named Safari Hotel, where they spoke of their mutual enthusiasm for the chase. Before leaving for home, Giscard visited the president's residence, where he was introduced to his host's numerous children and received gifts of diamonds and ebony carvings.[14]

A few years later, Giscard and some of his associates reserved for themselves a *chasse gardée* of about two million hectares between the towns of Rafaï, Zémio, and Djéma in the southeast. He was given a free hand in this hunting ground and could kill as he pleased. Anything that moved on the savannah was fair game – buffalo, antelope, rhinoceros – but elephants were his favourite target. Bokassa estimated that Giscard must personally have felled about fifty of the great beasts during the 1970s. It was impossible to tell for sure, since the French president was exempt from declarations and taxes. He simply shipped the tusks across the border to N'Djaména in Tchad, from where they were airlifted to France.[15]

Apart from these personal idiosyncracies, Centrafrique had a certain strategic value to France that could ill afford to be ignored, and the Giscard family had investments in the country that required protection. In 1930 Edmond Giscard d'Estaing (Valéry's father) had become a major shareholder in the Société financière française et coloniale (SFFC), a company with special interests in Indochina and elsewhere. The company had suffered in the crash of 1929, and it looks as if Giscard *père* seized the opportunity to buy up shares. He became its president in 1935 and retained that position until his retirement in 1973. Meanwhile, the company changed its name to the Société financière pour la France et les pays d'outre-mer (SOFFO). A major player in the world rubber trade (with connections to Michelin), it began to invest heavily in French Equatorial Africa after France's expulsion from Indochina, and by the 1970s it controlled 38 per cent of the Compagnie forestière de la Sangha-Oubangui, the old concessionary company that had exploited blacks in colonial days – and in which Giscard *père* had long been a shareholder.[16]

Taking all these factors into account, the close ties between Paris and Bangui during the Giscard presidency come as no surprise. The new cosiness was evident from the beginning. In September 1974 Giscard learned that Bokassa wanted to meet him at one of the châteaux he had purchased in France. The French president made the trip in a Puma helicopter and was invited to stay for dinner. Throughout the evening Bokassa stressed the need for a special relationship with France, complaining intermittently of the inadequacy of the flow of aid. Nonetheless, the conversation was relaxed and amicable, and it was agreed that Giscard's first official visit to Africa as president would be to Centrafrique.[17]

Giscard was given a rousing welcome when he arrived in Bangui on 5 March 1975 for the Franco-African summit. This was the annual get-together between France and its former African colonies, and Bokassa was thrilled to play host to the illustrious gathering.[18] It was not simply that he was the centre of attention for a few days, important though that was. Even more to the point was the fact that he could further cultivate his relationship with the French president and perhaps extract a promise of more aid. He raised the old question of the railway to the sea but Giscard would commit himself only to a feasibility study.[19] Even so, the summit was a grand occasion, and its highlight for Bokassa was the lavish banquet he threw for three thousand guests at the Palais de la Renaissance. On the day of his departure, Giscard had the honour of unveiling a bronze statue of Marshal Bokassa at an intersection that was renamed place Valéry Giscard d'Estaing.[20]

To Giscard it was all a political game in which the interests of his government and his family were paramount, and he was an adept player. Centrafrique's position in France's global strategy was small enough. But the African country harboured deposits of a valuable commodity that the politicians in Paris were anxious to keep at their disposal: uranium. France was not only a major nuclear power in the military sense (de Gaulle's *force de frappe*), but it was also developing a heavy dependence on atomic energy for industrial purposes. It had to have secure access to uranium supplies. Most of its uranium was imported in varying proportions from South Africa, Niger, and Gabon, the last two being former French colonies. Centrafrique was a possible fourth source.[21]

In 1963 France's Commissariat à l'énergie atomique (CEA) had estimated that the Central African Republic had uranium reserves amounting to about 15,000 metric tonnes. The deposits were difficult to exploit, however, since they were located in Bakouma, a swampy region 800 kilometres to the east of Bangui. From the moment he took power, Bokassa was determined to have this resource developed, and after many overtures a beginning was made in 1969. In that year the Compagnie d'uranium de Bakouma (URBA) was formed with start-up capital of 2.2 billion CFA francs. The Bangui government contributed 20 per cent of this investment, while CEA and the Compagnie française des minerais d'uranium (CFMU) each came up with 40 per cent. But the project foundered when it was discovered that a kilo of uranium produced at Bakouma cost more than the going world price for the stuff. In June 1971 the French partners in the consortium ordered operations to cease.

Bokassa was incensed and withdrew URBA's mining licence. The economic arguments for ceasing production left him cold. He was convinced that the European investors were not being forthright and that they wanted the resource to remain undeveloped until France's need became greater. He immediately sought alternative sources of investment, and U.S. President Richard Nixon was approached, but he declined the offer, fearing complications with Paris. Bokassa persisted, sending emissaries around the globe, and eventually, in 1974, Aluswisse, a Zurich-based company with no experience in mining uranium, agreed to take over the abandoned operation at Bakouma. This occurred around the time that Giscard came to power in Paris. The new president realized that Bokassa accorded great importance to the Bakouma mines and that France would have to play a role in their development to keep Centrafrique within its political orbit. Besides, it would be folly to permit a strategic resource such as uranium to slip into the grasp of another country. Aluswisse was happy to cooperate with the French, not having the know-how to work the mines itself. A further favourable omen was the rising price of uranium in the mid-1970s in response to the world energy crisis.

A leading role in the French machinations was played by Valéry's cousin, Jacques Giscard d'Estaing, a prominent industrialist with major interests in Africa. Jacques was the financial director of CEA; Valéry had given him the job as soon as he had entered the Elysée. By February 1975 a new agreement had been reached and a new consortium put in place. Uranium de Centrafrique (URCA) received 40 per cent of its capital from the Central African government, 30 per cent from Aluswisse, and 15 per cent each from the two former French partners, CEA and CFMU. Feasibility studies in 1977 were optimistic about the project's profitability, but there was still nothing underway by the time the regime collapsed.[22]

Bokassa's high hopes for his uranium resource were thus never realized. He made few personal gains from the Bakouma venture. In fact, the operation simply squandered scarce government capital. There was one positive outcome, however. The strategic mineral kept France friendly and allowed mutual interests between the president-for-life and the Giscard family to be cultivated. Bokassa came to be on good terms not only with Valéry and Jacques, but also with François Giscard, Jacques's brother, who was the managing director of the Banque française du commerce extérieur. François had received his appointment just two months after Valéry's election as president. It was he who organized his cousin's safaris and the payment of subsidies to client African presidents. He was made a commander of the Ordre de l'Opération Bokassa in January 1976.[23]

It is worth noting that on taking office Giscard dropped Jacques Foccart and set about dismantling his system of information gathering and manipulation, which he knew served the Gaullists. In its place he created his own system under René Journiac, who had been Foccart's assistant for seven years. The president's cousins, Jacques and François, played key roles in the new arrangement, ensuring that Giscardian interests remained to the fore.

If uranium did not fulfil its promise, the Central African Republic had another much-sought natural resource, one that did not disappoint its exploiters: diamonds. The precious stones had always been the country's most valuable product and its government's most lucrative source of revenue. During Dacko's regime the trade had been kept under reasonable control, but as soon as he was overthrown diamond dealers of dubious reputation flocked into Bangui believing that a free-for-all was about to begin. They were wrong. Timothée Malendoma, minister of economics in the new government, managed to convince Bokassa that the trade should be strictly regulated. The shady operators were expelled and a national diamond office was established with Malendoma in charge. A trading monopoly was then granted to a consortium made up of four foreign companies, one each from the United States, France, the Netherlands, and Israel. In return for its privileges, the group poured 40 per cent of its profits into the Central African treasury. Diamond production increased substantially under these arrangements, reaching 610,000 carats in 1968 – a value of 4.4 billion CFA francs (production had been a mere 110,000 carats in 1961).[24]

Bokassa succeeded in siphoning off some of the revenue from this source, but it was hardly sufficient to satisfy his wants. By 1969 he had saved only enough to purchase Villemorant, his first château in France. He knew that the diamond business offered him the surest road to vast wealth and he also knew that it would have to be deregulated to achieve this goal. Consequently, the all-too-honest Malendoma was shuffled out of the economics portfolio and the careful supervision of the trade began to lapse. In 1969 a new company, Centradiam, made its appearance on the Bangui diamond market. It was not part of the established consortium, whose monopoly was now terminated. Bokassa himself, it turned out, was a major shareholder in the new company, whose principal financial backing came from the Anagnostellis brothers – Greek tycoons with an unsavoury background. Andrée, the wife of Dmitri Anagnostellis, actually served as Bokassa's secretary between 1966 and 1974. Dmitri represented Arslanian, the Antwerp-based diamond company that was later known as Sodiam.[25] Centradiam paid no taxes, licence fees, or anything of the kind, and it took little imagination to figure out where much of the profit was going.

The diamond business became even more profitable early in the 1970s when Bokassa met and befriended Adrien Geddaï, a Lebanese wheeler-dealer with international criminal connections. Geddaï introduced the president to men of his own ilk, such as Adnan Khashoggi, the Saudi arms-dealer-cum-playboy, and René Tamraz, a Lebanese banker who was able to raise millions of "petrodollars" in the Arab world for deals of one sort or another. Geddaï and Tamraz were responsible for introducing another company, SADECA, into Centrafrique's diamond business – and Bokassa, naturally enough, profited handsomely from his collaboration in the venture.

It was generally understood that anyone trading in diamonds in Central Africa had to contribute generously to what the French call *pots de vin*. The usual way of doing this was to invite Bokassa to become a director or investor in one's firm. He contributed little, of course, and his exactions were considerable. He collected millions of francs from these companies – his dividends. The business concerns knew full well that he would not hesitate to seize their assets or cancel their mining permits if his demands were not met. This is what happened in November 1969 to the French and American interests that were part of the original monopoly consortium. When they resisted Bokassa's demand for hundreds of millions of CFA francs as a renewal fee for the mining permits, everything they owned was confiscated and their foreign personnel were expelled from the country.[26] The same thing happened in 1976 to SCED, a subsidiary of the American multinational, Diamond Distributors. Bokassa, on the pretext that the company paid its African employees poorly, cancelled its mining permit and helped himself to its hoard of gold and diamonds.[27]

Confiscations, kickbacks, and direct involvement in the smuggling of diamonds to the world's markets – these were the means by which Papa Bok enriched himself from his country's most valuable resource. His name is readily associated with the precious stones in one other respect: he always carried a fistful of them in his pocket (his "pot of jam") as presents for his hosts on his junkets abroad. On his first official visit to Paris in November 1966, he tried to give some to "Aunt Yvonne" (Madame de Gaulle) but was told that gifts of that sort were not appreciated. The Giscard family was not so scrupulous. Valéry, Jacques, François, and Valéry's wife Anne-Aymone all accepted the proffered gems. The tainted gifts were to come back to haunt the French president many years later.

Ivory was another lucrative source of revenue for Bokassa. He gave a free hand in the elephant tusk trade to La Couronne, a Spanish-based company, which had operations in many parts of Africa and a virtual stranglehold on the world market. One of the company's directors, Mme Gilberte Van Erpe, was the sister of one of his former wives. La Couronne's average declared export of ivory from Centrafrique was 150 tonnes – the equivalent of 5,000 dead elephants a year. The profits were enormous, and Bokassa took his share – one-third of the total. He admitted later that the country's elephant population had probably declined by 50 per cent during the 1970s.[28]

In spite of confiscations, policy fluctuations, and the search for alternative sources of aid and investment, the Central African economy remained firmly dominated by French interests. The lumber industry is a prime example. The export of hardwood lumber boomed during the Bokassa years. Until then, the forests, mainly located in Lobaye, had been relatively unexploited compared with those in Gabon and Congo/Brazzaville. The major players in this immensely profitable business were the Société d'exploitation forestière et industrielle (SEFI), controlled by the French Dujardin group, and the Société africaine forestière et agricole (SAFA), controlled by the Rivaud group and the Compagnie du Cambodge. The local brewing industry, too, was in French hands. Mocaf (Motte-Cordonnier-Afrique), a branch of the French company Motte-Cordonnier-d'Armentières, had established a brewery in Bangui to serve the local market in 1951 and started making money almost immediately. By 1975 it was employing one hundred and fifty African workers and a dozen or so European technical and managerial staff in its modern plant.[29] This pattern of African workers and expatriate bosses was typical of many industries in the country.[30]

Most of the major businesses were capitalized from abroad. French companies and banks were the main investors, but there were many joint ventures by different corporations, like that concerning uranium. The Central African government was often a minority shareholder, investing development funds supplied by French government agencies such as the Fonds d'aide de la coopération (FAC). Between 1973 and 1976 a total of 76,163,000 French francs were provided by FAC for investment in the country.[31] As a result of all this, there were few areas of productivity in which some profit did not accrue to the state and indirectly to Bokassa and his entourage.

Bokassa also had various sources of revenue that were reasonably legitimate. He described himself as his country's first peasant and first businessman. There was some truth to the latter claim, for he controlled an astonishing array of enterprises in Centrafrique. At his Villa Kolongo he had two factories turning out buttons and other odds and ends, while his principal residence of Berengo was a veritable hive of industrial activity. In this sprawling complex there were coffee and cocoa processing plants, an abattoir, a sawmill, a garment factory, a restaurant named Le Paysan, and the headquarters of the president's two airlines, Paysan Air and Centrafrique Charter Airlines. In Bangui he constructed two large apartment blocks: Pacifique 1, which was finished in 1969, and Pacifique 2, which was still incomplete when his regime collapsed. On the ground floor of Pacifique 1 he owned a store called Paysan 1, which sold clothing from Catherine's garment factory; and he had a small shopping centre adjacent to Pacifique 2, where furniture, stereo equipment, and other luxury items were sold.[32] Bokassa also created a semi-private public works company – SECIP – which, using state resources, took on major construction developments for his personal use. These projects included airstrips at hunting parks, villas around Bangui, and the Berengo complex. While all this was going on, the minister of public works had no materials with which to build roads, bridges, and other structures basic to the economy.[33]

Bokassa's enterprises were profitable because of dubious practices rather than business acumen. Wages were kept low and markets were virtually guaranteed. A large portion of the goods he produced were sold directly to the various branches of government, enabling him to fix prices to his own advantage. And he had no qualms about requisitioning the resources of the state – trucks, gasoline, and so forth – when it suited his needs. The exact details of these transactions and profits must remain a mystery, however, for he submitted no accounts of his activities. Nor did he pay any taxes. With nobody daring to ask questions, he was able to spirit his gains out of the country in the form of cash, diamonds, and gold. Much of this probably ended up in his Swiss bank account.

Even so, Bokassa was not content to hide all his fortune in a secret bank account just in case he was forced into exile. He was determined to enjoy his wealth and parade it ostentatiously. To this end he acquired extensive real estate holdings in France – not mundane apartment blocks, but châteaux. He believed that ownership of such palatial homes was a precondition to the dignity and recognition he desired. He would show the French that he could live as sumptuously as the best of them, and perhaps then they would respect him. The purchase of the châteaux, of course, was also part of the grand regal master plan with which he was becoming increasingly obsessed.

The château of Villemorant, near Neung-sur-Beuvron in Sologne, was Bokassa's favourite. A nineteenth-century creation, it contained twenty rooms and was surrounded by a private estate of twenty-three hectares. Not far away, at Neuvy-sur-Barangeon, was the château of Saint-Louis Chavanon, purchased in 1973. This was a much more substantial structure of about sixty rooms and was modelled on Louis XIII's palace. The grounds stretched for fifty hectares and featured a pool of shimmering beauty known as the Mirror. The other Sologne property was a large hunting domain called La Cottencière. It was nothing less than a four-hundred-hectare playground of ponds, woods, and meadows.

Close to Paris, in the Yvelines, Bokassa owned two more properties. The imposing château of Hardricourt, at Meulan, was the preferred lodging of his principal wife, Catherine. The other, at Mézy-sur-Seine, was rarely visited by the president-for-life, but his large family found use for it. Even this was not all. In the hills overlooking Nice, Papa Bok maintained a well-appointed villa, Le Patio; and at Romorantin, back in Sologne, he acquired a hotel-restaurant, Le Montauge, where he sometimes plied his cooking skills in the kitchen.[34]

The villas and châteaux were prestige properties rather than real estate investments in the normal sense. While they certainly increased in value over the years, the cost of maintenance was enormous. But Bokassa considered them essential for hobnobbing with the French ruling class and foreign dignitaries. Giscard was a regular guest at the social functions thrown at the châteaux, and the bonds of friendship between the two presidents grew accordingly.

Bokassa's ties with France were both sentimental and practical. His foreign policies may have zigzagged over the years, but he always felt that he could turn to the French in emergencies. With his friend Giscard in the Elysée, this expectation was stronger than ever, especially as he was in great need of funds at the time. By the summer of 1975, Bokassa's government was in serious financial difficulty. This was nothing new, but an unfortunate configuration of circumstances had made matters worse than usual. Low prices for the coffee and cotton export crops, rising prices for imported petroleum products, and the persistent mismanagement had brought the state to its knees. Another major factor was the drought of the early 1970s, which had reduced water levels on the Oubangui River, making it navigable for only about six months of the year. Approximately 95 per cent of Centrafrique's exports and imports used this river route, connecting with the ocean by the Brazzaville–Pointe Noire railway.[35]

In any event, the coffers were empty and public servants could not be paid. On 28 July Bokassa implored the French president to come to his aid before discontent among government employees boiled over. Giscard was sympathetic. But mindful of the French public's growing hostility to the African leader's well-known extravagance, he attached two conditions: that there be no more château purchases or personal investment abroad; and that a team of financial experts examine the administrative practices in the Central African Republic. These terms were agreed to, and the experts set out for Bangui on their tour of inspection. They were horrified at what they found. They discovered that the Central African government spent money without keeping proper records and without considering the budget, if indeed there was one. Every branch of the state apparatus was chaotic. There could be little doubt that the country was on the verge of bankruptcy.[36]

On receiving this news, Giscard felt obliged to refuse immediate aid. The government in Bangui limped along as best it could, leaving debts and public servants unpaid. Occasional morsels of help from abroad staved off disaster, but barely. All seemed grim, even hopeless, when the president-for-life chanced on a possible solution to his country's financial woes, a viable alternative to the niggardly French assistance. On 1 September 1976 he went to Libya for celebrations marking the seventh anniversary of the coup that had brought Colonel Muammar Gadhaffi to power.[37] The flamboyant Libyan strongman had by this time a well-established reputation as a troublemaker and eccentric. He had few friends left, save perhaps for the IRA, the PLO, and Uganda's President Idi Amin. To this fellowship he now welcomed Bokassa with extravagant promises. The ace up Gadhaffi's sleeve was his oil money. The vast wealth that gushed from the desert floor gave him the wherewithal to embark on ambitious international ventures, most of which ended in failure. Among these was the promotion abroad of his unique version of Islamic revolution. He probably thought that Bokassa was a fool – but a willing fool – one who would carry his message to Central Africa.

On his return to Bangui, the president-for-life transformed his cabinet into a Council of the Revolution modelled on that of Libya. He also announced his conversion to the religion of Mohammed. Soon afterwards, on 17 October, Gadhaffi arrived in Bangui, and at the mosque at Kilomètre 5 he looked on approvingly as Bokassa was officially initiated into Islam. The new convert was known as Salah Addin Ahmed Bokassa, and it was announced that the national flag would thenceforth feature a crescent next to its star. Members of the Council of the Revolution were encouraged to follow the example of their president, a resurrection, perhaps, of the old principle *cuius regio, eius religio*. A number of them refused, including the public works minister, Joseph Potolot. Others, with less scruples, went over to Islam and collected gifts of up to twenty million CFA francs apiece. Prime Minister Ange Patassé was among the converts and beneficiaries and was henceforth was known as Mustapha. Bokassa, of course, was rewarded more than all the others, collecting a cheque for one million U.S. dollars.

On the afternoon of 18 October, Gadhaffi addressed a large gathering at the Omnisports Stadium on his favourite theme – that Christianity was the religion of imperialism while Islam was that of liberation. He was guest of honour that evening at a banquet given at the Palais de la Renaissance, where he was seated next to his host and disciple, who was dressed for the occasion in the djellaba and calotte. When Gadhaffi departed on 20 October, he left behind a number of agents to teach the converts their new religion. Former president David Dacko, who by then was rehabilitated and acting as an adviser to the president-for-life, thought that the Islamic revolution was ridiculous – especially the sight of Bokassa and his ministers kneeling on white goatskins sent specially from Libya while they tried out their prayers under the gaze of Gadhaffi's agents.

Dacko attempted to reason with the president, pointing out that his conversion was a betrayal of the M'Baka, who had long been loyal to Catholicism.[38] Dacko had a point, of course. Even if Bokassa's conversion had been sincere and enduring, it is improbable that Islam would have made much headway in the country. Muslims were an insignificant minority of 20,000 in a population approximating 2 million. About 50 per cent of Central Africans adhered to Christianity, while the other half retained traditional beliefs. Besides, Islam was generally reviled as the religion of the hated Arab slave traders, whose commerce in human beings had ravaged the country for centuries until the French put a stop to it. The religion of liberation it was not, regardless of what Gadhaffi had to say.

It is worth noting that there was more to the Libyan overture than evangelical zeal. During Gadhaffi's visit to Bangui, he signed agreements for the establishment of four joint commercial companies with capital of more than three billion CFA francs.[39] Bokassa's conversion to Islam, therefore, served a number of purposes. He and his government received some badly needed money with which to pay their bills while additional funds were invested in the economy. In accepting help from such a controversial source, the president-marshal was probably hoping that the French would be prodded into a more generous attitude towards his country.

In the Central African Republic, as in many former colonies, the various contenders for prominence viewed the state as the most important source of personal and group advancement. In the struggle for control of scarce resources, it was in the governmental apparatus rather than the marketplace that real gains were to be made. This became possible through state regulation of, and intervention in, the economy by a variety of means: nationalization, marketing boards, joint public-private corporate ventures, state-owned companies, and the licensing of various forms of enterprise. The takeover of Librairie Hachette and the oil companies in 1974, the establishment of ONCPA,

CentraHydro, and SECIP, state investment in URBA, URCA, and the Libyan joint companies, and the licence fees demanded of Diamond Distributors and others are examples of such state involvement in the economy.

Confiscations and exactions caused resentment in the international business community and likely diminished the potential flow of investment money to the country. Yet the consequences were not all negative. Statism, as it is sometimes called, did allow for the accumulation of capital in African hands, something unheard of in colonial days.[40] Admittedly, the African beneficiaries were few in number and were limited to the Europeanized élite and the Bokassa family in particular. And much of the capital was poured into nonproductive investments (real estate, for example) or squandered on ostentatious living. But some of it did end up in the factories and workshops of Berengo and in the surrounding farms and plantations. African capitalism was making a modest start, and Bokassa's boast that he was his country's first peasant and businessman certainly had some justification.

CHAPTER SIX

La folie des grandeurs

Bokassa's concern with decorations and titles has already been noted. To be called Papa or Marshal was in keeping with the tradition of strong chieftainship. But he wanted more. He wanted to outdo his contemporaries in grandeur and rank. There was only one title that would accomplish this beyond doubt – emperor. Although emperors were a rare breed in the latter half of the twentieth century, there were still a few around: Japan's Hirohito, Iran's Shah Mohammad Reza Pahlavi, and, of course, Ethiopia's Haile Selassie, the Conquering Lion of Judah. Africa therefore already had one empire of note, and in fact Bokassa had been received and decorated at the Ethiopian imperial court, an honour that had had a profound impression on him.

Selassie's power began to wane in 1973 when a drought devastated part of his empire. His government, refusing to admit that it could not cope, stood idly by as 200,000 people starved to death. Chaos ensued, and in 1974 a group of army officers overthrew the regime. The soldiers locked Selassie in a wing of his palace, and for a time there were occasional reports of his deteriorating health. Then the reports stopped, and a rumour spread that the Conquering Lion was dead. No official announcement was ever made.[1] Meanwhile Bokassa, dismayed at the fall of Africa's last emperor, sought ways of sustaining the Ethiopian monarchy. He urged the French to rescue Selassie and his family and bring them to Bangui, where the imperial throne might be re-established in exile – but nothing came of it.[2]

In some ways, Selassie's downfall paved the way for Bokassa's own imperial dream. If Africa had lost its only empire, surely no one would object to the creation of another. In conceiving his grand design, Bokassa took little note of indigenous African monarchial traditions, such as those of Ethiopia and Swaziland. Nor did he show much interest in the resurrection or invention of native authenticity as practised, for example, by Zaïre's President Mobutu.[3] His model was Napoleon Bonaparte, the Corsican dynamo who had bent Europe to his will. Bokassa often spoke in glowing terms of the French emperor, and he had a huge library of books on the man. On visits to Paris he showed an inordinate interest in portraits of Napoleon and his marshals, noting in particular the details of their uniforms. At the francophone summit in Bangui in March 1975, he had planned to greet Giscard d'Estaing dressed as a marshal of the empire; but French officials dissuaded him from doing so, though only after strenuous entreaties.

Later in the year, at a dinner in his Château Villemorant, Bokassa presented Giscard with his idea of reviving the Napoleonic empire in Central Africa. Giscard was evasive and suggested that a traditional African ceremony, with as little expense as possible, might be more appropriate in the circumstances. The Central African Republic, after all, was virtually bankrupt, and dissatisfaction was widespread. But Bokassa would not listen. He would have his empire under the symbol of the Napoleonic eagle. It was necessary, he argued, to foster national unity and combat political destabilization. And he insisted on French aid for the affair, hinting that if this was not forthcoming, French access to his country's uranium might be jeopardized.[4]

Bokassa was confident that Giscard's unwillingness would eventually be overcome. His more immediate concern was how to get the imperial idea accepted at home. He could, of course, have exercised his absolute power and declared himself emperor, but that might have provoked opposition or, worse yet, mirth. It would be best, he reasoned, if MESAN, the only political party, took the initiative in establishing the empire and acclaiming him its ruler. Bokassa had already made a move that seemed to pave the way for such an initiative when, in January 1975, he had appointed Mme Elizabeth Domitien as his prime minister and vice-president of MESAN. Thus, Africa had its first female head of government. A heavy woman with a shrewd business sense, she had amassed a personal fortune through a variety of ventures. Her connections with the women of the marketplace were important to Bokassa, but her real value, or so it was said, was that she bore the name of a Roman emperor. Surely she would support an empire on the banks of the Oubangui.[5] But Domitien was in fact against the idea, fearing that it would cause embarrassment abroad. So in September she was ousted from the cabinet, and the post of prime minister went to the more accommodating and obsequious Ange Patassé.[6]

Captain Obrou's attempted coup in February 1976 banished from Bokassa's mind any lingering doubts he might have had about establishing an empire. He came to believe that the title "emperor" would in itself protect him from would-be assassins by intensifying the mystique about his person. He therefore went ahead with his plan to achieve his ambition through MESAN.

On 24 July he criticized the *parti unique* for failing to uncover the February plot. Then he announced that the party was to be reformed and that it would take on a new role: preserving the security of the state. What this meant in practice was a purge of MESAN's top officials and their replacement by people who were more unswervingly devoted to the president-for-life. The disgruntled Mme Domitien, for instance, in addition to being ejected from the cabinet, lost her job as MESAN's vice-president.

As the reforms proceeded, Bokassa made contact with the royal courts in Iran, Japan, and Morocco, which helped him put together the outline of an imperial constitution. The Gadhaffi visit, the conversion to Islam, and the establishment of the Council of the Revolution – all of which took place in the autumn of 1976 – in no way interfered with the unfolding imperial plans. It was at this time too that Bokasa rehabilitated David Dacko and made him a personal adviser. Dacko's main task was to maintain friendly ties with the French government. Relations had recently been cool as a result of the Islamic revolution. In late October, soon after Gadhaffi's visit, Bokassa sent Dacko to Paris to offer a deal: he would split with Libya if France would pay for his imperial project. The French quietly agreed.[7]

On 10 November Salah Addin Ahmed Bokassa, as he was still called, opened an "extraordinary conference" of MESAN at Bangui's Omnisports Stadium, telling the delegates that they were there to formulate a new constitution. He then told them what it ought to be like. A few days later the president-for-life left the delegates to their deliberations and set off on his first official visit to the People's Republic of China, with which he had re-established diplomatic relations in August. In Beijing he denounced the Gang of Four and recited other slogans popular in the post-Mao era. During the four-day stay, he met Chairman Hua Kuo-feng and signed a trade and cooperation agreement. And at a banquet in his honour on 15 November, Vice-President Li Hsien-nien praised his efforts to develop Centrafrique and his constant struggle against the imperialism, colonialism, and aggression of the superpowers in Africa.[8]

Meanwhile, the MESAN *congressistes* adopted a resolution to transform the republic into an empire. On 4 December 1976 the Central

African Empire was solemnly declared to exist with Bokassa I as emperor. The new constitution proclaimed that the empire was based on democratic principles. There was to be a National Assembly to enable the people to share power with the emperor. There were encouraging references to individual freedom and political liberty, the United Nations Charter, and the Universal Declaration of Human Rights. Less encouraging was the statement that the emperor himself would be the guarantor of these rights and freedoms.

Old friends immediately rallied round to proclaim their support. President Giscard was the first foreign head of state to send a telegram of congratulation. President Mobutu did even better. He turned up personally in Bangui on 4 December to hear the imperial proclamation. But most international reaction was muted. Meanwhile, there was speculation in the press that the emperor was in ill health and wished to rid himself of the day-to-day chores of running a government. In French government circles it was believed that he would stay in his palace and allow the country to be directed by Patassé and others. Some jurists who examined the constitution anticipated the emergence of an effective prime minister, a national assembly, and a supreme court, and they defended the imperial project on these grounds. It was also rumoured that Bokassa might abdicate in favour of his son Georges and then, with his family firmly entrenched in power, retire to one of his French châteaux.[9]

All of a sudden, revolutionary rhetoric of the Libyan variety, which had been briefly popular on Radio-Bangui, was silenced. Bokassa had tired of Islam, especially its prohibition on alcohol. And when the flow of Libyan aid proved inadequate, he abandoned the Koran without regret. In January 1977 he returned to the Catholic fold. This religious *volte-face* was precipitated by Bokassa's disenchantment with Gadhaffi's stinginess and his satisfaction about the secret deal with France. Besides, a "revolutionary empire" appeared somewhat contradictory. An important consideration, however, was his determination to be crowned emperor. It was not enough to have the title – Bokassa wanted an elaborate coronation like that of Napoleon, with the Pope presiding. Since His Holiness could hardly be expected to do the honours to a Muslim, a rapprochement with Rome made sense. The coronation was scheduled for 4 December 1977, exactly a year after the proclamation of the empire. In the intervening twelve months, the entire apparatus of the state was devoted to making the ceremony an unforgettable occasion.

On 13 March 1977, Catherine, *numero uno* among the emperor's wives, gave birth to Prince Saint-Jean de Bokassa de Berengo de Boubangui de Centrafrique. The state-controlled press applauded this addition to the already large royal family as a portent of good fortune. A week later, sixteen pages of the official newspapers were filled with the letters of congratulation that had inundated the Berengo court following the birth of *le petit prince*.[10] Catherine's production of yet another son gave her an advantage in an issue that was yet unresolved – which of Bokassa's wives would be crowned empress by his side. Gabriella, the Romanian, had been the favourite for a while, but Catherine was able to raise plausible arguments against her great rival: the empress should be a Central African and the mother of male heirs if a proper dynasty was to be created.[11]

Bokassa agreed, and under pressure from Catherine his visits to the Villa Kolongo became increasingly infrequent. Gabriella was now like a prisoner in her home, and she became bored and frustrated. As time went by, she discovered a kindred spirit in Martine N'Douta, one of the two nurses who attended her child. She confided in Martine, sharing her hopes, fantasies, and fears. She admitted that if her husband, whom she affectionately called Django, allowed her to go home on a holiday, she would never return. She was depressed, it seems, not just by Bokassa's neglect but because he had chosen Catherine as his empress.

Before long, Gabriella and Martine became sexually involved with the guards on duty at the villa. A servant girl who was not party to these goings-on informed the emperor and provided evidence in the form of nude photographs, which the women had taken of one another. On the evening of 28 September 1977, Bokassa and a squadron of soldiers turned up unexpectedly at Kolongo and put a prompt end to the revelry. The friends and lovers of the Romanian were handcuffed, blindfolded, and paraded around the edge of the nearby crocodile pond while Bokassa threatened to feed them to the reptiles. As it turned out, most of them met their end in a less macabre manner. Imprisoned in Ngaragba, they were taken out individually from time to time to face the firing squad. Only one of them survived until the end of the regime and regained his freedom. Gabriella was treated more leniently. She was sent back to Romania, which was what she wanted in any case. Her daughter stayed in Centrafrique.[12]

With the Romanian's fall from grace, Catherine could concentrate on another of her ambitions – securing the succession for one of her children. For much of 1977 the leading candidate for crown prince was Georges, the emperor's eldest son. Georges had been born in Brazzaville to Marguerite Green on 24 December 1949. At the age of sixteen he was reunited with his father and subsequently went to study in France and the United States. Since his return to Bangui in the mid-1970s, he had been serving in his father's cabinet. In spite of his prominence, Georges was not exactly imperial material. His speech was impaired by a serious stutter, and he spoke French with a heavy African accent. Worse still, he was a fairly decent character and often tried to mitigate his father's excesses of cruelty. Bokassa considered him weak.[13] In the end, therefore, Catherine prevailed. The emperor chose her second-youngest son, the four-year-old Jean-Bedel, Jr, as *prince héritier*.

International press coverage of these events was couched in unmitigated cynicism if not outright hostility. The pretensions of the poverty-stricken empire made an easy target for journalists seeking the sensational and exotic. As a result, many foreign newspapers and magazines were banned. Journalists from abroad were greeted with suspicion and were required to post a bond of four hundred dollars before being admitted to the country. Even so, a few intrepid newsmen made their way to Bangui, and two of them almost died as a result.

Michael Goldsmith was a British journalist who worked for Associated Press of New York. Jonathan Randall was a correspondent with the *Washington Post*. Together they covered the Organization of African Unity summit in Libreville, Gabon, and on 11 July they went on to Bangui to find out about the planned coronation festivities. They spent a few days talking to diplomats and officials but failed to get an interview with the emperor himself. On the afternoon of 14 July, Goldsmith telexed his report to the Associated Press office in Johannesburg. Part of the message became garbled, and the police, who intercepted it, assumed that a secret code was being used. Four hours later, the Englishman was arrested on suspicion of spying for South Africa.

The handcuffed Goldsmith was taken to Berengo and brought before Bokassa. He bowed, uttering "Majesté." The emperor was unmoved and then, without warning, struck the prisoner violently on the head with his *canne de justice*. Goldsmith fell to the ground under the force of the blow, an enormous gash on his forehead. He lost his glasses in the fall and Bokassa, spotting them lying on the floor, crushed them under his foot. Guards continued the beating until Goldsmith passed out. He regained consciousness the next day to find himself in a rat-infested prison cell. His clothes had been removed save for his shorts, and he was manacled hand and foot to the wall. He was in Ngaragba.

Meanwhile, Randall also had been arrested and had been thrown into a cell full of thieves. He was neither interrogated nor accused of any crime. On 21 July he was taken to Berengo handcuffed, barefoot, and unshaven. Bokassa awaited him seated at the end of a long table surrounded by cabinet ministers, courtiers, and members of the dip-lomatic corps. The emperor immediately launched into a long diatribe against the United States, which he blamed for all of Africa's ills.

"Their journalists are all spies," he said, "as well as their Peace Corps volunteers. Why cannot a great power control its journalists? I would never allow my journalists to do such a thing."

Bokassa then produced some notes that Randall had made about various imperial courtesans, and the verbal abuse continued. At the end of the rambling monologue, Randall was photographed, given his shoes and socks, and handed over to the U.S. chargé d'affaires. He left the country immediately and alerted Mrs Goldsmith to her husband's fate.

Roxanne Goldsmith now appealed to the emperor to release her husband. President Bongo of Gabon also interceded on behalf of the prisoner, having been asked to do so by Andrew Young, U.S. ambas-sador to the United Nations. These representations and others had an immediate effect. Goldsmith was unchained, moved to a larger cell, given medical atttention for his wounds, and fed European-style meals from a nearby hotel (water and manioc had been his diet until then). On 12 August he was taken once more to Berengo, where a group of cabinet ministers read him an exchange of telegrams between his wife and the emperor. Bokassa then appeared and lec-tured the journalist without interruption for more than two hours. He accused Goldsmith of espionage and of making insulting remarks in his dispatch to Johannesburg. In spite of this, he said, he had decided to be compassionate and release him – but only because of the devotion and persistent appeals of his wife, Roxanne. Goldsmith spent a couple of happy nights at the Safari Hotel and was scheduled to catch a flight to Paris on Sunday, 14 August. But just before leav-ing, he was taken once again to Berengo, where he was forced to sign a "confession" that had been prepared. Bokassa then became friendly, embraced Goldsmith, and invited him to say nothing of his unpleasant experiences. Shortly thereafter, the journalist was safely aboard his plane, his month-long nightmare over.

Goldsmith's story was widely publicized, bringing further dis-credit to the empire.[14] Rather late in the day, Bokassa realized that journalists, even hostile ones, would be indispensable to the success of his forthcoming coronation. It was one thing to be criticized; it was quite another to be ignored. It would be nothing less than cata-strophic if the media stayed away. In the months that followed, he was therefore on his best behaviour, and in a television interview in the autumn he was almost contrite. When asked if he had beaten up prisoners and cut off thieves' ears, he replied, "I admit I did these things in the past, but I've stopped. It won't happen again."[15]

Meanwhile, the empire was mustering every resource to ensure the success of the coronation. Special committees were established to supervise various aspects of the work. The committee in charge of accommodation had the task of finding suitable rooms for an anticipated 2,500 foreign guests. To this end it began to commandeer apartments, houses, and hotels for the duration of the festivities, renovating them in a fitting manner. Another committee was responsible for making the capital look its best, especially those areas that would be involved in the coronation ceremonies. Streets were scrubbed, buildings painted, and beggars driven out of sight. The empire's textile industry was kept busy producing hundreds of new suits for local guests. Strict rules of protocol dictated the colours: white for schoolchildren, navy blue for middle-management people in the private and public sectors, and black for cabinet ministers and senior officials.[16]

While all this was going on, a number of international artists were commissioned to honour the emperor in their respective genres. Painter Hans Linus of Murnau, West Germany, did two large portraits of His Majesty. One showed him bareheaded, wearing a white uniform; the other showed his crowned head. The latter was featured on a commemorative postage stamp that was issued for the coronation. A French composer provided an "Imperial March" and a companion "Imperial Waltz," and a poet wrote a coronation ode of twenty quatrains, four of which (in translation) went as follows:

Do you know where breathes today
The Christian spirit of France?
Of ancient Rome and Byzantium?
It's in Bangui, la Coquette.

The successor of Clovis the Great
Of the heroes of Greece and of Gaul
Of Charlemagne and Saint Louis
Of Bonaparte and de Gaulle.

It's Bokassa, Caesar Augustus
The most illustrious of the French!
Let's prostrate ourselves before his bust
Let's celebrate everywhere his favours.

Bokassa, the new Bonaparte
Bangui, his illustrious city
Eclipses Rome, Athens, Sparta
By its brilliant beauty.[17]

French craftsmen produced the most memorable items associated with the coronation. Sculptor Olivier Brice became involved in November 1976, when he was approached confidentially by an official of the Central African embassy in Paris. Bokassa wanted the versatile artist to decorate Bangui Cathedral, where he hoped his coronation would take place. Brice did such a good job that he was invited to do the throne and the carriage as well.

The throne was in the form of an eagle sitting upright with wings outstretched. The gold-plated bronze structure weighed 2 tonnes and was 3.5 metres high and 4.5 metres wide. Brice built a special workshop near his home in Gisors, Normandy, where thirty craftsmen executed his design. A local upholsterer, Michel Cousin, was hired to do the red velvet seat – in effect, a cavity in the bird's belly. The golden eagle cost the equivalent of $2.5 million. Meanwhile, Brice bought an antique coach in Nice and refurbished it with appropriate velvet, gold trim, and eagle symbols. This was to be the imperial carriage that would transport the emperor on the day of his coronation. Eight white horses were found in Belgium to pull it, and a few dozen Normandy greys were acquired to carry the escort of "hussars" that was to accompany the carriage. In order to ensure that all went well on the day, a troop of Central African soldiers spent the summer of 1977 near Lisieux, also in Normandy, learning equestrian skills.[18]

The costumes, too, were French creations. The 200-year-old firm of Guiselin, which had designed Napoleon's uniforms, was called on to create Bokassa's coronation attire. First there was a floor-length toga decorated with tens of thousands of tiny pearls. Matching pearl-covered slippers went with it. Then there was a mantle: nine metres of crimson velvet, embroidered with gold imperial emblems and trimmed with a wide ermine border. The total cost of the emperor's costume was $145,000. A gold lamé gown highlighted by 935,000 sequins was made for Catherine, who was to be crowned empress next to her husband. The bill from the House of Lanvin was $72,400. The empress also had a flowing mantle similar to that of the emperor but of more modest dimensions.[19]

The imperial crown was the work of Arthus Bertrand, the Saint-Germain-des-Prés jeweller. It was traditional in design: a heavy gold frame resting on an ermine headband with a crimson velvet canopy on top. Golden prongs curved over the velvet to join together in supporting a golden eagle. The eagle was perched, wings outstretched, on a blue orb representing the earth, on which a map of Africa was etched in gold. The crown was encrusted with diamonds, the largest of which, displayed prominently in front, weighed eighty carats. The entire crown was valued at $2.5 million. There was also a gold crown for the empress which featured a diamond of twenty-five carats. The crowns, along with the imperial sceptre, sword, and other bits and pieces brought the total jewellery bill to around $5 million.

The emperor wanted his guests to enjoy themselves throughout the festivities. More than 240 tonnes of food and drink were flown in from Europe for the post-coronation banquet. The wines, 40,000 bottles in all, included cases of Château Lafite-Rothschild and Château Mouton-Rothschild 1971, vintages that were selling in the United States at the time for $25 apiece. Of course, the occasion demanded champagne – 24,000 bottles of Moët et Chandon – and Chivas Regal scotch whisky, Bokassa's favourite, was there in abundance. Finally, in order to take the guests around Bangui in style and comfort, sixty brand-new Mercedes-Benzes were ordered from Germany. The cars were shipped to Cameroun, from where they were air-freighted to the land-locked empire. The air freight charges alone amounted to $5,000 per car.

When everything was added up – throne, clothes, jewellery, liquor, cars, and so on – the total cost of the coronation came to around $22 million. This was an enormous sum considering the state of the national economy. It approximated one-quarter of the empire's annual budget. France paid for most of it, as it had promised to do in return for Centrafrique's break with Libya, but there were also local contributions. Throughout 1977, Bokassa put considerable pressure on the empire's private sector to make appropriate donations. For instance, it was made known to companies trading in coffee, cotton, and diamonds that their generosity would largely determine the future of their business operations. They bowed to the inevitable. Many of the gems adorning the imperial jewels were gifts from Bangui's diamond merchants.

One of these firms, Diamond Distributors, which had suffered crippling confiscations in the past, succeeded in avoiding major exactions by a clever ruse. The company president, Albert Jolis, baulked at the prospect of having to donate a "very large diamond" to the emperor, as he was asked to do. A solution to his dilemma appeared when one of his assistants handed him a chunk of black bort weighing nearly seventy carats. Normally, this poorly crystallized stone would have been crushed to make industrial abrasives. But Jolis, suspecting that Bokassa knew nothing about diamonds, believed he could dazzle him with the bort, which, by a happy coincidence, resembled Africa in shape. He ordered the large stone cut, polished, and mounted on a ring. He then had a one-quarter carat white diamond set in its centre, approximating the location of Bangui on a map of the continent. The ring was placed in a presentation case with a certificate declaring that it represented Africa and was unique in the world. A week later Jolis flew into Bangui and presented the gift, with understandable apprehension, to the emperor. Bokassa was delighted with his "unique diamond." Diamond Distributors' mining concession was safe, at least for the moment. The emperor wore his black diamond ring during the coronation ceremony, and the world press, not knowing any better, reported that it was worth over $500,000. It had cost Jolis about $250.[20]

Had Bokassa had his way, the coronation would have taken place at Bangui's Cathédrale de Notre-Dame with Pope Paul VI presiding. The emperor was familiar with the incident in Paris 173 years previously in which Napoleon had taken the crown from the hands of Pope Pius VII and placed it on his own head. He wanted to recreate this scene and asked the local archbishop, Monseigneur Ndayen, and the papal nuncio, Oriano Quilici, to persuade the Pope to come. The churchmen resisted, and in June 1977 the nuncio explained that Paul VI was too old to make the journey. Besides, the Vatican was no longer in the business of crowning royalty or of handing emperors their crowns. The best the archbishop could offer was a mass in the cathedral after the coronation ceremony. The nuncio promised that the Vatican would send a prominent envoy, Monseigneur Domenico Enrici, who had represented the Pope at the crowning of Spain's King Juan Carlos.[21] In the end, the coronation was scheduled to take place at the Palais des Sports Jean-Bedel Bokassa, on avenue Bokassa, not far from Université Jean-Bedel Bokassa. The chosen venue was in fact a basketball stadium built by the Yugoslavs. Olivier Brice was to decorate it in an appropriate manner.

As preparations progressed, Bokassa's major concern was to ensure a respectable turnout of international dignitaries. His fellow emperors, Japan's Hirohito and Iran's Shah Reza Pahlavi, were the first to be invited, but they declined. The rest of the world's reigning monarchs were also on the official guest list, and one by one they too refused. The only aristocrat to accept was Prince Emmanuel of Liechtenstein, a relative of the little country's sovereign. The prime minister of Mauritius, Sir Seewoosagur Ramgoolam, turned up – the most prominent politician to do so. No presidents came. President Ould Daddah of Mauritania sent his wife and most other African countries either were represented by their ambassadors or boycotted the affair. Even old friends like Mobutu, Bongo, and Idi Amin found excuses to stay away. "They were jealous of me because I had an empire and they didn't," Bokassa later told an interviewer.[22] He may have been right.

Giscard d'Estaing, to the surprise of many, decided not to attend but sent a sabre "from the Napoleonic era" as a gift on behalf of his government.[23] Paris was represented by Robert Galley, minister of cooperation, and by René Journiac, presidential adviser on African affairs. François Giscard d'Estaing, who had arranged most of the payments, was also there. Galley, in response to attacks in the French press on the extravagance involved, said, "Personally, I find it perfectly abnormal to criticize what is to take place in Bangui while finding the Queen of England's Jubilee ceremony all right. It smacks of racism."[24] In all, 2,500 guests were invited from abroad and 600 accepted. They included 100 journalists, who were apparently undeterred by Michael Goldsmith's encounter with His Imperial Majesty. The $400 bond normally required of foreign newsmen was waived for the occasion. Media coverage of the coronation was thus assured.

By 7:00 AM on the great day – 4 December 1977 – Mercedes limousines were busily conveying guests along the boulevards of Bangui to the coronation palace. By 8:30 they were all in their places – a multitude of 4,000 in all. The emperor was due to arrive at 9:00, and in the interim recorded music blared from loudspeakers to maintain a suitable atmosphere. Brice had done a good job in disguising the harsher elements of the stadium's drab socialist architecture by hanging rich tapestries and banners in the national colours all around. At one end, in a sea of blazing red carpet and drapes, stood the golden eagle throne on a raised platform. To the right stood the empress's throne – a green velvet creation covered by a four-postered golden canopy. On the left was a stool of gold-trimmed crimson velvet for the crown prince.

Nine o'clock came and there was no sign of the emperor. The French marine band, which had been sitting in silence for over an hour, began to play "Chevaliers de la table ronde," an ancient drinking song. The air-conditioning was not working and the temperature, already in the high thirties, was beginning to take its toll on the formally attired guests. Some were fanning themselves with coronation programs; others were mopping sweat from their brows. At last, at 10:10 AM, a marching band was heard in the distance. The emperor was approaching in his horse-drawn carriage. Bokassa and Catherine had begun their procession at the Palais de la Renaissance several kilometres away, but they had found the heat in the enclosed carriage unbearable and had transferred to an air-conditioned Mercedes. They returned to the carriage only for the last few hundred metres.

By 10:15 AM the imperial cortège began to enter the stadium and the ceremonies were underway. The first to appear were two guards dressed in Napoleonic military uniforms bearing the national flag and the imperial standard. They carried these emblems up the carpeted aisle and stationed themselves on either side of the gilded throne. Then came the heir apparent, four-year-old Prince Jean-Bedel. The crown prince was attired for the occasion in a white naval uniform with gold braid and a matching visored cap that was too big for his head. The crowd stood in polite silence as he marched up the aisle and perched himself on his assigned stool. The Empress Catherine appeared next. Tall, slim, and elegant, she was resplendent in her shimmering dress of gold lamé. On her head sat a wreath of golden laurel leaves. Ladies-in-waiting in white evening gowns and broad-brimmed floppy hats held up her short train as she proceeded slowly towards her throne. Meanwhile, the marine band played the "Imperial March." Light and yet majestic, it was certainly appropriate, though not everyone thought it sufficiently ponderous.

A brief moment of silence followed. Then the drums rolled and a voice announced over the loudspeaker, "Sa Majesté, Bokassa Premier, l'empereur de Centrafrique." The band struck up the "Imperial March" once more, and the emperor strode into the stadium. His well-built body was clad in the ankle-length coronation toga, which gleamed with the silver-grey lustre of pearls. Around his waist hung a sash in the national colours – blue, white, green, yellow, and red. On his chest were two of his favourite medals. His head was adorned, Roman style, with a wreath of golden laurels, his feet with slippers of pearl. On his hands were gloves of white antelope skin. The occasion called for solemnity, dignity, and a serious demeanour, and he rose to the challenge. As he made his way up the aisle, his countenance radiated an expression of triumph like that of a military hero returning from great conquests.

As the emperor reclined in his winged throne, a number of functionaries in Napoleonic uniforms began to carry the coronation paraphernalia into the stadium. They approached His Majesty, who rose to greet them. First they gave him the sword, which he buckled on. Then came the sceptre – a two-metre ebony staff encrusted with precious stones – which he grasped in his right hand, holding it upright like a bishop's crozier. Next they placed one end of the nine-metre-long velvet and ermine mantle on his shoulders, allowing the rest of it to cascade down the steps of the platform to the left. Finally, there was the crown. Bokassa removed his laurel wreath and, lifting the crown from the cushion on which it rested, he planted it firmly on his head. A twenty-one-gun salute then boomed forth, rattling the windows of the stadium; and the audience, which had been standing throughout, applauded politely. The emperor now took an oath to the nation: "We, Bokassa I, Emperor of Central Africa, by the will of the Central African people ... do solemnly swear and promise, before the people, before the whole of humanity and before history, to do everything possible to uphold the constitution, safeguard national independence and territorial integrity ... and serve the Central African nation in accordance with the sacred ideals of the national political party." Following the oath, the audience joined in singing the national anthem in Sango.

With the singing at an end, it was Catherine's turn to be invested. Her mantle was carried up the aisle and placed around her shoulders. She then knelt before the emperor, who rose from his throne and placed her crown on her head. Photographs recording the scene bear an uncanny resemblance to Louis David's painting of Napoleon's coronation that hangs in the Louvre. A few choral renditions wrapped up the ceremony. Bokassa then led the way out of the stadium in full imperial regalia, a coterie of attendants struggling with his cumbersome mantle. The empress was next, assisted by her ladies-in-waiting. Then came the crown prince, followed by the emperor's other progeny, all dressed in white for the occasion, who had been seated close to the throne. It was shortly after 11:00 AM. The coronation had taken about an hour.

From there, it was on to mass at the cathedral, about two kilometres away. A troop of hussars in the now-familiar Napoleonic garb led the way on horseback. The emperor and empress once more suffered the stifling heat of their carriage, while the crown prince travelled in a horse-drawn open landau. Along the way the imperial cavalcade passed under a number of concrete triumphal arches and banners bearing the letter B, while large crowds listlessly lined the boulevards. There was no evident enthusiasm among the onlookers for the unusual spectacle, no spontaneous outbursts of "Vive l'empereur!"

Archbishop Ndayen awaited Their Majesties at his red brick cathedral and led them to a couple of thrones arranged at the front. The heir apparent had a stool to sit on, as at the stadium. Some pews were reserved for high-ranking guests, but most had to fend for themselves and many were left standing. The archbishop officiated at the mass, which was conducted in French, Latin, and Sango. His sermon was full of dignity, and he wished the emperor well, though he avoided the praise and flattery that was evidently expected. Ndayen's attitude was simple: his church was open to all – even dogs wandered in unmolested, he had once remarked. It was now early afternoon, and the tropical heat and humidity were at their most oppressive. Yet Bokassa sat impassively through the mass under the weight of his full coronation regalia. In a surprising move, the archbishop had the collection plates passed round, and their heaping appearance testified to the shrewdness of his decision. A *Te Deum* brought the service to an end.

Later in the afternoon the emperor held a reception for the most prominent guests. Others were free to cool off as best they could, the air-conditioned bar at the Rock Hotel being a popular destination. All four thousand guests were invited to a banquet that evening at the Palais de la Renaissance. Tables were set outdoors in the extensive courtyard where, less than two years earlier, Fidèle Obrou and his fellow conspirators had spent their final hours. Everything was in place by 9 PM when the meal was supposed to begin, but as usual the emperor was late. This time his tardiness was not so irritating. The sun no longer blazed overhead, and the tables were liberally supplied with wines and liquors. A pleasant cocktail hour ensued until the arrival of the host and hostess at 10 PM. Bokassa had by then shed his heavy coronation robes and was dressed in a Napoleonic marshal's uniform. On his head sat a cockaded hat with ostrich plumes, on his finger the black diamond ring. Catherine was in a long evening dress of Parisian *haute couture*.

A fine dinner with some local flavour was served. Beginning with Iranian caviar, the tables were loaded successively with *chaussons aux écrevisses* (crayfish pastry roll), *suprême de capitaine à l'oseille* (sturgeon), *antilopes sauce grand veneur* (antelope in huntsman sauce), *foie gras*, and *gâteau impérial*. The seven-layer imperial cake decorated in green icing sprang open at the top to release a half-dozen doves. When all the guests had had their fill and the plates were being cleared away, Bokassa turned to Robert Galley and whispered, "You never noticed, but you ate human flesh!" It was chance remarks of this sort that later gave rise to the rumours regarding the emperor's eating habits.

A thirty-five-minute firework display followed the meal. Then there was entertainment, some of it provided by a song-and-dance group made up partly of former Saigon bar girls. This brought back happy memories for His Majesty. The French marine band was also on duty. When it struck up the "Imperial Waltz," Bokassa and Catherine led their guests onto the dance floor. The *soirée* came to an end around 2:30 AM when the imperial couple departed.

A parade was scheduled for the following morning on one of Bangui's main boulevards, where a special reviewing stand had been erected for the emperor and his guests. Bokassa arrived at 10:00 AM, an hour late as usual. He was once again in his marshal's uniform. Catherine had chosen a garden-party dress and a wide-brimmed lavender hat for the occasion. Crown Prince Jean-Bedel was dressed in his admiral's outfit. The main feature of the parade was the empire's thousand-man army, which marched by first. Then came groups representing civic, youth, student, and athletic organizations, while traditional African dancers brought up the rear. Bokassa gazed at it all with evident pleasure. Catherine's enthusiasm, if any, was less obvious. The crown prince fell asleep. Sports events filled the afternoon. A basketball tournament, known as the Coronation Cup, was particularly popular and the emperor himself was in attendance. There were more parties and receptions that evening, and then the festive mood faded. Before long, guests and journalists alike were homeward bound and Bangui returned to normal.[25]

Bokassa had wanted to be noticed, and he certainly had been. The world press diligently reported his moment of glory, though without the accolades or acclaim that he expected. His crowned image was flashed around the globe, usually accompanied by mocking commentary. The reaction in Africa alternated between embarrassment and rage. Kenya's *Sunday Nation* referred to Bokassa's "clowning glory," while Zambia's *Daily Mail* deplored his "obnoxious excesses." The coronation was seen to epitomize the worst Western stereotypes of the continent, and it was said to play into the hands of the white supremacists in Rhodesia and South Africa, who insisted that blacks were childlike, irresponsible, and incapable of ruling themselves.

The European coverage was just as contemptuous, especially in France. French journalists dismissed the coronation as a tragicomedy and masquerade; they scoffed at its wastefulness and at its pseudo-historical trappings; and they denounced their own government's hypocritical support for it all. President Giscard's response was more positive. Watching the coronation on the television news that evening, he found the images beautiful, with a certain dignity. He was especially moved by the sight of Catherine receiving her crown: "The new empress ... a former student of missionary schools, playing a role similar to that of Josephine, personified both modesty and allure."[26]

Bokassa's coronation has been condemned for its extravagance, and with much justification. Yet it was a relatively modest affair compared with similar celebrations in other countries. Consider, for example, the $100 million spent by the Shah of Iran in 1971 to celebrate the 2,500th anniversary of the founding of the Persian Empire, an event that allowed him to pose as a successor of the Emperor Darius.[27] Bokassa was certainly not alone in stage-managing self-glorification and spending money for such ends. It might also be noted that although the Napoleonic symbols and pageantry caused the coronation to be ridiculed for its inauthenticity, they were not inconsistent with the practice of cultural and institutional adaptation that characterized Africa's interaction with Europe. Just as European education had become highly prized as the key to modern knowledge, so too European clothing symbolized status and prestige. That Bokassa should adopt costumes and uniforms from French models for the coronation is not at all surprising. Moreover, since Centrafrique's political institutions and practices were largely borrowed from France, it could be argued that a Bonapartist monarchy was no less authentic than a republic.

CHAPTER SEVEN

Oui, Majesté impériale

Bokassa's imperial court was situated at Berengo, eighty kilometres southwest of Bangui, and was connected to the capital by the country's only paved highway. It bore no resemblance to any of Europe's royal residences or even to the futuristic palace of Gabon's President Bongo. In an important sense, Berengo reflected Bokassa's practical side – his description of himself as peasant and businessman as well as emperor. The imperial court complex had begun as his private farm and had evolved over the years as factories and workshops sprang up in the vicinity. By the time Bokassa established the empire, Berengo consisted of the farm, factories, an airport, and a compound of comfortable modern houses surrounded by a security palisade. It was very much like a model village and had a population of nearly three housand. There were farmers, workers, servants, wives, mistresses, children, and the ever-present security guards.[1]

Security was Berengo's most compelling *raison d'être*. Bokassa had always been fearful of potential assassins, and with good cause, especially after Captain Obrou's attempted coup. The imperial guards, one thousand men in all, were his principal source of protection. Highly trained and well armed, they were drawn from his own M'Baka people. The M'Baka, as a minority in the empire, knew that their privileges depended on Bokassa staying in power. The guards were therefore intensely loyal, and their presence around the imperial court gave it the appearance of a military camp. The Central African army, by contrast, was poorly trained and usually without ammunition; it would have been no match for the guards in the event of a confrontation. The imperial guards had been trained by the former Israeli general Samuel Gonen, who had been relieved of his command because of blunders in the Yom Kippur War of 1973.[2]

Bokassa was determined to enjoy his new role to the full and to give his court some of the trappings of imperial pomp and splendour. To begin with, life at Berengo freed him from the everyday chores of running the government, at least at the beginning. This task now fell to his prime minister, Ange Patassé. The prime minister was authorized to greet visiting heads of state on their arrival at Bangui. Later, they were taken to Berengo to be formally received by the emperor. This routine gave Bokassa a great advantage in the constant manœuvring for position and precedence that marks encounters between international leaders. Visitors were obliged to come to him on his terms and to conform to the behavioural expectations of the court.

All communication with His Majesty was circumscribed by strict rules of protocol. A bulletin of 8 December 1976 explained the required etiquette. Persons approaching the supreme ruler were to stop at six paces, salute, and bow their heads. Then, in responding to questions, they were expected to utter, "Yes, Imperial Majesty." Should an answer in the negative be in order, a blunt "no" was to be avoided. This code of conduct, which had been borrowed from the court of Haile Selassie, even applied to the Empress Catherine.[3] Bokassa defended it by saying that he was trying to remind foreigners that Africa had had its own kings and traditions of protocol long before the arrival of Europeans. He was not, he insisted, putting a distance between himself and his people.[4] There was some truth to this, for Berengo was no Buckingham Palace, and although Bokassa sought dignity and respect, he was no stuffy monarch. By nature spontaneous and gregarious, he was far more likely to embrace visiting dignitaries than to keep them at a distant six paces.

An important accessory to the imperial pomp was the new letterhead paper, on which the words "Cour Impériale Empire Centrafricain" surrounded Bokassa's coronation crown done in gold and red. The crown hovered over the golden imperial sun, on which was embossed a white eagle. Underneath were the words "unité, dignité, travail." The paper bore a watermark of His Majesty's head wearing a laurel wreath in the Roman manner.[5]

Although the emperor's power was absolute, it did not extend very much beyond the Bangui-Berengo corridor. There were prefects and other government officials in the larger provincial towns, but they were usually ignored by the local populace. If trouble erupted, as it did early in 1979, troops had to be rushed in from the capital to restore order. In smaller centres, traditional village councils and secret societies continued to regulate everyday life, independent of imperial directives.

Bokassa rarely visited the provinces except to go hunting, and after his coronation it was unusual for him to spend much time even in Bangui. At Berengo he built an office for himself, a room for the Council of Ministers, and accommodation for visiting heads of state. Then he created an imperial cabinet of a dozen members that met regularly at Berengo. It functioned independently of the prime minister's cabinet in Bangui, and Patassé soon came to understand that the imperial cabinet was where the real power lay. Although he had the position of prime minister, he himself was not running the country.[6]

It was a confusing system of government for all involved, but confusion had always been the norm in administrative matters in Centrafrique, whether as a republic or empire. Rational bureaucratic procedures had never become well established. The idea behind the two cabinets was apparently to enable the emperor to wield real power while giving him a scapegoat if things went wrong. The prime minister could always be held responsible for the many ills of the country, and these continued to be enormous.[7]

One of Patassé's most pressing tasks was to maintain the flow of aid to the empire. International donors were understandably reluctant to provide funds after the coronation and its accompanying bad publicity. The Carter administration in the United States tied its aid programs to good marks on human rights, and in December 1977, in reponse to the mistreatment of the journalists Randall and Goldsmith, it had ended its assistance to Bangui. Patassé tried in vain to get the decision reversed and even invited a delegation of congressmen to the empire to see things for themselves.[8] Some European countries had fewer scruples, however. France and West Germany were considering collaboration in Centrafrique's single most important project – the Bangui-ocean railway. But opposition groups in both countries were against it, and strong objections were voiced to any European investment in the empire. In mid-1978 a member of the European Economic Community's commission in Bangui revealed to the headquarters in Brussels that 60 million CFA francs of aid had recently been misappropriated by the imperial government. The commissioner was expelled from the empire as a result of his disclosure, and attitudes in Europe hardened.[9]

The pressure of work soon proved too much for Patassé, and in March 1978 he suffered a serious heart attack. He went to France, where he spent several months recuperating in hospital. During his absence Bokassa dissolved Patassé's government and appointed Henri Maïdou, the former minister of education, in his place. The emperor kept a close eye on his two cabinets. Consequently, they could achieve very little when he was abroad – and he was frequently abroad, especially in 1978. Bokassa had always enjoyed the international stage, and now that he was a crowned head he expected more attention than usual.

In fact, Bokassa's new status caused some embarrassment in diplomatic circles. Other emperors, such as Hirohito of Japan and the Shah of Iran, were normally accorded places of special honour at international gatherings – ahead of mere kings and presidents. Would this protocol now be extended to Bokassa I? The initial test would be the Franco-African summit that was to be held Paris in May 1978. The French tried to solve the problem by persuading His Majesty not to make the journey and to send his prime minister instead. Bokassa would not hear of it. He arrived in Paris more than a week before the summit was due to start, having just visited North Korea, where he had signed a treaty of peace and friendship with President Kim Il Sung.

When the summit opened on 22 May in the Salon Napoléon III at the Elysée Palace, Bokassa found to his dismay that the order of precedence had not changed since his coronation. He still ranked behind the Ivory Coast's Houphouët-Boigny, Senegal's Senghor, and Mauritania's Ould Daddah; and in the course of the meetings and speechmaking, only one of the other fourteen heads of state, Gabon's Omar Bongo, referred to him as "Majesté impériale."[10] Bongo, who had imperial ambitions himself, had apparently been hoping that Bokassa's coronation would create a climate of acceptance for his own. But judging by the attitudes displayed at the Paris summit, there would be no further African empires for a while.

Bokassa returned to France for a private visit in June and dropped in to see his old regiment in Fréjus. It was the wettest and coldest June the country had experienced in a century, but that did not stop the distinguished visitor from doing the rounds. One day a cortège of limousines pulled up at André Viol's gas station at Bar-sur-Aube. A black man, soaking wet from the rain, emerged from one of the cars and asked if he could take a shower and change his clothes. Viol indicated the door of the public washroom, but then another approached and explained that the drenched one was Emperor Bokassa. His Majesty had been reduced to this state while paying homage at the grave of Charles de Gaulle at Columbey-les-deux-Eglises nearby. The garageman suddenly became more helpful and invited the emperor to his own apartment. After showering and putting on dry clothes, Bokassa sent to his car for a bottle of whiskey, which he shared with his host. He had never lost the common touch.[11]

Relations remained cordial with President Giscard, who was in Centrafrique on another safari in August 1978. Giscard had been visiting President Mobutu of Zaïre at his residence in N'Gbadolité and had flown straight from there to Rafaï, where he shared a *chasse gardée* with his friend Marc Péchenart, a manufacturer of cattle feed. He was greeted on arrival by a group that included a Catholic missionary priest and the local *sous-préfet*. While taking some refreshments in the missionary's cabin, he heard another plane coming in to land, a rare enough event in remote Rafaï. The *sous-préfet* took off immediately in his Peugeot van, returning in a few minutes with a passenger. It was His Imperial Majesty, who had made the three-hour trip from Bangui in a small plane.

"I know that you came for a holiday and that you don't wish to be disturbed," he declared, "but I couldn't let you come to my country without greeting you."

Giscard at first thought that Bokassa was going to join him on the hunting trip, but after fifteen minutes His Majesty rose and announced, "I don't want to delay you, because you want to get there [to the hunting camp] before nightfall. As for me, I'm returning to Bangui. I asked President Malloum and General Mobutu to come to Bangui when you return. You will meet the three of us to take stock of the situation in Tchad."[12]

Giscard believed in active French military intervention in Africa in support of friendly regimes, and 1978 was a particularly busy year in that respect. In May the legionnaires had descended on Kolwezi, in Zaïre's Shaba province, to put down a rebel outbreak and protect the expatriate population. Paris was strongly behind Mobutu as the only man who could hold his country together – a myth which Mobutu himself carefully cultivated. Tchad was more complicated and required a more extensive and sustained French military presence to prevent it from disintegrating or falling under Libyan influence. In 1978 the government of Félix Malloum was seriously threatened by Frolinat, a northern rebel army backed by Gadhaffi. France put almost two thousand troops in the field to save the Malloum regime and subsequently became involved in negotiations for the formation of a government of national unity.[13] The French military base at Bouar in the Central African Empire was a key logistical point in these manœuvres. Consequently, on 17 August, Giscard stopped in Bangui en route to Paris to discuss the situation in Tchad as Bokassa had suggested. The emperor enjoyed such occasions, especially if he could emphasize France's indebtedness to him in implementing its African policies. It underlined the special relationship he had with Giscard.

Bokassa was back in France on 20 September, staying until 18 October. He was received at the Elysée two days after his arrival, and on 2 October he hosted Giscard at Villemorant. Bokassa spent most of his visit at his Sologne properties. By this time, he was a well-known figure in the region. In spite of the hostile coverage of his activities in the French press, he and his entourage were popular with the businessmen and petty officials in the surrounding towns. The inhabitants were pleased to have such a famous neighbour and were not above pandering to His Majesty's appetite for flattery.

Even as Bokassa was enjoying himself in his French châteaux, his eldest son, who had once been tipped as his successor, was struggling to make ends meet in a dingy Paris apartment. Georges had run afoul of his father during the summer of 1978 for attempting to interfere in the ivory trade. He and his wife, a Camerounian *métisse* whose father was French, had been kept under house arrest for seventeen days in September, given little to eat, and even denied medical treatment for their sick child. Then, on the eve of the emperor's visit to France, they were put on a plane bound for Paris. On arrival, Georges tried to avoid the French press, but without much success, and when the newsmen persisted he made some critical comments about the political repression in his father's empire.[14]

Georges was right. Two years after the declaration of empire and a year after the coronation, there was no improvement in civil liberties and human rights in Centrafrique. The guarantees written into the imperial constitution were meaningless. There was still no assembly or independent judiciary. Ngaragba remained crowded, and the execution squads were as busy as ever. But the French government remained strongly behind Bokassa and dismissed as unworthy the critical remarks of Prince Georges and the swelling ranks of disaffected exiles. The flow of aid from Paris to Bangui continued. This was just as well. The imperial regime, like its republican predecessor, could not have survived for long without it. Yet in the final analysis, this dependence on French handouts would prove to be the emperor's Achilles' heel.

CHAPTER EIGHT

Autumn of the Patriarch

On 16 January 1979 Iran's Shah Mohammad Reza Pahlavi boarded a Boeing 707 at Mehrabad Airport, Teheran, to leave his turmoil-ridden country for good. The overthrow of the Peacock Throne launched a year that would go down in history as the Twilight of the Tyrants. In Nicaragua, Cambodia, Uganda, and Equatorial Guinea, brutal and reviled regimes were swept away one after another. This prompted political pundits to engage in an intriguing guessing game: which despot would be the next to go? From the beginning, the name of Bokassa I was on everybody's lips, for on the very day that the Shah took flight, disturbances erupted in Bangui – disturbances that proved difficult to quell and eventually brought the Central African Empire to its knees.

To all appearances, the Bokassa dynasty seemed secure enough. The Central African army was such an impotent force – unarmed and untrained – that it could never hope to take on the emperor's loyal guards with any success. The prospect of a military coup from within the country was virtually nil. Certainly, there were opponents of the regime living abroad – in France, the Republic of the Congo, and elsewhere – but they were divided into rival factions and were not taken very seriously. The conventional sources of opposition were thus dispersed, divided, and powerless.

The first blows that shook the empire came from an unexpected quarter: the *lycées*, or secondary schools. The *lycéens* were the sons and daughters of the privileged class of civil servants, so their challenge to the status quo was in some respects surprising. Yet because of the very nature of their education, they were one of the few social groups able to develop a political consciousness. They came to accept neither the desirability nor the inevitability of one-man rule. In combination with the university students, who possessed a similar awareness, they emerged in 1979 as a formidable force.

Bokassa liked to pose as a champion of education, though deep down he distrusted it. He had sponsored the establishment of a number of *lycées*, one of which bore his name, and in 1970 he had laid the foundation stone of the Université Bokassa. The university gave prestige to Bangui, but it had a practical purpose as well. Central Africans often pursued their advanced studies abroad, where they could acquire dangerous political ideas. It was safer to educate them at home, where a close eye could be kept on things.

Relations between the dictatorship and its students were frequently strained during the 1970s. *Lycéens* in Bangui, Bambari, Berbérati, and Sibut went on strike in 1971 and 1972 to protest the poor conditions in their schools. The strikes were considered acts of rebellion and were forcibly put down by the military, using beatings, arrests, and detentions. In February 1974 students at the Université Bokassa boycotted classes in response to the dismissal of some professors who had been accused of discussing political matters in their courses. Repression inevitably followed, and the leaders of the student organization, the Association nationale des étudiants centrafricains (ANECA), were detained for a few days and given the customary rough treatment. There was more trouble at the university in October 1975, when students demanded the prompt payment of their bursaries. The government reacted by conscripting the protesters into the army.

In March 1976 the gendarmerie arrested a teacher at the Collège d'enseignement général in Bria for raising political issues in his class. What followed was predictable: protests by the students and repression by the security forces. As well, the college was closed down and the students were forbidden to enrol in other educational institutions. To ensure that the problem was put to rest for good, a government decree ordained that no teacher, whether Central African or foreign, was to discuss politics or criticize the state; and the minister of national education was instructed to conduct an inquiry into the morality of all teachers in the country. Strict surveillance of the various branches of the educational system then became the rule. ANECA, the student organization, was considered a breeding ground of seditious dissent and was suppressed in 1977. Students were then more or less forced to join the Jeunesse révolutionnaire of MESAN, an obsequious body, or risk losing their bursaries.[1]

Many of the teachers in the *lycées* and institutions of higher learning were French *coopérants* (technical assistants on tours of duty in former colonies), and it was inevitable that they would expose their students to Western political traditions and notions of human rights. In spite of repression, surveillance, and espionage, these ideas found fertile ground in the schools, and intellectual opposition to the regime began to smoulder beneath the surface. Students came to conceive of democratic alternatives to the neofeudal notion of leadership.

The major confrontation between the students and the state in 1979 had its origins in the emperor's dissatisfaction with the results of the 1977 baccalaureate – the challenging French-based examination that faced *lycéens* at the conclusion of their studies. Henri Maïdou, minister of education at the time, felt that the fault lay with the *coopérants*, whose attitude betrayed a lack of sympathy for their culturally different students. His solution was to get rid of the French teachers and Africanize the school system. Bokassa, a firm believer in France's civilizing influence, could not agree. He thought that certain subjects could be taught effectively only by *coopérants*. The disappointing "bac" results were due, he surmised, to laziness and lack of discipline in the schools. The troublesome behaviour of the students over the years was surely proof of that. The emperor had his own solution: school uniform. During his visits to China and other communist states, he had been favourably impressed by the parades of identically attired children marching and drilling. A military man at heart, he loved the order and discipline of these spectacles, and he had convinced himself that a touch of barrack-room precision and uniformity would restore purpose and direction to his schools.[2]

Accordingly, on 2 February 1978, the education ministry announced that as of 1 October, uniforms would be required clothing for all elementary and secondary students in the empire. The cut, colour, and style of the apparel was explicity prescribed. Girls were to wear navy blue dresses with collars and belts of light blue. The boys' outfits were to consist of dark blue pants and light blue short-sleeved shirts featuring two pockets and epaulettes. Accessories of a personal nature, such as jewellery and distinctive hats, were expressly forbidden. The announcement specified that those failing to abide by the new dress code would be excluded from class after the effective date. It soon became clear that the emperor had an additional motive for bringing in the dress code: the ensembles were to be made by the Compagnie industrielle oubanguienne des textiles (CIOT), formerly a French-owned enterprise, which since 1976 had been controlled by the Bokassa family; and the clothes were to go on sale in Bokassa's retail stores. He would reform the school system and turn a profit at the same time.

The uniform requirement was poorly timed, to say the least. The economy was in rapid decline, with diamond, coffee, and cotton production continuing to fall. The budget deficit between 1970 and 1977 had been rising by from 1 to 6 billion CFA francs annually. The trade deficit alone in 1978 was 2 billion CFA francs ($8 million). The national debt stood at 70 billion CFA francs ($280 million) or about five years of national revenue. Meanwhile, galloping inflation was eating away at whatever income people managed to earn. In one year the price of sugar had tripled while that of meat had quadrupled.[3] The imperial government was bankrupt and had not been able to pay its civil servants for over two months. And now these same civil servants were being asked to find between 4,000 and 5,000 CFA francs ($16–$20) to dress each of their children for school. In normal circumstances the requirement would have imposed grave hardship on families with several children, but when parents had not received the wages owed to them, it was demanding the impossible.

By 1 October thousands of uniforms lay untouched in Bokassa's stores. The schools opened and the students arrived, but only a handful sported the requisite attire. Nothing happened at first, except for a sense of unease in the classrooms. Nobody was sent away, and school carried on as usual. Meanwhile, the unsold uniforms gathered dust on store shelves. But on 15 January 1979, Lycée Boganda, one of the largest secondary schools in Bangui, suddenly refused admission to students who were not in uniform. The same thing happened at Lycée Bokassa the following day. Student leaders protested to the government but were rebuffed. They then sent emissaries to all the schools in the city calling for a major demonstration on the eighteenth.

Around 8 AM on the appointed day, students from Lycée Boganda gathered on avenue Bokassa and began to march towards the centre of town. They were joined along the way by lycéens from other parts of the city, swelling the crowd to about two thousand. As the demonstrators made their way down avenue Boganda, they paused briefly to insult Bokassa's statue with shouts of "Pay our bursaries and our parents!" Apprised of the march, Bokassa ordered a couple of military units to the city centre to assist the gendarmerie in confronting the students. The soldiers and policemen broke up the demonstration with their rifle-butts and batons, but the lycéens were not prepared to give up. That evening they gathered at the Université Bokassa, where they persuaded the university students to make common cause with them. Radical elements at the university saw the revolutionary potential of the movement – perhaps it could win popular support and bring down the regime. Students from the Ecole normale supérieure and Ecole nationale d'administration et de magistrature also agreed to ally themselves to the cause, and a mass demonstration for the following day was decided on.

The demonstration of 19 January involved about three thousand students aged between fourteen and twenty-five. Gathering at the university, they marched towards the city centre. By this time the news from Iran had filtered in and another slogan was added to their repetoire: "After the Shah, Bokassa!" Shortly after 10 AM, the demonstrators were outside the Palais de la Renaissance and were facing a menacing cordon of soldiers. Once again the soldiers broke up the demonstration, and the students retreated along the broad boulevards that radiated north and west from the city centre. On their way they smashed the windows of shops and offices that were associated in some way with the regime, and when they came to Pacifique 2, the emperor's store at the junction of avenues Boganda and Bokassa, they ransacked it thoroughly.[4]

By 11:30 AM the police and military had restored order in the downtown area, but much of the suburbs were beyond their control. The students sought refuge in Kilomètre 5, the popular market area in the west end, and in the *kodros* of Gobongo, Fou, Miskine, Malimaka, and Boy Rabé, which form the city's northern periphery. Here, their numbers swollen by disaffected workers and *godobé* (the professional thieves), they found themselves in the vanguard of a virtual insurrection. Repression was sure to follow, of that they were certain, but in the meantime they busied themselves blocking the main arteries with barricades of tree-trunks and overturned cars.

At 4 PM Bokassa, who had remained in Berengo throughout, sent orders to smash the barricades and retake the suburbs. The task fell to troops stationed in Bangui under the command of Generals Josephat Mayomokola and François Bozize. They received live ammunition for the first time but were cautioned to fire into the air and use tear gas grenades when confronting the troublemakers. As the soldiers moved into the afflicted neighbourhoods, they encountered stiff resistance. Poorly trained and inexperienced in the use of live ammunition, they were clearly unequal to the task. The generals, who at one stage were almost taken captive by the students, called for reinforcements.

Bokassa now decided to send his elite imperial guard into action, and around 6 PM an airlift began, taking the guards from Berengo to the capital. About 135 men in all, heavily armed with Kalashnikov assault rifles and dressed in battle gear, they occupied Bangui airport and spread out into the northern suburbs. The emperor also donned combat gear and drove to the scene of the trouble to take command.

He ordered his men to restore order using every means possible, and he vowed to burn Gobongo and the adjoining neighbourhoods to the ground if the troubles persisted. At midnight he addressed the nation on the radio, calling for the return of peace and admonishing parents to rein in their children.

In the early hours of the morning the imperial guard went into action, aided by two Soviet-built tanks and a number of armoured cars mounted with machine-guns. By the early afternoon of 20 January they had regained control of Bangui, and by 6 PM a strict curfew was in effect. Throughout the day the radio gave no report on the troubles. It continued to play military music, with periodic interruptions as Bokassa appealed for calm and proclaimed the curfew and the introduction of martial law. He also announced that the school uniform regulation would no longer apply. Later, the government admitted that six people had died and that sixty had been injured in the fighting. These figures were far from the truth. The death toll was probably closer to one hundred and some estimates were considerably higher.[5] Meanwhile, as the student movement in the capital was crushed, minor troubles flared up in the provincial towns of Bouar, Bossangoa, and Bouca. The arrival of soldiers from the capital restored order.

The events of January shook the Central African Empire but never threatened to bring it down. Bokassa's first instinct was to blame the French, whom he suspected of sending *agents provocateurs* among the students in order to stir them up and destabilize his regime. Prime Minister Maïdou was another suspect, since he had been absent from the country at the hour of crisis and his son had been among the demonstrators. Police informers infiltrated the schools and colleges but could find no evidence of a plot. In truth, there was none. The student revolt had simply been a spontaneous reaction to a difficult, indeed impossible, situation.

The Giscard government still backed Bokassa, and ultimately that was all that mattered. In January, Paris welcomed Maïdou and readily signed three agreements for the development of agriculture, transportation, and the long-neglected uranium deposits at Bakouma. And in February, by which time the recent repression had become common knowledge, Giscard offered a loan of one billion CFA francs to his embattled client. At the same time, Kuwait provided a credit line of three million U.S. dollars.[6] The money enabled the emperor to pay his soldiers, policemen, teachers, and other civil servants and to give the students their bursaries. As a further measure of appeasement, he allowed the revival of ANECA, the student organization.

But it was too late for conciliation. To parents, students, and teachers, the bloody reprisals of January could not easily be forgotten or forgiven. What had begun as a protest directed against a specific grievance was now developing into an organized, clandestine opposition whose aim was nothing less than the overthrow of the regime. Evidence was not hard to find as pamphlets began to circulate calling for a general strike and the abdication of the emperor. One of the documents listed His Majesty's real estate holdings abroad, making the obvious inference of corruption and profiteering. The pamphlets were distributed covertly and were usually destroyed after being read.

Schools and colleges opened again before the end of January, but the classrooms never returned to normal. The problem was to get the students back to class and to find instructors to keep them busy. Many Central African teachers and professors heeded the pamphleteers' call to strike and refused to report for duty. It was the French *coopérants* (who were forbidden to interfere in the internal affairs of the country) who kept the system going. As the unrest continued, Bokassa grew increasingly disturbed. Since conciliation had not worked, he resorted to repression once more. On 9 March he ordered the arrest of three prominent individuals whose loyalty to the regime was suspect: Alphonse Blagué, director of the Ecole normale supérieure; Nicholas Gotoas, principal of Lycée Boganda; and Daniel Nditifei, manager of the Central Bank. As well, at the beginning of April, a number of *lycéens* were taken into custody, one of them after a subversive pamphlet had been found in his house.

On Monday, 9 April, the schools were scheduled to reopen after the Easter recess, but word had spread among the *lycéens* that they would boycott classes and gather at the university in a show of solidarity with their incarcerated comrades. The university students came too, and it was clear that their organization, ANECA, was taking on an important leadership role in a new round of agitation. At the meeting it was decided to press for the release of the detainees and, failing that, to call for a general strike of all schools. A delegation led by ANECA president Albert Ndodé met with the education and interior ministers that afternoon, but the government refused to budge. A message then spread through the student network encouraging them to boycott all classes until their comrades were released.

Whereas in January it had been the *lycéens* who had played the leading role in organizing defiance of the government, in the April agitation it was the university students who were to the fore. They used the immediate issue of the prisoners as a rallying point for a program of fundamental political change. Their rhetoric became increasingly revolutionary and marxist in tone as they called for the re-establishment of the republic, radical social change and an alliance with the proletariat and peasant masses.[7] As the classrooms of Bangui emptied, the schools were transformed into meeting places for student rallies. Bokassa's spies informed him of the mounting unrest, and he resolved to act quickly to avoid a repetition of the January troubles. On 12 April he ordered all schools closed and sent in an army unit to occupy the university. The police arrested approximately sixty students, but Albert Ndodé, their principal target, eluded them and went into hiding, a price on his head.

The students continued to meet, but furtively now, in their own homes. After a few days, they began to test the waters by holding small rallies outside churches and at the Boganda monument. But the emperor's patience was wearing thin. On 17 April a student rally at the Bofia church in Boy Rabé was broken up by security forces under General Mayomokola and many arrests were made. A curfew was proclaimed for that evening, and at midnight soldiers and policemen embarked on a house-to-house search in the capital, detaining students of all ages. News spread of the dragnet, and an estimated 150 young people sought refuge in the town of Zongo, across the Oubangui River. Those unable to escape were taken to police commissariats. There the police noted their identities, interrogated them and roughed them up a little. By the morning of the eighteenth, the commissariats were filled with prisoners, and many were sent to Ngaragba.[8]

On arrival at the prison, the students were stripped naked and forced to lie on the ground while guards pounded them with their batons. Mokoa, the prison director, ordered thirty of them to be stuffed into one of the Safari cells, twenty into the other. These cells measured a mere 2.5 by 3.0 metres each and were designed for one person at a time. The remaining prisoners, about twenty in all, were put in the comparative comfort of the Birao block. Conditions in Safari were unbearable and the weaker students found it impossible to breathe. At 5:30 in the morning, when the doors were opened, many of them were dead. Thierry-Jacques Gallo, in prison for his part in the Obrou plot, watched as common criminals loaded the cadavers onto a truck to be taken away for secret burial. He counted eighteen bodies.[9]

A true picture of those twelve hours of terror remains elusive, since eye-witness accounts do not agree. The major dispute concerns Bokassa's personal involvement in the brutality. French jurist André Baccard, who is anything but an apologist for the emperor, denies that Bokassa was present at Ngaragba on the fatal night. He bases his conclusion on the testimony of the witnesses to whom he spoke.[10] There are other witnesses, however, who claim that Bokassa was present. Informants told Bernard Loubat, a French journalist who visited Bangui in June, that the emperor turned up at the prison at 8:00 PM on 18 April. He was in a rage and joined in the beating of the students. He allegedly returned at 11:45 PM and entered the cells to administer another thrashing, this time gouging out one student's eye with the end of his cane. At 3:00 AM he was back again, drunk as well as furious, and lashing out once more at the young prisoners.[11]

During 19 April, parents began to turn up at the Palais de la Renaissance demanding to know the whereabouts of their children. Government spokesmen denied that mass arrests had taken place and said the youngsters were probably across the river in Zaïre. Only forty-eight prisoners had been taken, they explained, and those were mainly *godobé* caught in the act of looting. While it is impossible to tell with any accuracy the full extent of the arrests and deaths, we can be reasonably certain that at least eighteen people died on the night of 18–19 April in the confines of Ngaragba. There were probably many more deaths, some in the notorious prison, others elsewhere. The emperor's personal participation in the violence must remain an open question,[12] but there can be no doubt about his responsibility. Soldiers, policemen, and prison guards were all acting under his orders, and rough treatment of the regime's opponents was standard procedure.

Bokassa moved quickly to distance himself from the repression. He went on radio and declared 20 April to be a "national day of peace for the Central African Empire." On the same day he addressed a meeting of MESAN officials at Château Boganda at which he pronounced himself "the father and protector of all the children who represent the future of the country." He also announced an ordinance for "the protection of Central African youth." The ordinance forbade the arrest and detention of young people, especially students, except for infractions of common and criminal law.[13]

There were some immediate benefits for Ngaragba's unwilling guests. On the "national day of peace" the university students were separated from the others and put into the Birao cells, where they remained until their release on the twenty-eighth. Meanwhile, the *lycée* students, about thirty in all, were placed in the relative comfort of a common room behind the prison office. On the twenty-first they were allowed to wash themselves and retrieve their clothes. Their watches, money, and other personal effects had all disappeared. Around two o'clock Mokoa assembled them in the courtyard and warned them that if they were ever brought back to Ngaragba for any reason, they would be unlikely to survive the experience. Then they were set free. They emerged from the prison gates to the waiting arms of their parents, who had maintained a nervous vigil outside for several days.

The student revolt was over, but it had not been in vain. World opinion was soon to take up the cause and pressure Bokassa to account for his actions. One of the most vigorous agitators was Amnesty International, which had been founded in 1961 to champion the cause of human rights.[14] Early in May 1979 reports of the Bangui repression began to reach Amnesty's headquarters in London as visitors from the empire bore news of the events. Their accounts were disturbingly similar. On 11 May Amnesty telegrammed Bokassa protesting against the arrests and deaths, and demanding a public inquiry to determine who was responsible. There was no reply, so on the fourteenth Amnesty released a report on the events of April, outlining in detail the conditions under which the students had died and citing the survivors who claimed that Bokassa had participated personally in the carnage.

The report caused international outrage, especially in France, where the emperor's name was a household word. The French media pilloried him as "the bloody clown" and hastened to note its government's continued support for him. Similarly, the weekly *Jeune Afrique* condemned the muted response of world leaders, especially those in Africa, and called for an impartial inquiry into the massacre. The disclosures were, of course, an embarrassment to the Giscard regime, which tried to fend off criticism with vague statements about the need for an inquiry. They were an even worse embarrassment to Bokassa. On 16 May, Prime Minister Maïdou rejected the claims made in Amnesty's report. He conceded that fifty students had been arrested in April but said that all had been over sixteen years of age and all had been released on the twentieth. Those who had disappeared had not been killed, he insisted, but had fled across the river to Zaïre. The following day, Bokassa reiterated Maïdou's explanation and confirmed his regime's support for the Universal Declaration of Human Rights. Neither performance was convincing, and the shadow of suspicion continued to hang over the empire.

On 20 May Bokassa arrived in Kigali, Rwanda, for the annual Franco-African summit. At the inevitable news conference on arrival, he admitted that deaths had taken place, but he denied that schoolchildren as young as eight had been among the casualties. The demonstrators had been adolescents, he asserted, and had been led by marxist agitators in violent confrontations with the authorities.[15] During the conference, Bokassa detected an unaccustomed coolness among his fellow leaders. Giscard, in particular, was not his amicable self. The French president tried to avoid being alone with Bokassa, and when they did meet there were no warm embraces or exchanges of hunting lore as in the past. Moreover, it was Giscard who was most insistent that the Bangui bloodshed be investigated by an international commission of jurists.

The establishment of such a commission of inquiry became the major subject of discussion at the conference. Giscard championed the idea and won Houphouët-Boigny, Senghor, and Gnassingbé Eyadéma (of Togo) to his side. Other leaders baulked at the notion, since it seemed to represent interference in the internal affairs of a member country, which could be a dangerous precedent, but they went along with it when it was made clear that the purpose was not to condemn or depose Bokassa but to exonerate him. France could not continue to support him otherwise. Some French representatives at the summit even encouraged the emperor to execute a few of his subordinates who had been directly involved in the killing and in this way pose as an upholder of justice.[16] But Bokassa resisted betraying his close collaborators and initially rejected the commission of inquiry. During a long *tête-à-tête* on the evening of the twenty-first, President Mobutu made some progress with him. He pointed out that Paris demanded an inquiry because of pressure from the French media and the political opposition. If France cut off aid, the empire would be in serious trouble. The inquiry would be a mere formality, which would clear the emperor's name, and then life could go on as usual. Finally, in a closed-door session that carried on into the night with all delegates present, Bokassa, feeling completely isolated, gave in and agreed to cooperate with the proposed investigation.[17]

The next morning, just as the delegates were preparing to leave, surprising news arrived. Sylvestre Bangui, the Central African ambassador to France, had held a press conference in Paris to announce that he was resigning from the imperial service and relinquishing his rank of general. His reason: the emperor's participation in the massacre of schoolchildren. The facts had been revealed to him by numerous reliable witnesses, he declared, and he could no longer serve such a bloodstained regime.[18] The *J'accuse* stunned Bokassa, who was already faltering under the strain of the summit. Sylvestre Bangui was one of the few surviving comrades from his early days in power and a member of his own M'Baka *ethnie*. He had a sense of being deserted, perhaps betrayed, by his old friends. The fundamental weakness of his regime, its heavy dependence on French aid, was now painfully apparent. There was little he could do but await the verdict of the commission of inquiry.[19]

Bokassa still had friends and admirers abroad, however. Veterans of France's colonial wars in Indochina and Algeria, especially those with right-wing inclinations, tended to be sympathetic. They rallied round their fellow *ancien combattant* and defended him against the charge of child beating. One of them, Roger Holeindre, even conducted his own investigation into the matter. Holeindre arrived in Bangui late in May and spent several days in the city. He toured the streets, bars, and dance halls, talking to dozens of residents, and claimed not to have found one mother who was missing a child. Nor could he find any trace of a mass grave. In other words, there was no proof that the said massacre had taken place.

Holeindre was granted an exclusive interview with the emperor and he published the text of their conversation, along with the results of his inquiry, in *Paris Match* on 1 June. In the interview Bokassa played down the seriousness of the disturbances that had rocked his empire. There had been demonstrations, followed by skirmishes with the security forces as they attempted to maintain law and order, he said. That was all. And the demonstrations would never have occurred if they had not been fomented by foreign subversives. He blamed Amnesty International for exaggerating the gravity of the situation. The human rights organization had given undue credence to the lies and falsehoods passed on to it by Central African students in Paris, he said.[20]

At the beginning of June, Bokassa's most pressing concern was the commission of inquiry to which he had so reluctantly agreed in Kigali. Would it come to the same conclusion as Holeindre? Would it exonerate him of wrongdoing as Mobutu and others had suggested? Or was it part of a widespread conspiracy to bring him down? He could not be sure, but he knew that he was increasingly isolated, and his nervousness became all the more pronounced as arrangements for the investigation were put into place.

The commission of inquiry, or, to give it its correct title, the Mission de constatation des événements de Bangui, was to be headed by Youssoupha N'Diaye, a prominent Senegalese magistrate. A youthful forty-one years old, N'Diaye had abandoned a successful career in professional football in the 1960s for an equally successful career in law. The other members of the mission were the magistrates Tia Kone of the Ivory Coast, Fulgence Semineca of Rwanda, and Atsu-Koffi Amega of Togo. There was also one female member, who was also the only anglophone, Mrs Angie Brooks-Randolph of the Supreme Court of Liberia. The mission was accompanied by a secretariat of three.

When the investigators arrived in Bangui on 12 June, they received a message from the emperor that he wished to meet them before they began their inquiry. An audience was arranged for 9:40 AM the following morning. When the magistrates arrived at Berengo at the appointed hour, they were shown into the council room, where Bokassa was seated in the company of the Empress Catherine, Prime Minister Maïdou, and Joseph Potolot, president of the Supreme Court. N'Diaye's first impression of His Majesty was favourable, and he found it hard to conceive of him killing anyone. Bokassa was charming, courteous – almost obsequious – and punctuated his remarks with "Merci, monsieur le président," "Mille mercis." He agreed to cooperate fully with the inquiry, telling his visitors that they could go wherever they chose and speak to whomever they wished. Furthermore, he offered them free accommodation at the OCAM Palace[21] and the use of government limousines and chauffeurs. The investigators turned down these offers, fearing that they would compromise their independence. Moreover, they suspected that OCAM might be bugged and that the free transportation was intended to keep track of their movements.

Bokassa spent much of the meeting giving the official version of the unrest. The January disturbances, he said, had resulted in thirteen dead and sixty injured among the security forces. On the side of the rioters, there had been sixty injured; that was all. The situation had been one of "veritable war." Army officers had come to him saying that the country was going up in flames and begging him to go on the radio to restore order. He had made the broadcast and peace had returned. In dealing with the April troubles, the emperor similarly claimed that his words had been enough to calm matters. As soon as the problem appeared, he had arranged to address a public meeting at Château Boganda to which leading diplomatic and political figures had been invited. Students also came along, declared themselves satisfied with the promises he had made, and returned peacefully to their homes, renouncing their political demands. To these implausible accounts of the recent unrest, Bokassa added equally implausible explanations. He apportioned much of the blame to one of his ex-wives, a Frenchwoman whom he had divorced after only two years of marriage. She was furious at the breakup of the union, he alleged, and sought revenge by spreading monstrous lies about him to Amnesty International and the French press.

The mission left Berengo perplexed at Bokassa's performance. The emperor had been a most gracious host, but his words left many questions unanswered. The magistrates now had the task of testing the official story against the testimony of other informants. The truth-according-to-Bokassa was adhered to faithfully by his ministers and officials. Shortly before the mission's arrival, His Majesty had created an ad hoc committee of Central African magistrates under Potolot's direction to conduct its own "independent" inquiry into the disturbances. This committee met with the mission and provided the officials with the answers to their questions. Potolot and his collaborators denied that there had been any deaths in April except those of policemen who had infiltrated the student movement and had been exposed. The students who had disappeared were said to be across the river in Zaïre and would eventually return. The mission interviewed the prime minister, the ministers of the interior and of national education, the directors of MESAN, and a number of policemen, all of whom gave the same response: there had been no massacre, just a campaign of vilification in the international press.

N'Diaye and his fellow investigators then crossed over to Zongo to inquire into the fate of the students who had sought refuge there. Local officials informed them that a total of 115 students, including 38 Zaïrois, had come over during the April crackdown. The Zaïrois had stayed, but all the Central Africans had returned to the empire within a few days. The official story was beginning to lose its credibility. Back in Bangui, the investigators met doctors and Red Cross workers who were able to testify personally to the deaths and injuries in January. They also interviewed priests, nuns, and teachers in the education system whose students had been manhandled or had disappeared. Most of the informants asked to remain anonymous for fear of reprisal. N'Diaye observed that terror appeared to be widespread in the empire. Consequently, it was often necessary to interview witnesses in secret, and meetings were arranged in bars and other places where Bokassa's agents would be unlikely to find them. Most critical of all to the inquiry was the willingness of students to come forward and tell their stories. Several of them claimed to be survivors of the April terror in Ngaragba, and their accounts were highly influential.

On 18 June the mission visited the notorious prison and was shown around by Otto Sacher, the assistant director. Sacher denied that there had been any deaths there in April, but he refused to allow his guests to enter certain cells, and these may have contained key witnesses. Thierry-Jacques Gallo, for instance, who had seen the students' bodies loaded on the truck on 19 April, was in one of the cells from which the mission was excluded. N'Diaye found the visit to the prison painful – nothing less than a nightmare. Moreover, the restrictions placed on the investigators while in Ngaragba were a violation of the promise of full cooperation made by the emperor. Similarly, they were denied permission to interview Barthélémy Yangongo, a former minister of information who had been imprisoned since April for alleged subversion. These actions by the imperial authorities suggested a growing unease as the inquiry progressed.

Bokassa's personal apprehension was clear when the members of the mission visited him on 21 June just before concluding the Bangui stage of their investigation. The encounter started badly when the jurists refused his invitation to dinner or even to a round of cocktails. The emperor drank throughout the interview and spoke continually of plots and war, and of enemies massing behind the Congolese frontier to attack him. And once again he tried to blame all his misfortunes on his scheming French ex-wife. N'Diaye found the performance pathetic. He thought Bokassa was a frightened man, and a devious one too. The emperor had been able to conceal his crude side behind a smokescreen of charm during their first meeting, but he now knew that much had been revealed to the mission, and this made him lose his *sang-froid*.

The following day, the mission left Bangui for Abidjan. A subcommittee of three then spent 25–30 June in Paris and London collecting further evidence. In Paris, they interviewed Albert Ndodé, the student leader, who had slipped out of the empire on 11 May. They also spoke to Bokassa's would-be successors, Sylvestre Bangui and Ange Patassé, who readily denounced the emperor's atrocities. Patassé had stayed in France after recovering his health and now opposed the regime. Georges, Bokassa's estranged son, also came forward to condemn his father. In London, Amnesty International officials shared their documents and correspondence on the subject with the investigators. Finally, between 1 and 10 July, all the mission members were together again in Abidjan, sifting the often contradictory evidence and writing their report.[22]

Bokassa needed defenders now more than ever, and he was prepared to pay good money to the right people. Jean-Pierre Dupont, a French businessman who had helped organize the coronation ceremony, suggested the name of Jacques Duchemin. Well schooled in African politics, Duchemin had worked for the governments of Algeria and Niger and had served as adviser to Moïse Tshombe, the Katangan separatist, as well as to François Tombalbaye, president of Tchad. He is believed to have served as an agent for France's SDECE on many of his African assignments. Duchemin arrived in Bangui in June as the Mission de constatation was doing its work. He impressed and flattered Bokassa during a series of interviews and received the appointment he had hoped for, becoming minister plenipotentiary to the imperial court with a generous salary, diplomatic passport, and other appropriate privileges.[23]

During the months that followed, Duchemin was a regular visitor to France. He contacted old friends in the media and attempted to influence their hostile coverage of the empire and its ruler – but to little avail. His shady reputation as a man for hire was well known, and he was not taken very seriously. At the beginning of September *Jeune Afrique*, which mockingly described him as "the saviour of Bokassa," interviewed him at length about his role as imperial factotum. Duchemin insisted that the Bangui troubles had been deliberately instigated by foreign agents who had bribed the police to behave brutally in order to discredit Bokassa. "I have affection for and a good opinion of the emperor," he said. "I consider him to be completely sincere."[24] As it turned out, Duchemin was anything but sincere. After the collapse of the empire, he capitalized on his connection by writing *L'empereur*, a scurrilous book about the fallen potentate which emphasized the bizarre and the macabre.[25]

Bokassa found a more reliable defender in the French journalist and writer Roger Delpey. Like the emperor, Delpey had fought in Indochina in the 1950s. Later, he wrote a book about the experience, *Soldats de la boue*, in which he praised the gallantry of the French forces and the justice of their cause. Among his other writings was *Adolf Hitler, l'affaire* (1975), in which he argued that the Führer and Eva Braun had not died in their Berlin bunker in the spring of 1945 but had somehow slipped away – an enduring right-wing fantasy.

Delpey's admiration for Bokassa was genuine and was based on the latter's twenty-three years of service in the French armed forces and on his military decorations. He arrived in Bangui in July with a *carte blanche* from the emperor to conduct his own inquiry into the events of January and April. He came to the conclusion that Bokassa was in no way responsible for whatever brutality had taken place in the previous months. Moreover, he came up with his own explanation for the troubles: the emperor was a victim of an insidious campaign of disinformation organized and executed by the SDECE. A plot was afoot to discredit His Majesty as a prelude to disposing of him.[26]

Delpey interviewed Bokassa a number of times during July and August and lent his voice to the movement to defend the embattled emperor that was emerging in Paris. The movement was led by businessmen who had profited from the imperial largesse over the years and wanted the good times to continue. Jean-Pierre Dupont, for instance, was active in the campaign and circulated a petition among his fellow profiteers in support of Bokassa.[27]

By July Bokassa was unsure of the French government's position, though the fact that some of its officials were referring to his empire as the *République centrafricaine* was not reassuring.[26] He wanted to believe that Giscard was still behind him and that the coolness the president had shown was simply a reaction to pressure from the press and the socialist opposition. Bokassa had not lost his confidence in Robert Galley and considered him a faithful friend. He remembered the minister of cooperation's spirited defence of the coronation ceremony and his declaration to the press at the end of May that a man should be presumed innocent until proved otherwise.[29] Yet there was mounting evidence of betrayal, of defection, of subterfuge. Officials at the French embassy began to act suspiciously, and so did some of the senior officials in the imperial service. This time it was not Bokassa's paranoia – moves were indeed afoot to undermine him.

The most prominent conspirator was Henri Maïdou, the austerely intellectual prime minister. In May 1979, in response to Amnesty International's report, Bokassa had forced him to read public statements denying that any massacre had taken place. Maïdou began to fear that the people would turn against him and that he would fall victim to their wrath if the regime collapsed. It was time to seek collaborators in an act of treason. He found a fellow conspirator in David Dacko, the former president. Since becoming a personal adviser at the court in December 1976, Dacko had been forced to live in close contact with the emperor, but since the April repression he had sought to distance himself from the regime. Like Maïdou, he was concerned for the future.

Maïdou and Dacko approached the French embassy and sent a message to Paris that a popular revolt led by themselves was imminent. All they needed were troops to overcome the imperial guard. The French, who had their own sources of information, were not convinced. Nor were they prepared to intervene openly at that stage. They would wait first to see what the Mission de constatation revealed. But Dacko could not wait. In mid-July he arrived unannounced at Bangui-M'Poko Airport and succeeded in boarding a plane bound for Paris. Bokassa only found out about his adviser's unauthorized departure when the aircraft was already in the air. He sent a message ordering the pilot to return, but the pilot conveyed the message to Dacko, who replied that to be taken back would mean certain death. The pilot believed him and continued on his northward flightpath. In Paris, the fugitive maintained a low profile, kept an eye on developments in the empire, and was in regular contact with the French authorities.[30]

Dacko's defection was another blow to a regime that was clearly faltering. His presence in Paris added to the list of those who had once supported the emperor but now, from the comparative safety of exile, sought his overthrow. Bokassa could take some small comfort from the fact that his emigré opponents were badly divided amongst themselves, each aspiring to the presidency of a restored republic. There would be no cooperation while personal ambition guided their actions. To further their claims, they began to organize their own political movements and to solicit support among expatriate Central Africans, especially among the student population in Paris.

Sylvestre Bangui created the Front de libération des oubanguiens (FLO) in seeking to promote his claims to the succession. Ange Patassé's organization was the Mouvement de libération du peuple centrafricain (MLPC), while the Front patriotique oubanguien (FPO) supported Abel Goumba. Goumba was almost a forgotten figure by this time. One of Boganda's close associates in the dying days of colonialism, he had attempted to form an opposition party to Dacko and MESAN at the time of independence. Dacko had suppressed his party and thrown him in jail. Released in 1962, Goumba had gone to France, where he completed his medical studies. In 1979 he was working for the World Health Organization in Benin. In many ways he was the most credible of Bokassa's would-be successors, for he alone had not been compromised by association with the imperial regime.[31]

The opposition movements were only a minor irritant to the emperor. Without substantial support in the homeland or from the French government, they were powerless. They could never hope to shake the imperial throne, let alone topple its occupant. Far more worrisome were the ongoing deliberations of the Mission de constatation. Informal discussions of the matter at the Organization of African Unity summit in Monrovia in July left many delegates convinced that a report implicating Bokassa in the deaths of children would bring irresistible international pressure on him to abdicate. France, it was believed, would take the lead in bringing the pressure to bear.

Late in July, President Bongo phoned Bokassa asking him to come to Gabon, where a representative of the French government would bring him an important message from Giscard d'Estaing. The emperor was immediately suspicious. If Giscard had a matter of such moment to discuss, why did he not send his representative directly to Bangui? He had been advised for some time now not to leave his empire if he wanted to avoid unpleasant surprises, and he had not ventured abroad since the beginning of June. But Bongo pleaded, and such was the sense of urgency he conveyed that Bokassa agreed to make the journey to Franceville, a mining town deep in the Gabonese forest, where the meeting was scheduled for 1 August.

Giscard's emissary was René Journiac, his technical adviser on African affairs. Journiac knew the continent and its politics well. A master of intrigue, he worked in the shadowy world of conspiracy, sabotage, and assassination, turning up to protect French interests whenever and wherever they were threatened. When African leaders were received at the Elysée, his elegant silhouette was always in the background, his finger on the pulse of the situation, his whispered advice at the ready should the president require it. Courteous and charming, inscrutible and machiavellian, he was tailor-made to direct France's underhanded politics in its former colonies.[32]

Bokassa had known Journiac since 1968 and distrusted him. Indeed, relations between the two men had been openly strained for over a year. When His Majesty emerged from his Caravelle in Franceville on the morning of 1 August, he detected that something was amiss. Bongo and Journiac were there to greet him, and the latter's smile was forced, his handshake cold. The three sat down together, and Bongo explained that his role was that of mediator between the emperor and the Elysée. Journiac's message was blunt and unambiguous: the report of the Mission de constatation, which was soon to be released, had implicated Bokassa personally in the Bangui massacres and, as a result, Giscard was demanding that he give up the throne. The discussions went on all day, but Bokassa refused to give in. He would not abdicate. Even a personal telephone call from Giscard next morning failed to move him; it simply made him so angry that he slammed down the receiver. As he returned to Bangui, he knew that his dear cousin had abandoned him.[33]

There was now nothing to do but wait for the release of the Mission de constatation's report. Since the emperor had been apprised of its central conclusion, he had every reason to be apprehensive. On 16 August the report was at last released for all to see. It was 133 pages long and contained 18 appendices consisting of photographs, death certificates, and a complete list of those killed by the security forces. Most of it consisted of verbatim transcripts of witnesses' testimony, the most devastating being that of six students who had survived Ngaragba in April. Three of them said that they had seen Bokassa at the prison on that night of terror and that he had joined in the maiming and killing.

The authors of the report estimated that at least 150 people of all ages had died in the January troubles. They were particularly appalled at the shooting of an eight-year-old student by General

Mayomokola and at attacks on the Red Cross by soldiers. Their investigation of the April disturbances established that children of a very tender age had been arrested, beaten up, and thrown into crowded cells. Of the 250 who had been detained, they estimated that between 50 and 200 had died. Their summary conclusion, which was readily quoted by the international media, was as follows: "In conclusion, the Mission de constatation considers that in the month of January 1979, in Bangui, disturbances were repressed brutally by the security forces and that in the month of April 1979, the massacre of about 100 children was carried out under the orders of Emperor Bokassa and almost certainly with his personal participation."[34]

The Empress Catherine, who visited France shortly afterwards, could see for herself how things had changed. She spent the long weekend of 26 to 29 August at the Château Hardricourt making preparations for her children's return to school. Normally, she would have passed some time in the neighbouring village, shopping or chatting with the inhabitants. But now it was different. The villagers shunned the people from the château, and some of them had aired their animosity in graffiti whose message was unmistakable: "Bokassa assassin" ... "Year of the Child – give the bayonet to Bokassa."[35]

Mismanagement, profiteering, and waste had ultimately undermined the Central African economy. Shrinking resources had stalled the patronage system, left civil servants unpaid, and fostered unrest at all socials levels, especially in the lower and middle levels of the state bureaucracy and the modern sector. The school uniform incident had been the spark that had ignited a potentially explosive situation. The economic and moral crisis of the Bokassa regime in 1978–79 had caused the governing élite to fragment, and an increasing number of its most prominent members were now opposing Bokassa from abroad. The ruler, isolated and desperate, had few options open to him. Coercion brought only temporary respite, and if he found himself unable to pay his soldiers, he would be finished.

Bokassa's unwillingness to relinquish power, even when offered a safe haven in France, may have been due to a realistic appraisal of the plight of some of his fellow dictators who had been driven from office that year. The Shah of Iran was almost constantly on the move, seeking a country that would guarantee not to extradite him; Uganda's Idi Amin, who had fled his country in April, was under protective custody in Libya; and Equatorial Guinea's Macias Nguema, overthrown in August, had been executed after a summary trial. Clinging to power was the best guarantee against vengeful enemies.

CHAPTER NINE

Barracuda

Emperor Bokassa was now a serious liability to President Giscard, and the well-known friendship between the two leaders was a source of mounting embarrassment. The leader of the French socialist party, François Mitterrand, who was hoping to unseat Giscard in the 1981 presidential election, was making the most of his rival's discomfiture. The French media, too, were following developments closely and were calling on the Elysée to withdraw support from the "Butcher of Bangui."[1]

After Franceville it was clear that Bokassa would not relinquish power voluntarily. Giscard pondered the alternatives. A direct invasion by the French army would bring the empire down, but at enormous cost. Bokassa and his guards would probably resist and there was no telling how many lives would be lost. Nor would it do for France to become involved in a guerrilla campaign in the forests of Lobaye. In any case, direct military intervention would cause an international outcry and much annoyance in diplomatic circles. Using the power of the purse was another possibility. France could sever financial aid and withdraw its 3,500 *coopérants* who were working in the empire. But what if Bokassa prevented the evacuation of the French citizens and held them hostage? What if economic and political collapse ensued and radical forces hostile to France seized power in the general confusion? There was also the danger that Gadhaffi might step into the breach once more with a barrelful of oil money. Cutting the financial jugular was just too risky.

Giscard and his advisers ultimately settled on a compromise solution, one that combined elements of the military and economic. Two days after the release of the report of the Mission de constatation, Paris announced that it was ending its program of aid to the empire with the exception of humanitarian projects. The *coopérants* were to stay – their critical role in the educational, health, and technical domains was considered humanitarian.[2] This part of the plan was designed to put pressure on Bokassa as well as to appease the French media and opposition. A military invasion was also prepared, but it was to be put into effect only when the emperor was abroad. Paris believed that the imperial guards would be less inclined to fight without their leader.[3]

There was much to be done as the French watched and waited for Bokassa to leave his empire. The details of the military intervention were worked out by René Journiac and Alexandre de Marenches, head of the SDECE. They presented their plan to a special meeting of the national defence committee chaired by Giscard himself. The commander-in-chief of the armed forces, General Guy Méry, Defence Minister Yvon Bourges, and Foreign Minister Jean François-Poncet were also present. Robert Picquet, the French ambassador in Bangui, and Olympio Mazza, military attaché at the embassy, were informed of the plans from the beginning. They were busily gathering intelligence to ensure that the invaders encountered no obstacles upon arrival.[4]

Getting rid of the emperor was only part of the task; it was equally important to choose his successor carefully. Such a critical detail could not be left to chance – or to democracy. The French were going to hand-pick the president of the restored republic and install him in power. Moreover, they were determined to select someone who, above all else, would best serve their interests. But when Giscard and his intimates surveyed the various pretenders to the succession, they found them wanting.

Abel Goumba was immediately discounted. He had spent too many years in exile and was virtually unknown to Central Africans. A more serious objection was his avowed marxism. If put in power, he would probably steer the country in Moscow's direction. Nobody around Giscard wanted him, least of all Journiac. Ange Patassé was almost equally suspect. He had once been a member of the Oubanguian communist party, formed after the *loi-cadre* of 1956. His leftist sympathies had subsequently waned, and he had served in Bokassa's cabinet for thirteen years, but during that time the only political ideology to which he had subscribed had been self-interest. The Elysée considered him untrustworthy and too nationalistic. It was also worried by his occasional resort to leftist rhetoric and his friendliness with Mitterrand. Giscard had never been on good terms with him, and this was decisive. Sylvestre Bangui also was discounted. Since he was a M'Baka – of Bokassa's ethnic group – his chances of rallying the country behind him were slim. In any case, the Elysée considered that he lacked "the right stuff" to be president. Worse still, he was known to be close to Jacques Chirac, leader of Rassemblement pour la république and one of Giscard's major political rivals.

This left Henri Maïdou and David Dacko. The former was favoured by René Journiac. Maïdou was intelligent, well educated, serious, had an air of authority, and was a lover of France. But his continuing role as Bokassa's prime minister and his public pronouncements denying the massacre of Bangui youngsters had impaired his credibility. Dacko, too, was far from being the perfect choice. He was a M'Baka, suffered from bad health, and was weak and ineffectual. But he had once been elected president of Centrafrique – albeit as the only candidate of the only political party – and while in power he had usually shown a willingness to accommodate French interests. After much soul-searching, Giscard and his advisers settled on a compromise solution: Dacko would be made president of the restored republic and Maïdou vice-president.[5] There was only one problem with this formula: David Dacko was reluctant to serve. Although he wanted the empire to fall, he was terrified of Bokassa and unwilling to raise a hand against him unless success were assured. Nor did he completely trust the French – he suspected that they had wanted him ousted back in 1965. He was relieved to be in Paris, away from the turbulent politics of his homeland. He had not felt so safe and secure since that fateful night of Saint-Sylvestre.[6]

Journiac and de Marenches visited Dacko often, pouring on the charm and flattery, appealing to his better nature, and stressing that his people needed him now more than ever. Gradually, Dacko's resolve began to weaken and, being short of money, he agreed to participate in the coup conceived by the French. De Marenches then helped him prepare the statement he would read over the radio on his return to power.[7] It was already September and Dacko was moved into an apartment on the rue de Berri, just off the Champs-Elysées, where he was kept under close surveillance by security guards. He had to be ready to leave at any time. As these arrangements were being put in place, Giscard felt it advisable to consult with some of the major francophone African leaders. Bongo, Houphouët-Boigny, Mobutu, and Senghor were told of France's intentions and all gave their approval.[8]

As the noose tightened around his neck, Bokassa did what the French had feared all along: he played the Libyan card. It was not easy to approach Colonel Gadhaffi after all that had transpired between them since 1976, especially the short-lived nature of Bokassa's conversion to Islam. But the colonel was willing to overlook the past as long as he could get what he wanted – and the empire had two things that interested him especially: the military base at Bouar and the Bakouma uranium deposits. Bouar, his priority, had an excellent runway and was often used as a refuelling stop by French military aircraft en route to other African countries. Gadhaffi wanted it as a means of shipping supplies to the forces he supported in the Tchadian civil strife, and he wanted the French, who were checking his ambitions, to leave.

Bokassa had already approached Libya in June in an effort to mend fences, and Gadhaffi had welcomed the overture and agreed to send between 150 and 200 military advisers to the empire. As well, 400 Central African soldiers were sent to Libya for their training. Tripoli also offered some loans, but not nearly enough to keep the imperial government solvent. Gadhaffi was holding out for Bouar and was determined to keep up the pressure until he got it. Bokassa knew that the colonel would drive a hard bargain this time, but by the beginning of September he had little alternative. French aid was but a trickle, and his government was bankrupt. There was no money to pay soldiers or civil servants, and chaos loomed on the horizon. Libya was his only hope.

Discussions with the Libyan ambassador in Bangui, Bachir Salah Bachir, revealed that Gadhaffi expected Bokassa to go to Tripoli in person, where the details of an agreement would be worked out. The emperor was reluctant to leave, fearing what might happen in his absence, but he knew that he had little choice in the matter. He would have to make the journey to Tripoli. On Friday, 14 September 1979, Bokassa sat down with Prime Minister Maïdou and drew up the list of delegates who would accompany him. There were twenty-three in all: Alphonse Koyamba, vice-premier in charge of finance; Joseph Potolot, president of the Supreme Court; Jean-Jacques Ngoma, imperial court adviser; Eugène Katouka, protocol adviser; Colonel Gbongo, aide-de-camp; Commandant Mamelemokokwa, security chief; Mme Delannon, secretary of the imperial cabinet; Ali Hijazi, friend and business partner of the emperor; Bachir Salah Bachir, Libyan ambassador; also an employee of the Libyan embassy, a nurse, a radio operator, a photographer, two servant boys, and eight security agents. Only Bokassa and Maïdou knew the time and date of departure; the others were told just forty-eight hours in advance.

At 8:30 AM on Wednesday, 19 September, the imperial Caravelle took off from Berengo carrying Bokassa and his delegation. During the flight, Ambassador Bachir informed His Majesty that Gadhaffi would not be at the Libyan capital on their arrival but that they would meet him the following day at Benghazi. They landed at Tripoli International Airport later in the afternoon and were led in an official cortège to a castle that had once belonged to King Idris's son. Bokassa busied himself for the remainder of the evening studying the speech he was going to deliver to his host and benefactor the next day and reviewing the file on his empire's financial needs.

The next morning the Central African delegation flew on to Benghazi, where they were accommodated in a luxury hotel. Bokassa now learned that his meeting with Gadhaffi was scheduled for much later that evening, and he spent the intervening hours going over his notes and files. Just before 9:00 PM word came that the motorcade that was to take him to the colonel's house was waiting outside. By then, Bokassa had been kicking his heels in Libya for more than thirty hours. Gadhaffi had been playing a waiting game – reminding him that any new arrangement between them would be according to Libyan rules.

Brought eventually before Gadhaffi, Bokassa produced his prepared speech and began to read, beginning with "Very Dear Brother." After the predictable platitudes about fraternity and eternal friendship, he got to the heart of the matter:

The Central African Empire is having the most difficult time in its history. In effect, since the new direction of its foreign policy, resolutely African and nationalist, the neo-colonialist and imperialist powers, with France and the U.S. at their head, have unleashed and orchestrated in their mass media a low and violent campaign of denigration against Our Person. They have decreed, in the most hypocritical manner, an economic blockade against our country, already severely penalized by nature. Trampling under foot the basic principles of national sovereignty and of non-interference in the affairs of other countries, these powers demand Our resignation in order to place their own puppets at the head of the country.

Bokassa went on to say how wonderful it was to observe that the great Libyan people had not abandoned him in difficult times:

And that is why, freely, the Central African Empire has decided to adopt the revolutionary ideas of the Libyan Arab Jamahirya, authentically African and nationalist, and which has always checked the imperialist and racist designs of France, the U.S. and their lackies.

He then asked for assistance in saving the Central African economy and concluded his speech with cries of "Long live Gadhaffi," "Long live Libya," and "Long live the fraternal love between our two countries."

The rhetoric was familiar to Gadhaffi. He had heard it all before in 1976 when Bokassa had needed a handout. He smiled nonetheless and stepped forward to embrace his visitor, saying how happy he was to see his brother, Salah Addin, again.

They sat down together and the emperor quickly explained what had happened in January and April and how his country had been paralysed politically and economically ever since. The terms of an agreement, which was to be good for two years, were worked out with little difficulty. Gadhaffi undertook to pay the salaries of the empire's soldiers and civil servants, as well as its students' bursaries. This was to be done directly through the Libyan embassy in Bangui. In return, he was to be given control of the military base at Bouar. Ali Treiki, the Libyan minister of external affairs, who was taking notes during the discussions, was instructed to prepare a document outlining the terms of the agreement which the two leaders were to sign in the morning.

The hour was late as Bokassa left for his hotel. He was delighted with what had transpired. His financial woes were over, his grip on power secure. At the hotel he found the members of his delegation gathered in the dining room finishing their meal. He paused briefly to let them know of his success. Eugène Katouka joined him as he took the elevator to his suite. Food had been brought to his room, and he helped himself while Katouka kept him company. By 1:00 AM he was asleep, oblivious of what was happening in the distant empire.[9]

On the evening of Wednesday, 19 September, Henri Maïdou had telephoned Paris with the news that the emperor was already in Tripoli. This was the signal to launch the military invasion known as Opération Barracuda, which had been in preparation for about two months.[10] Two French strike forces poised within short flying distances of Bangui were immediately placed on full alert. The first of these was a company (200 men) of the Third RPIMA (Régiment parachutiste d'infanterie de marine). These troops had been in Zaïre's Shaba province between 12 and 17 September on joint military manœuvres with Mobutu's men. At the end of the exercise they had returned to their base in Libreville, Gabon, and they had barely settled back in when the alert came. The second strike force consisted of two companies (400 men) of the Eighth RPIMA, which were stationed in N'Djaména, Tchad. The French had 2,500 troops supporting the government in that wartorn country.

At 9:30 AM on Thursday, 20 September, a grey Citroën came to a halt opposite David Dacko's apartment on the rue de Berri. An SDECE agent stepped from the car and entered the building to fetch the president-in-waiting, who had been confined to his apartment for the past week, bodyguards watching his every move. He was taken to a nearby air base, and from there was flown to Tarbes, near the Spanish border, where a military expedition was ready for take-off. On the runway were two c-160 Transalls – long-distance military transport planes. On board were 130 men of the élite First RPIMA, commanded by Brigadier-General Jacques Guichard. These were France's finest – the shock troops who were to spearhead the invasion of the empire. Dacko was by now losing his nerve and virtually had to be forced into one of the Transalls before the convoy took off. Along the way, the paratroopers played cards and studied detailed maps of Bangui while Dacko sat silently in a corner of the cockpit.

The invading forces stopped briefly in N'Djaména for refuelling and consultation with the troops who were to follow them into battle. Shortly after 11:00 PM they were over Bangui. The airport was already closed for the night and there were only a few security guards on duty, but two SDECE *barbouzes* (secret agents) were on the ground, and they guided the planes in with flashlights. Minutes later, the paratroopers were in the terminal building challenging the astonished guards, who put up no resistance.

With the airport safely in their hands, the paratroopers moved out in their armoured cars to occupy strategic locations in the city.[11] Dacko remained at the airport, but once news came that Bangui was in French hands he was taken under armed escort to the radio station. There, at 11:50 PM, he made the following announcement: "This is David Dacko speaking ... The regime of Bokassa I has disintegrated. Its final act was the massacre of a hundred children bringing universal condemnation and ultimately bringing the regime down. For fourteen years the country has been exploited by the man who proclaimed himself emperor and dragged our image in the mud by his excesses and delusions of grandeur."[12] As this message was being broadcast, support troops of the Third and Eighth RPIMA were coming in to land. The invasion met no resistance. The Central African soldiers around Bangui threw down their weapons and surrendered at the sight of the French. The imperial guards out at Berengo remained at their posts for a few hours, but then, fearing a shoot-out with the invaders, they left for their villages, abandoning their arms and uniforms along the way. The Central African Empire had fallen without a shot being fired in its defence.

Bokassa learned of his overthrow at 2:30 AM when the Libyan minister Ali Treiki awakened him in his Benghazi hotel room. There had been unconfirmed reports on the radio of a coup in Bangui supported by the French. If the reports were true – and Bokassa suspected that they were – he faced some difficult decisions. First, he asked to see Gadhaffi to discuss his dilemma, but a few hours later he was told that the Libyan leader had left the city – a clear indication of no support from that quarter. Later in the morning he telephoned the Empress Catherine, who was staying at the Château Hardricourt in France. She urged him not to return to Centrafrique, which he was considering, and he promised to make no rash moves until there was more specific information from the homeland.

Before long, the radio began to broadcast the first detailed accounts of the coup. Official reports claimed that Dacko had organized the coup and that once it was underway he had called on French assistance. Bokassa did not believe this. He knew too well that Giscard had betrayed him and that Dacko, whom he considered a weakling, was acting on France's behalf. He sought solace in the illusion that his people continued to love him, that it was not they who had cast him out but the colonialist invaders. In his own mind he was still emperor, and his entourage treated him accordingly. He could never accept being Citizen Bokassa.

Dignity, or pretensions thereto, had to be maintained. Nevertheless, Bokassa was above all a practical man and he realized that he now had to decide either to stay in Libya or leave – and if the latter, where to go? Staying did not appeal to him. Idi Amin was spending his exile near Tripoli, a virtual prisoner in his villa. Bokassa wanted better that that – he wanted room to manœuvre, the freedom to plot a comeback. The solution was obvious: he would go to France, where several châteaux awaited him. He envisaged no problem in doing so. Was he not a French citizen and a decorated veteran of the French army? Moreover, had not Journiac offered him sanctuary there during their meeting at Franceville? It all made perfect sense.

At 9:00 AM Bokassa gave instructions to his entourage, and they set out for the airport. They boarded the Caravelle and took off in a westerly direction, stopping at Tripoli to refuel. There, Ali Hijazi decided to disembark. All the others stayed with the fallen emperor. At no stage did the Libyan authorities impede their movements or interfere with their departure plans. In truth, Gadhaffi was happy to see them go. By mid-afternoon, the Caravelle was charting a course across the Mediterranean en route to Paris. Bokassa was lost in thought. Delpey had been right all along, he concluded. The SDECE had paved the way for his overthrow with its campaign of disinformation. He recalled an old French proverb which he believed was applicable in his case: "When you want to kill your dog, accuse it of having rabies."

The downfall of the Central African Empire had been planned meticulously. Indeed, de Marenches boasted that it "ought to be taught in schools of special warfare." Until now, everything had worked with precision – it had been the very model of the flawless, bloodless coup – but all of a sudden France faced an imponderable, an embarrassing, development which it had not anticipated: the ex-emperor's plane had entered its airspace and was heading for Paris.

Bokassa was made brutally aware of how his status had changed as the Caravelle approached Orly Airport. The message from the control tower was unmistakable: permission to land denied. It was the same at Roissy Airport. But when Bokassa threatened to land on a highway, something had to be done. Roissy made an urgent call to the Elysée and received word that the Caravelle be instructed to land at Evreux military base, west of Paris. The message was passed on, and at 7:50 PM the aircraft touched down on French soil as it had been directed. Armed soldiers immediately rushed forward and took up positions around it. The base commander appeared and announced that nobody could disembark and that, after refuelling, they would all have to return to Libya.

The fugitive ex-emperor and his companions spent the next few hours in silence listening to French radio broadcasts. That was their only source of information. Word of their arrival had spread, and news bulletins were describing the event as a major crisis for the Elysée. Official government communiqués on the matter were typically vague and curt. They pronounced Bokassa an undesirable and noted that his presence in France was temporary. Around 10:00 PM the radio observed that Georges Bokassa had turned up at Evreux but had not been allowed aboard the Caravelle to see his father.[13] As they settled down for the night, they learned that local communists were demonstrating outside the base with chants of "Bokassa murderer! Giscard accomplice!"

The morning of Saturday, 22 September, broke in a cool, grey drizzle over Evreux. It had been a cold and uncomfortable night for the fugitives on the quarantined Caravelle, especially for those who had never been to Europe before and were unaccustomed to its chilling clime. The air inside the plane had turned stale and foul-smelling. The Central Africans could not shower, shave, or change their clothes; their suitcases were locked in the baggage compartment. They were also out of food, and since it looked as if they would be there for some time, meals were passed in from the base canteen.

Meanwhile, the arrival of the ex-emperor – and, in particular, his claim to French citizenship – was causing a major headache for the

Giscard regime. If Bokassa could establish his citizenship, he would have to be allowed to stay. Legal experts were consulted and they did a quick analysis. To be recognized as a French citizen, a "colonial" would have to meet one of the following criteria: (1) to be resident in France at the time of one's country's independence; (2) to have a spouse or ancestor born in France; (3) to be resident in France and to have made, before 1 August 1973, a declaration to choose French nationality. The experts concluded that Bokassa did not qualify on any of these counts.[14]

Now began the delicate diplomatic task of finding a country that would take the deposed ruler. The Elysée approached Argentina, Brazil, Mexico, and several African countries but met blank refusals from them all. When Justice Minister Alain Payrefitte, a distinguished historian and member of the Académie française, was asked by newsmen what the government would do if no country would accept Bokassa, he replied sardonically, "It would then be necessary to send him to St Helena if, of course, the English agreed."[15] It was going to be a long and tiresome weekend for Giscard and Journiac. It was even more tiresome for those trapped in the immobilized Caravelle. They spent much of their time listening to the radio, which continued to be their only window on the outside world. They learned that the communists were again demonstrating outside the base and that journalists and curiosity seekers were milling around in growing numbers. As well, they heard that the question of Bokassa's citizenship had sparked a major brouhaha.

By Saturday evening, Bokassa was prepared to accept that neither France nor a growing number of other countries would take him in. This he had learned on the radio. In view of this rejection, he demanded to be returned to Boubangui, the village of his birth, under the protection of French troops. If this was done, he said, he would abandon political activities and live the life of a simple farmer. There followed another cold and uncomfortable night aboard the Caravelle. Bokassa did not sleep much, and long before dawn his ear was to the radio. There was news from Bangui: Dacko would not accept Bokassa's return to Centrafrique. With this door slammed shut, the fallen monarch tried another tack. At 5:30 AM he dictated a communiqué to the French government in which he asked to go to Zaïre if President Mobutu would have him. Failing that, he was prepared to go to Tripoli.

At midday the radio announced that the government had still not found a country willing to open its doors to its unwelcome guest. Moreover, the two countries on which Bokassa had been counting, Zaïre and Libya, had both refused. Gadhaffi had excused himself on the grounds that he already had Idi Amin on his hands. Mobutu owed Giscard a favour after the Shaba invasion, but even so he baulked at offering refuge to Bokassa. His principal excuse was that he wished to develop good relations with the newly installed Dacko regime in Bangui. Besides, he suspected, with some justification, that the former emperor would use Zaïre as a staging ground for a return to power. Despite these refusals, matters were at last reaching a conclusion. That evening, the base commander ordered everyone to leave the aircraft, surrendering their weapons as they did so. Bokassa and his companions were thoroughly searched, their identity papers were confiscated, and they were taken to sleeping quarters. All members of the entourage were then asked if they wished to accompany their leader into exile. Only two of them, Katouka and Gbongo, agreed.

At 3:50 AM on Monday, 24 September, a military aircraft left Evreux for Abidjan, capital of the Ivory Coast, with Bokassa on board. Félix Houphouët-Boigny had responded to Giscard and Jouralniac when all others had turned them down. He had agreed to take in the homeless former emperor on humanitarian grounds. When Bokassa arrived in Abidjan at 10:00 AM, he was taken by helicopter to Houphouët-Boigny's residence. There, the Ivorian president assured his guest that he was nobody's prisoner but warned that he was not to engage in political activities. An hour later, the former emperor was taken to his new home – a spacious mansion overlooking the lagoon in one of Abidjan's wealthier suburbs. Thus ended the long odyssey that had begun five days earlier in Berengo.[16]

CHAPTER TEN

Operation Revenge

While Bokassa was at Evreux, his enemies were helping themselves to everything of value he had left behind in Centrafrique. On the morning of Friday, 21 September, four Puma helicopters of the Barracuda invasion force brought a squadron of paratroopers to Berengo. First, the soldiers raided the imperial residence and took away the coronation paraphernalia as well as quantities of cash, diamonds, and jewellery, the total value of which it is impossible to estimate. Then they sought out the government records stored in the Council of Ministers building nearby. Bokassa had been in the habit of keeping his personal papers in sturdy binders covered with green leather, and two hundred of these were seized at the Council of Ministers. Filing cabinets filled with other important documents were emptied – imperial decrees, memoranda, and a dossier of forty letters from President Giscard addressed to "mon cher parent." There were items of a nostalgic nature too – a scrapbook of newspaper cuttings on the coronation, and the emperor's guest book.

All day long, the Puma helicopters were busy transporting the imperial archives and treasures from Berengo to the French embassy in Bangui. At the same time, another contingent of soldiers was combing the Villa Kolongo with similar instructions. Here they came on a safe containing two superb diamonds, one weighing twenty carats, the other, eighty. Next to the stones lay two gold watches with faces encircled in diamonds. Bokassa had transformed one room at the villa into a personal museum that featured souvenirs of his youth, his military career, his trips abroad, and his family. The jewellery, the memorabilia – everything – was taken away.[1] What happened to it all? Most likely, this imperial treasure trove was ultimately sent to France, and it probably remains there today in the care of the secret service.[2] Even now, more than a decade later, the French authorities refuse to discuss the matter.

In the looting of his homes, Bokassa lost a fortune as well as invaluable mementos of his eventful life. And there was more bad news to come. One of the first acts of the restored Dacko regime was to declare the confiscation of all his properties in Centrafrique. Gone at the stroke of a pen were the villas, factories, plantations, and shops in which he had invested so much. Gone too were the air-conditioned limousines – the Mercedes-Benzes, Rolls-Royces, and Cadillacs – in which he had delighted. In just a few days, his net worth had plummeted by an incalculable sum. He still had his European properties and bank accounts, but their future too was far from secure.

As the Barracudas were combing through the Villa Kolongo, they discovered two cadavers trussed up in the walk-in freezer awaiting the attentions of the imperial cook – or so they claimed. One of the bodies was identified by the tattoo on its chest as that of the math teacher Gaston Wengue. The arms, one leg, and head were missing. The deceased's niece, Albertine Kettego, aged sixteen, said that he had been arrested on 11 August near one of Bokassa's residences on a minor traffic offence. The other victim was Jean-Robert Massanquet, twenty-five years old, who had been detained on 26 August on suspicion of involvement in the student unrest.

Civilians, who were now arriving at the villa to join in the looting, killed the crocodiles occupying the L-shaped pond near one of the entrances. Later, the Barracudas drained the pond and allegedly found on the bottom the bone fragments of thirty humans who had perished in the reptiles' jaws. The soldiers were told that others had been fed to lions that were kept nearby in a cage built into an artificial hill. Inevitably, journalists learned of these stories, and lurid headlines soon filled the international press.[3] When pressed by reporters about Bokassa's eating habits, President Dacko readily conceded that human flesh had been a regular item on the Berengo menu. Moreover, it had been served to visiting dignitaries. The French press was naturally intrigued at this revelation and quickly identified Robert Galley as one who had partaken of the grisly fare. Galley retained his sense of humour, and when asked if he had dined on the remains of Auguste M'Bongo, a Bokassa cabinet minister who had disappeared, he replied, "Yes, and he tasted just like veal."[4] But the news from Papa's *chambre froide*, and in particular the way it was played up in the First World media, annoyed many Central Africans. The allegations of cannibalism, they felt, were insulting not only to Bokassa but to the entire nation. Some saw the stories of cadavers and crocodile pits as a smear campaign to justify Opération Barracuda, and they began to resent the French troops as agents of neo-colonial control.[5]

Even so, the downfall of the regime was greeted with widespread enthusiasm. For several days, gangs of youths kept busy pulling down Bokassa's numerous statues and images. On finding the imperial throne still sitting in the coronation stadium, they ripped out its velvet upholstery and plucked its golden feathers. The feathers were later sold to souvenir hunters for four francs apiece. They found the imperial carriage in one of Bokassa's many villas and pulled it through the streets of Bangui to the kicks and blows of jeering spectators. Afterwards, twisted and broken, it was abandoned and became a children's plaything in the La Kouanga residential quarter, just west of the downtown core. Before long, there were few reminders of the imperial age, save the three concrete triumphal arches that had been constructed for the coronation.[6]

As all this transpired, His Former Majesty was settling in to his new quarters at 5 boulevard de la Corniche, in Cocody, the posh residential district of Abidjan. The villa, three stories high, offered a magnificent view of the lagoon, the port, and the commercial centre of the bustling Ivorian capital, but the splendour of it all meant little to the fallen tyrant. He remained indoors, a victim of depression and despair. He passed the hours, whiskey bottle in hand, listening to military music. "Fanfares et pompoms rouges," a recording by the French marine band, never left the turntable. The same band, playing many of the same tunes, had entertained the guests at his coronation feast. The accommodation was provided free of charge by President Houphouët-Boigny, and for that Bokassa was grateful. Meals were also free and were delivered to the villa daily from a nearby hotel. Some of Bokassa's favourite things made up the usual fare: steak, fried potatoes, Camembert, and Beaujolais. Whiskey was not among the regular provisions, but local bootleggers ensured a steady supply.

Initially the former emperor lived alone, save for the companionship of Katouka and Gbongo, who had accompanied him into exile. He missed his family greatly, especially Catherine. Apart from the obvious comfort that her presence would have provided, she was an accomplished tarot card reader, and Bokassa had become attached to her revelations. He wrote frequently, urging her to join him in Abidjan, but she refused. Moreover, he heard that she was living it up in Europe, and the jealousy he had always felt about her added to his gloom. Nor did it help to learn that all the other women whom he had maintained as wives and mistresses had abandoned him too. Those of foreign nationality took the first flight out of Bangui as soon as the dust had settled after Opération Barracuda. Those of Central African origin stayed where they were and accepted the protection of the new government from the wrath of the people. The emperor's sister, Catherine M'Balanga, was not so fortunate. She had played too much at politics and made too many enemies. She was arrested and thrown in Ngaragba.

Most of Bokassa's children were busy with their studies abroad when the Barracudas dropped from the skies. Two of the older ones, Nicaise and Saint-Cyr, happened to be in Bangui as the empire was overthrown, but they went into hiding and later succeeded in leaving the country and making their way to France. The real Martine also escaped. She was in Paris at the time, purchasing equipment for her Vietnamese restaurant, and she never returned to Bangui. But her husband, Dr Dédéavodé, who had stayed behind, was among those detained by the new regime.[7]

Every visitor to the Cocody villa seemed to bear depressing news – of family or friends dispersed and humiliated, of property lost or spoliated. Bokassa had been in his new home only a few weeks when he was called on by a man he had never heard of before, whose message was alarming. The stranger was Bernard Tapie, a young French businessman endowed with voracious ambition and an ego to match. Tapie was undoubedly one of a kind. He had grown up in the tough working-class suburb of Le Bourget, north of Paris, and had achieved some success in an early career as a pop singer. Later, he went into business, picking up bankrupt firms at bargain prices, and by 1979 he had built up a modest printing empire called Le Groupe Bernard Tapie.

Like many others, Tapie had been fascinated by the lurid press reports of Bokassa and the Central African Empire, and when public figures began to call for the confiscation of Bokassa's properties in France, an idea occurred to him. Thus, on 1 October, Tapie stepped off a plane in Abidjan with the intention of meeting the fallen emperor. The Ivorian authorities were carefully screening visitors to their infamous guest and were at first uncooperative, but a few well-placed bribes secured Tapie the opening he wanted. At 11 AM on 6 October he and two advisers were received at 5 boulevard de la Corniche by a dispirited Bokassa, who was still in shock from his overthrow. The young entrepreneur quickly explained why he had come. Pressure was mounting in France, he said, for the confiscation without compensation of the imperial châteaux. To avert such a calamity, he proposed to purchase the properties for the sum of 12.5 million francs. The Elysée and Houphouët-Boigny had discreetly approved the deal, he added.

Bokassa was hardly in a position to refuse. His two properties in Switzerland had already been expropriated. One of them, which had served as the Central African embassy in Berne, had been seized by the Swiss government in lieu of debts run up by a former ambassador. The other, an apartment block, had been claimed by the Dacko regime, and Switzerland had obliged. Even the Caravelle that had carried him to Evreux had been claimed and returned to Bangui. With the loss of everything in Centrafrique, Switzerland, and now France, Bokassa was facing the grim prospect of destitution. Since arriving in Abidjan, he had been unable to make withdrawals from his European bank accounts and had been living on the generosity of Houphouët-Boigny and on his monthly pension of six thousand francs from the French army. The Tapie deal was a gulp of oxygen to a suffocating man, and he decided to accept it even though he knew that the properties were worth at least twice the price offered. By 7 PM that evening the official documents had been drawn up and signed, and soon afterwards Tapie was on his way back to Paris.

Bokassa was no longer a property owner. The man who a month earlier had possessed more than a dozen villas and châteaux on two continents now had no place to call home. But he had cash – at least, the cheque was in the mail. But a week went by, and then another, and there was still no sign of the first payment. More ominously, the French newspapers began to publish disturbing accounts of the deal. Tapie was going around Paris saying that he had cheated the former emperor of his châteaux. He had done it not for personal gain, he assured the press, but for the betterment of humanity. He planned to sell the properties and offer the proceeds to charity. In fact, he made a trip to New York, where he met Henry Labouisse, director general of UNICEF, promising him the profits once he had unloaded the various properties.[8]

Alarmed at these reports, Bokassa phoned Tapie in Paris asking for his money but heard only mocking laughter at the other end. Realizing he had been swindled, he contacted Houphouët-Boigny. The Ivorian president, who had been totally unaware of the real estate dealings and had certainly not approved the contract with Tapie, immediately put his lawyers on the case seeking cancellation of the contract and damages of one million francs.[9] The legal team sought an injunction in Paris to prevent the disposal of the property, and Tapie (who was already trying to sell some of the imperial limousine fleet) was duly notified. The case opened before the Tribunal de grande instance in Abidjan at the end of December, and it was ultimately decided in Bokassa's favour. The court annulled the sale, which it agreed had been marred by misrepresentation, and it awarded damages of 100,000 francs. Tapie refused to pay, and the case passed to the French judicial system. Two years later, on 10 December 1981, the court in Paris upheld the Abidjan decision.[10] Tapie had been made to look foolish throughout. He was forced to admit that his scheme had never had the approval of either the French or the Ivorian government, and his claim to have been motivated by the "most basic humanitarian ethics" was greeted with scepticism, especially when he confessed that he had hoped that the publicity would launch him on a political career.[11]

Apart from the Tapie affair, Bokassa's name was never far from the headlines in the weeks following his flight to Abidjan. The French political opposition was not slow to press its advantage in embarrassing the government over its relations with the former emperor. In the National Assembly, socialist leader Mitterrand condemned Giscard's big game hunting in Centrafrique and his terms of endearment for its former ruler. There were calls for a parliamentary inquiry into France's role in supporting the empire and demands for the abolition of the Ministry of Cooperation.[12] It was just the beginning of the political fallout and a modest one at that. The Bokassa story was far from over.

The Canard enchaîné is a unique newspaper by any standard. Specializing in biting satire and shocking exposés, it has long been a thorn in the side of the French establishment.[13] On 10 October 1979, its headline proclaimed, "When Giscard was pocketing Bokassa's diamonds." On an inside page was a copy of a document dated March 1973 signed by Bokassa, requesting the Comptoir national du diamant, in Bangui, to prepare a plaquette (presentation tray) of diamonds, thirty carats in all, for Giscard d'Estaing. The accompanying article alleged that Bokassa had been in the habit of showering Giscard with gifts during the latter's frequent visits to Centrafrique. The custom had begun, it said, as early as 1967 when elephant tusks and objects carved from ivory had been given; from 1970 onwards, diamonds had been the usual gift. Bokassa's generosity with the precious stones had also extended to Giscard's brother Olivier and to his cousins Jacques and François. Other recipients named in the article included Robert Galley, René Journiac, and the minister of defence, Yvon Bourges. The Canard went on to say that the Barracudas had seized the archives at Berengo precisely because they contained compromising documents respecting the Giscard regime's relations with the empire.

The article caused a sensation, and Giscard immediately consulted his advisers on the best tactics to quell the "Diamondgate Scandal," as some were already calling it. They decided on a two-pronged strategy: to prevent further revelations by getting at the source of the document, and to play down the importance of the affair to the media. The Direction de la sûreté territoriale (DST), which was given the task of finding the *Canard*'s source, had little initial success. It was several months and many published documents later before they got their man. Meanwhile, the Elysée launched its public relations campaign. At 7:50 PM on the evening of 10 October, Pierre Hunt, a presidential palace spokesman, met the press and issued the following statement: "The exchange of presents of a traditional character, particularly on the occasion of visits by members of the government to foreign states, have in no case either the character or value mentioned by certain publications concerning Central Africa.[14]" In reply to questions, Hunt added that he did not think it "very dignified for the office of president to have to justify or reply to information savouring more of defamation or an orchestrated campaign, rather than real news." The Elysée was trying to dismiss the whole affair as barely worthy of comment. At the same time, Jacques Wahl, a close Giscard adviser, telephoned the directors of the major French television stations, playing down the *Canard* story and suggesting that the document published in the satirical weekly was probably a fake.

Nevertheless, next day the highly respected *Le Monde* gave the diamond scandal major coverage. It reprinted the *Canard*'s allegations and criticized the Elysée statement of the previous evening. To dispute the value of the tainted gifts was not the same as to deny that they had been received, it pointed out. Editor Jacques Fauvet asked whether the diamonds had been returned and demanded a parliamentary inquiry into France's relations with Bokassa's empire. What most infuriated Giscard was a two-page spread attacking his family for its business interests in Africa, especially since Fauvet had been his guest two evenings before at a dinner for Portuguese President Ramalho Eanes. He seriously considered seizing *Le Monde* but resisted the temptation (though he later regretted not having done so).[15] The diamond business continued to fill the newspapers during the following week, and the foreign press soon picked up the story. Giscard was compared unfavourably with de Gaulle, who had refused all gifts, regardless of the source; some elements in the Union pour la Démocratie française (UDF), Giscard's party, suspected a plot by the Gaullists or the socialists to sabotage the president's re-election chances in 1981.

On 17 October the *Canard* documented Bokassa's generosity to his "dear cousin" more precisely than before: in 1970, after a safari, one beautiful diamond; in 1972, a *plaquette* of small diamonds; in April 1973, the *plaquette* of thirty carats cited the previous week and estimated to be worth one million francs; in March 1975, the occasion of the Bangui summit, a *plaquette* of twenty carats, including one stone of exceptional beauty. There was no hope of smothering the scandal now. Pierre Hunt met the press the same day and assured them that the president would respond fully to the allegations at "the appropriate time" (which turned out to be more than a month later).

Meanwhile, Roger Delpey, who would soon figure prominently in the scandal, was visiting his friend Bokassa in Abidjan. Delpey, it will be recalled, had been in Centrafrique a couple of times during the summer and had had lengthy interviews with the emperor. He had been planning to write a book about the massacres of January and April in order to exonerate His Majesty of all wrongdoing and thereby stymie those who were plotting his downfall. But events had moved too quickly for the writer-adventurer, and the Barracudas had secured the future before he could complete his work. He still hoped to write the book if only to clear Bokassa's name.

In his interviews with Delpey in Abidjan, which went on for the best part of ten days, Bokassa talked in detail about the events surrounding his overthrow – his trip to Libya, his sojourn at Evreux, and so forth. He was bitter at the French for having engineered his fall and was still incredulous that they could have done such a thing. When asked if now, having lost all, he would have changed anything, he was vague.

"When I took over from Dacko," he mused, "the state was bankrupt and nothing worked. How could I possibly put it all right in thirteen years? Nor did France or other African countries help me very much. Then I had to fight corruption and laziness. I promoted the status of women ... I banned dowries and female circumcision."

He tried to blame his subordinates, on whom he said he could never rely. Henri Maïdou was "an opportunist – a little Judas." Sylvestre Bangui was another opportunist and was all the more detestable since he was a fellow M'Baka. Ange Patassé was power-hungry and appeared to be mad. In his conversations with Delpey, Bokassa proclaimed his innocence of all the crimes of which he had been accused. The allegations were lies and fabrications – he had fallen into a trap set by his enemies. "I am not afraid to face justice, true justice," he declared.

Delpey left on 27 October promising to return a few weeks later. In the meantime, on 14 November, Bokassa had another, quite unexpected, visitor from Europe: the former Empress Catherine. He was delighted to see her, but his joy faded when she refused his advances. In explanation, Catherine produced from her handbag a medical certificate signed by a surgeon at a clinic in Neuilly, a suburb west of Paris, requiring her to abstain from sexual activity for several months, though it did not say why.[16] Dark thoughts flashed across Bokassa's mind. In the months and years that followed, the episode continued to haunt him, driving him to jealous rage and wild speculation.

The rest of the afternoon was a tense affair. They discussed the children, and Catherine agreed that some of them should come to live in Abidjan. They discussed business, and it transpired that she had emptied his bank account in Romorantin of its contents – 400,000 francs in all. She had also taken an undisclosed sum from his Swiss bank account and had helped herself to some of his most prized cars: two 1978 Rolls-Royce Silver Shadows, each of which was valued at between 350,000 and 400,000 francs; a 1978 Daimler worth 150,000 francs; a Jaguar, and several more. She had accomplished all this, if we are to believe Bokassa, with the close co-operation of Giscard d'Estaing and his family.

The next day Delpey returned for another series of interviews. Bokassa was depressed and brooded over his betrayal by Catherine, accusing her of collusion with Giscard in plotting his overthrow. Yet he did not hold her fully responsible: because of her youth, naïveté, and complete ignorance of politics, she had been led astray by devious and unscrupulous men. Bokassa railed against Bernard Tapie for trying to swindle him of his châteaux; he had harsh words for Jacques Duchemin, who had spread the rumour of cannibalistic feasts at Berengo; and he ridiculed David Dacko – a spineless coward who dreaded ever having to meet him again face to face.[17]

In spite of his misfortunes, Bokassa had the satisfaction of watching Giscard squirm uncomfortably as he tried to extricate himself from the growing scandal surrounding his relations with his former hunting companion. On the evening of 27 November, the very day that Delpey left Abidjan, Giscard was interviewed in an Antenne 2 television broadcast called "An Hour with the President of the Republic." When the question of Opération Barracuda was raised, he defended it firmly, arguing that if his government had not intervened they would now be facing an Iran-type situation.[18] He tried to minimize the significance of the diamond business, pointing out that the exchange of gifts was a normal protocol between heads of state. The objects he had received had either been given to museums or to charity or were being kept at the Elysée Palace, he said. In any case, the diamonds at the centre of the furore had nothing like the value attributed to them in the media. When asked about his long silence on the issue, he replied, "It has something to do with my character and with the idea I have of my role. One must allow base things to die of their own poison."[19] Giscard was a polished television performer and could often be charming and persuasive, but when placed on the defensive he became touchy and sought refuge in the dignity of his office. His retreat to lofty heights served him poorly on this occasion. The Antenne 2 broadcast did nothing to dispel the clouds that were gathering over the presidency.

The *Canard* continued to make damaging revelations and was prospering as a result. Its circulation was now 586,000, up by 200,000 from a year earlier.[20] But what if it were sued? When he took office, Giscard had promised never to prosecute the press, regardless of what it printed about him. It was a decision he had often come to regret, but for the sake of the dignity of his office he had kept his word. There were times, however, when his patience was sorely tried, especially by the *Canard*. Over the years, the satirical weekly had needled him mercilessly, poking fun at his aristocratic pretensions and his love of the chase. Its cartoonists invariably depicted him with a crown atop his bald head or standing, smoking gun in hand, astride a landscape littered with the carcasses of slaughtered animals. Safari Valéry, it called him.

Towards the beginning of December, it was revealed that the president's cousins François and Jacques Giscard were suing the *Canard* for defamation. They accused the paper of implying that they had received Bokassa's diamonds in return for funnelling money to Centrafrique to pay for the imperial coronation and for placing an excessively high valuation on the empire's uranium deposits. The legal action was interpreted in the French press as a clumsy attempt to silence a newspaper that had embarrassed the ruling family. The Giscard clan was trying to settle a score with the maverick weekly.

Bokassa now had much to be cheerful about. He was delighted at the *Canard*'s revelations and at the unease these were causing his "dear cousin." His newly found confidence brought back the old aggressiveness. He vowed to get even with those who had betrayed him, and he entered wholeheartedly into a campaign for revenge which he had been formulating with the active encouragement of his friend Roger Delpey. On 9 February 1980, Delpey came back to Abidjan and stayed for three days. His discussions with the fallen monarch ranged over familiar terrain: Catherine, Tapie, Giscard and the diamond scandal, the imprisonment of former members of the imperial government in Bangui, and René Journiac, who had been killed a few days before in an air crash in Cameroun. Then the conversation turned to an interview with Henri Maïdou published in a recent edition of *Jeune Afrique*. Maïdou, now vice-president of the restored

Central African Republic, claimed that he and Dacko had never really supported the imperial regime; they had gone along with it out of sheer terror.

"Some terror," snapped Bokassa, "with loads of CFA francs, beautiful cars, beautiful villas, beautiful women, and beautiful business. Look at him [Maïdou] in the photograph, with the face of a *bon vivant* and playboy. Look at the photographs of Dacko and all the others. Well nourished and well dressed. With decorations, golden jewels and diamond rings. Where was the terror?"

This was the world the fallen emperor had lost, and he was understandably bitter. But it was not irretrievably lost, and Delpey had drawn up the details of a plan which he believed could set things right again. The plan involved clearing Bokassa's name and ensuring the defeat of Giscard d'Estaing in the 1981 presidential election. Giscard's successor, it was assumed, would not oppose the return to power of a rehabilitated ex-emperor. The tactical details of what was termed Operation Revenge were as follows:

1 International lawyer Raymond de Geouffre de la Pradelle (a friend of Delpey's) presents Bokassa's case to the United Nations.
2 Bokassa writes to all heads of state in francophone Africa asking for the creation of an impartial commission of inquiry into the crimes levelled against him.
3 He writes to French government ministers and political leaders explaining the nature of his dispute with Giscard.
4 He writes to French army commanders and presidents of veterans' associations pleading his case.
5 He writes his memoirs – giving special attention to his relations with Giscard – and publishes them before the French presidential election of 1981.
6 Delpey publishes a book based on his investigation into the Bangui massacres in order to combat the lies told by the Mission de constatation. The book is to be sent to prominent politicians and jurists all over the world.
7 Delpey leaks documents to French newspapers proving that Giscard accepted diamonds and other gifts from Bokassa.[21]

Some aspects of the plan were already in operation. Delpey was busily working on his book and it was he who had been providing the *Canard enchaîné* with its Diamondgate material.

Circumstances excluded Bokassa from taking a direct role in Operation Revenge. Confined to his villa, with his visitors, telephone calls, and correspondence all carefully monitored, he had to rely on

Delpey to send out the various letters that were part of the plan. With this in mind, he supplied his friend with blank letterhead paper to which his signature was already appended. Back in the comparative safety of France, Delpey was to type in the agreed messages and send the letters on to their destinations. Needless to say, Operation Revenge was going to cost money. Delpey came up with a figure of between one and two million francs. This posed an immediate impediment, since the former emperor had lost almost everything. One of Delpey's roles was to raise the money for the plan.

It is certainly possible – even likely – that at least some of the documents leaked to the *Canard* were forged by Delpey with Bokassa's cooperation. This is what Giscard and the French secret service came to believe.[22] Delpey claimed he had been given the documents while at the Berengo court in August 1979, but he never explained why. He said he had hidden them in a Swiss safety deposit box, withdrawing them in little batches from time to time to keep the scandal simmering.

On 12 March the *Canard* published more documents provided by Delpey. This time the targets were François and Jacques Giscard d'Estaing, who were already locked in their court battle with the paper. The documents were memoranda signed by Bokassa indicating the number of stones received by each of the president's cousins. Jacques had evidently been given one *plaquette*; François, six. Each *plaquette* contained either fifteen or twenty cut diamonds. Another document, dated 15 June 1978, showed that François had been granted Central African citizenship. He had been a loyal subject of His Imperial Majesty.

Delpey was also producing letters over Bokassa's signature for various people of influence. The message addressed to General Gnassingbé Eyadéma, president of Togo, was typical of those sent to African leaders. In it Bokassa blamed all his misfortunes on differences he had had with the French president – differences over political and economic matters, but also respecting the privileges which the Giscard family wanted in the empire. Giscard had engineered his downfall, Bokassa alleged, in order to replace him with someone meek and servile. His only wish was to clear his name, regain his honour, and be reunited with his family. He urged Eyadéma to meet Delpey, who would provide him with proof of all of this, before the opening of the Franco-African summit scheduled for Nice on 8–10 May. The assembled statesmen could then press for his return to Centrafrique, with or without power.[23]

Bokassa seemed to believe that the francophone presidents would rally to his cause once the evils attributed to him were exposed as falsehoods. It was a fragile hope at best. Eyadéma, Bongo, and the others could ill afford to offend the French, and none felt an obligation to the fallen emperor, whom they had often considered an embarrassment to Africa. Delpey shared Bokassa's illusions, and at his home near Paris his typewriter rarely rested as the weeks went by. Raising money continued to be a problem. Hoping for support from an old Bokassa supporter, Delpey visited the Libyan embassy on 17 April and again on 3 May. The Libyans were apparently noncommittal but suggested that he come back once more after they had made inquiries.

A few days later, Giscard was at Nice's waterfront airport to greet the francophone African leaders who were arriving for the summit. Some of the visitors brought along the letters they had received from Bokassa via Delpey and passed them on to their host. The president now had confirmation of what he and the secret service had suspected for some time – that Delpey was acting as Bokassa's *agent provocateur* in France.

On Saturday, 10 May, Delpey was arrested when leaving the Libyan embassy on the rue Charles Lamoureux and was taken to DST headquarters on the rue des Saussaies. There he learned that he was being held on suspicion of violating article 80 of the penal code, an edict that forbids activities that threaten the external security of the state. More specifically, it applies to anyone "who communicates with agents of a foreign power for the purpose of or having the effect of damaging France's military or diplomatic position." In peacetime a guilty verdict can bring a prison sentence of from one to five years and a fine ranging from 60,000 to 500,000 francs. Delpey had never heard of article 80, but he was to have plenty of time to study it in the privacy of his cell.

Later in the day the DST agents took Delpey to his home in Chatou-Croissy, where they confiscated his files on Bokassa. They showed a particular interest in a dossier labelled Operation Revenge and a reference it contained to a collection of 187 documents which the former emperor had allegedly given his friend. The agents pressed Delpey to surrender the documents, assuming that they were connected with Giscard and the diamonds, but he remained obdurate. He insisted that he had no intention of damaging the country's security; he simply wanted to clear the name of Bokassa, a man who had been unjustly maligned.[24]

News of the arrest spread quickly among the French media, and on Tuesday, 13 May, a Ministry of Interior spokesman confirmed to journalists that Delpey was being questioned by the DST on suspicion of attempting to discredit France "at the highest level." Most

French newspapers printed the official government story – that Delpey was a spy. According to *Le Figaro*, the writer-adventurer had been planning, with Libyan help, to manufacture fake documents in order to embarrass France and destabilize francophone Africa. On Friday, 16 May, Delpey was taken before the State Security Court, a secretive judicial body.[25] The charges against him were read, and he was taken to the Prison de la Santé on boulevard Arago. There he stayed all summer, except for occasional appearances before the court, during which his lawyers argued vehemently that he was neither a spy nor a politician, just a writer. They urged his immediate release. They also pressed to have Bokassa called as a witness, since only he could explain the accused's visits to the Libyan embassy. The court would not budge on either count.

As the months went by, some French newpapers became increasingly sceptical of the government's motives in the affair. *Le Monde* suggested that the state had acted to silence Delpey and Bokassa in order to prevent the publication of more embarrassing documents. It also criticized the political nature of the State Security Court. As a result, the newspaper was prosecuted for "casting discredit on the courts." The action was initiated by Justice Minister Alain Peyrefitte, a law-and-order zealot. The case was dropped after the presidential election.

Bokassa would not be silenced, and on 9 September he telephoned the *Canard* editorial office from Abidjan. In an hour-long interview, he defended Delpey from the charges of threatening state security and confirmed that he had given diamonds to President Giscard, to the president's wife Anne-Aymone, and to his cousins François and Jacques. Bokassa's purpose in calling had been to help his friend Delpey and to give new momentum to his anti-Giscard campaign. But he also wanted to complain of his straitened circumstances and of the low blow that had brought him there. He had been confined to his house for a whole year, he grumbled, under guard by Ivorian troops. His only wish now was to go back to Centrafrique, even if he were no longer head of state: "I want to return to my home, in my country, in my native village, to look after my children, to practise agriculture."[26] The *Canard* published excerpts from the interview on 17 and 24 September. It was another scoop for the maverick weekly and another setback for Giscard.

Meanwhile, in his Santé Prison cell, Roger Delpey observed the revival of the scandal with growing satisfaction. His wife kept him supplied with a great variety of newspapers, and he was pleased to learn that in some journalistic circles he was being portrayed as a martyr for freedom of speech. He was discouraged, nonetheless, at his case's lack of progress before the State Security Court. Although there were appearances, interrogations, and examinations of evidence from time to time, there was no trial as such. Delpey came to believe that he was the victim of deliberate procrastination, that the authorities planned to keep him behind bars until after the presidential election of April/May 1981.[27]

To Giscard and his advisers, Delpey posed a problem that defied resolution. If the prisoner was released he could do untold damage during the election campaign with his cache of Bokassa documents. He might also finish his book on the overthrow of the empire, and no one could tell what it might reveal. On the other hand, keeping him locked up was proving to be even more troublesome. The press, both at home and abroad, had taken up the prisoner's cause. *Time* magazine, the *Guardian*, and other respected publications in the English-speaking world had harsh words for the president who threw his critics in jail. Worse still, members of the European Parliament were taking an open interest in the case and so was Amnesty International.

Faced with choosing the lesser of two evils, the president decided to rid himself of the man who was now widely referred to as "Giscard's prisoner." It would have been foolhardy to enter an election campaign saddled with such a burden. On 28 November Delpey was released from prison. Now a minor celebrity, he readily provided the press with his version of the fall of the Central African Empire, and he promised further revelations based on a cache of documents which he claimed to have stored in a Swiss vault.[28]

In February 1981, Delpey's long-awaited book, *La manipulation*, appeared, but it proved a disappointment. It contained none of the elusive documents which the author had promised. He explained this by claiming that his Swiss associate refused to release the documents because of a death threat against him.[29] Apart from the author's own account of the Bangui repression, the book was little more than a transcription of the interviews he had held with Bokassa in Berengo and Abidjan. Few French readers put much faith in the fallen emperor's version of events. Consequently, the book did not derail Giscard as Bokassa and Delpey had hoped, but it did serve to remind the president that he had a fight on his hands.

Meanwhile, Giscard's cousins' suit against the *Canard* was not going well. The case was eventually concluded on 23 December 1980 when the Paris court of appeal ruled that the newspaper had indeed slandered François and Jacques. But it awarded only symbolic damages of one franc each. Both sides claimed moral victory. In the same month Giscard discreetly arranged for the sale of the troublesome diamonds to Paris jewellers. His return was 111,547 francs. Later, on 4 February 1981, he made out a cheque for this amount in favour of the Central African Red Cross and a number of other charities, and mailed it to President Dacko.[30] On 10 March, in a televised interview during the election campaign, he was able to announce the sale of the diamonds and the charitable donation. He also took the occasion to chide the newspapers for making such a fuss of it all – their insinuations had been base and cowardly.

The presidential election campaign had begun tentatively in the spring of 1980, had gathered momentum during the summer, and by the autumn, as the major candidates declared themselves, it was fully underway. Giscard's performance was uninspiring, and he seemed to have nothing new to offer the electorate. His *protocole égotique*, his arrogance, and his apparent indifference to the rising tide of unemployment contributed to his growing unpopularity. The Bokassa diamond scandal had further impaired a reputation that was already seriously flawed; it had reinforced the image of Giscard as a man lacking in principles and good judgment, and it contributed to the moral crisis of his regime in the final months of its mandate. On 10 May 1981, when the results of the second round of the election were announced, François Mitterrand was the country's new leader.[31] Crowds gathered on the streets of Paris chanting, "Giscard au chômage!" ("Giscard out!"), a sentiment shared by the exiled emperor.

For some months now, Bokassa had been given more freedom by the Ivorian authorities. He was allowed to leave his house once in a while and became somewhat of a fixture in the fashionable bars and nightclubs of Abidjan's Treichville quarter. At first he was not so easily accepted, and many of the bargirls refused to sit or dance with him because of his reputation as a cannibal and child killer. But despite his complaints of poverty, he had money to spend and was soon considered a good client. Sometimes he became drunk and uncontrollable and lashed out at members of his entourage as if nothing had changed and he was still omnipotent. After one such scene in a Treichville nightclub, he gave up the bottle entirely and did not touch any liquor for several months. Then came Giscard's defeat. It called for a celebration. The Chivas flowed again as in the old days, and the former emperor's depression lifted. "He betrayed me. Now we are on the same footing ... He is unemployed like me," he was heard to remark.[32]

CHAPTER ELEVEN

The New Republic

In the restored Central African Republic, Jean-Bedel Bokassa was not forgotten. Although he was thousands of kilometres away, he remained an ever-present force in the political fortunes of his homeland and a source of unease for the country's new rulers. On the morning after Opération Barracuda, a new government was put into place in Bangui. In accordance with arrangements worked out beforehand in Paris, David Dacko became president and Henri Maïdou vice-president. The "government of public well-being" was composed in the main of Bokassa's former collaborators. Bernard Ayandho, in disgrace for a number of years, was appointed prime minister, and there were cabinet posts for Sylvestre Bangui, former ambassador to France, François Bozize, former imperial general, and Alphonse Koyamba, former imperial finance minister, to name but a few. The old familiar faces left those who had wanted real change disappointed.

The passing of time had failed to transform David Dacko into the kind of leader his country needed. Weak and indecisive as ever, he was now saddled with the additional burden of being the "parachuted president" and the "puppet of Paris." French advisers never left his side, and French troops guarded his person. When asked about the soldiers, he said that they could stay in Centrafrique for a hundred years if they so wished – a comment deeply resented by those with nationalist inclinations. For the time being at least, it was clear that the Barracudas were necessary, since the Central African security forces had largely vanished with the collapse of the empire.

The new president thought he could temper the antipathy towards him with popular gestures. He released political and common prisoners – and was applauded for doing so. He promised democratic elections – and was greeted with scepticism. (His high-handedness with opposition groups between 1960 and 1966 had not been forgotten.) In a further attempt to court popularity, Dacko tried to distance himself from the previous regime – no easy task for someone who was a M'Baka and a cousin of Bokassa, and had been an adviser at the imperial court for several years. Undaunted nonetheless, Dacko announced that he would seek Bokassa's extradition from the Ivory Coast to face charges of murder, embezzlement, and cannibalism.[1] This extradition demand was a shrewd and calculated move and helped improve Dacko's image. But in truth, neither he nor the French wanted Bokassa in the dock. They preferred him to remain where he was without a public platform from which to make damning revelations and accusations. The gambit paid off; Houphouët-Boigny refused to hand over his guest.

Dacko had been in office only a few days when there was a serious challenge to his leadership. The challenger was Ange Patassé, who was incensed that the French had overlooked him in choosing Bokassa's successor. On the morning of Wednesday, 26 September, the air and frontier police at Roissy Airport stopped Patassé as he was trying to board an Air Afrique flight to Bangui. One of the reasons given was that his passport said Empire centrafricain, and the empire no longer existed; the other, that he was carrying two pistols inside his coat. That evening, a crowd of three thousand assembled at Bangui-M'Poko Airport to await Patassé's return. When news came that their hero had been detained in France, the crowd took to the streets in riotous mood. Dacko called for calm but could do little else.

The next day, the French authorities relented and told Patassé that he was free to leave. Instead, he sought refuge in the Libyan embassy where he asked for political asylum. From there, he called on his countrymen to rise up against Dacko and his French protectors. On Friday, 28 September, he flew to Tripoli, where he announced details of the policies he would pursue on taking his "rightful place" as president of the Central African Republic: socialism, better baccalaureate examination results, economic prosperity with Libyan aid, cultural cooperation with noncolonialist Frenchmen, and the extermination of the M'Baka in punishment for their support of Bokassa.[2] These promises appealed to some of the radical student elements in Bangui and to Patassé's own ethnie, the Sara, who dominated the region bordering on Tchad, but they did not please everyone.

Flirting with Gadhaffi tarnished Patassé's image as a popular leader, and nobody heeded his call for a general uprising. When he stepped off the plane in Bangui on 4 October, only a small gathering of young people chanting anti-French slogans was at the airport to greet him. Undeterred, he set about organizing his political movement, the MLPC, and promoting his policies. In the weeks that followed, there were clashes between his supporters and the security forces, and these disturbances alarmed the government. On 3 November, with the backing of his French advisers, Dacko acted. He had Patassé and several other prominent members of the MLPC arrested and thrown in Ngaragba.

Dacko also had to face the problem of those directly implicated in Bokassa's reign of terror. Within a few days of Operation Barracuda, demonstrators began to call for retribution. "The dog is gone, the pups remain" was a slogan that appeared on public walls with a frequency that could not be ignored.[3] Partly to court popularity, partly to distance himself from the provious regime, Dacko ordered the arrest of thirty-four of Bokassa's closest collaborators. They were duly rounded up and were put on trial in February 1980. Most of the accused received prison terms for their crimes, but a number of death sentences were handed down. Among the condemned were Dr Dédéavodé, found guilty of poisoning the baby of Fidèle Obrou and the fake Martine; General Mayomokola, for shooting demonstrators in January 1979; Captain Mokoa, for the Ngaragba massacres of April 1979; and Colonel Inga, for miscellaneous murders. The death sentences were appealed to the Supreme Court, which overturned them on a technicality in August. Another trial was hastily organized, which produced the same verdict as the first. Even so, the expected executions were not immediately carried out. The condemned men lingered in Ngaragba throughout the year, never knowing when they might be called out to face the firing squad.

Meanwhile, Dacko was growing accustomed to the exercise of power. Politics in Centrafrique was what it always had been – the gateway to making money. The president soon had several lucrative ventures going. Coffee plantations and other enterprises confiscated from Bokassa fell into his hands, and he also became involved in the notorious ivory trade. During the first six months of 1980, about 120 tonnes of ivory left Bangui, usually accompanied by "exceptional authorizations" signed by Dacko himself. The tusks were shipped through Paris, and their arrival in the French capital created embarrassment for the Elysée.[4] The slaughter of elephants during the Bokassa era was well known in France, and now it seemed that the emperor's successor was behaving no differently.

Although Dacko was beginning to enjoy the privileges of power, his position was far from secure. The French insisted that he hold a multicandidate presidential election, and he knew that this would be his greatest test. Paris wanted him to win, of course, and thus legitimize Opération Barracuda, but he was not confident that he could woo a majority of voters in a fair contest. He therefore set about vanquishing his rivals so that by polling day his victory would be assured. On 24 November 1979 he dissolved MESAN and created in its place the Union démocratique centrafricaine, which was proclaimed the new political party for all Central Africans. There was something ominous in the choice of words, and many feared that a new one-party system was being introduced. This is apparently what the president had in mind, but he refrained from the anticipated step of suppressing rival movements.

Dacko's more immediate problem was how to remove those within the government who aspired to his job. Henri Maïdou was the most obvious contender. The vice-president made no secret of his ambition and boasted that it was he who had engineered Bokassa's downfall. Moreover, he claimed that since he was not a M'Baka, he was better suited than Dacko to bring about national reconciliation. On 10 August 1980, when he openly declared his intention of running for president if a free election was held, Dacko had him arrested on the pretext that the country could not have two heads.

Some weeks later, Dacko removed Ayandho as prime minister, and shortly thereafter Sylvestre Bangui resigned from the government in protest. The president had succeeded in eliminating his rivals, but he was completely isolated. Moreover, supporters of Patassé, Maïdou, Ayandho, Bangui, and Abel Goumba (who was still in exile) were talking of forming a united opposition front. Dacko now realized that he had gone too far, and under pressure from Paris, which was growing increasingly irritated by his strong-arm tactics, he released his political prisoners on 1 December 1980. He then announced that there would be a constitutional referendum and free presidential elections early in the new year.[5]

The race was now on, and Dacko resolved to use his position as president to every advantage. One of his better ideas was to put Bokassa on trial in absentia. It was risky in some ways, since it would likely alienate the M'Baka. On the other hand, it would serve to distance the president further from the imperial regime and might at the same time tarnish the reputations of Patassé and Maïdou by reminding the public of the two men's long association with the fallen emperor. When news reached Bokassa in Abidjan of his pending trial, he made it known that he wished to return to his homeland to defend himself, and he sent letters to his supporters in Bangui protesting his innocence and demanding a fair hearing. There was no chance, however, that the Dacko government would agree to such a thing. Justice was simply not the issue.

Bokassa's trial in absentia opened in Bangui on 19 December 1980 in the stadium where three years earlier he had been crowned emperor. The principal charges were the attacks on personal liberty, and the beatings, murder, embezzlement of funds, and cannibalism. The trial was plagued with irregularities from the start. First, there was the question of jurisdiction. Bokassa was charged in the criminal court as if he were a common criminal, yet these were no ordinary crimes. In any case, they had been committed while the accused was in power. The trial was clearly political in nature, and this should have been recognized. Then there was the question of procedure. There were no cross-examinations and no lawyers for the defence. In an almost festive atmosphere, the witnesses, fifty in all, were given free rein to say whatever they wished without fear of contradiction. Many simply recited the more fantastic stories that had been printed in the French press following the fall of the empire. They knew that thousands of their fellow citizens were tuned in to the radio broadcasts of the proceedings, and they vied to outdo one another in entertaining this vast audience with bizarre tales.

Few of those who testified were honest, forthright, or convincing. Many who had been in His Majesty's service were patently preoccupied with salvaging their own reputations and distancing themselves from the horrors of the imperial age. They chose their words with studied care. Koyamba mentioned how Bokassa "was sent every week about 20 million CFA francs deducted from special funds," but he had little more to say. Patassé talked vaguely of how the emperor had been obsessed with the profits of his diverse enterprises. Maïdou seemed tongue-tied and simply deplored the absence of the accused. Madame Domitien repeatedly claimed that she alone had opposed Bokassa's excesses.[6]

While everyone agreed that the emperor had enriched himself greatly over the years, no one could say for certain how much he had accumulated. Nor could anyone produce documentary evidence on this count. The charge of embezzlement remained far from proven. On the question of murders and beatings, it was much the same. Many who testified told of the midnight trials at the Villa Kolongo and the victims dispatched to the crocodile pond and the lion cage. Yet it was all very vague. Names and dates remained elusive. Perhaps the most credible witness was Captain Mokoa. The former security chief at Ngaragba had been under a death sentence for the best part of a year and realized that he had little to lose in being forthright.

"I had executed at Ngaragba prison from 1976 to 1979 dozens of officers, soldiers, diverse personages, thieves, students – under instructions from Bokassa," he told the court. He mentioned Lingou-pou and others who had been beaten to death with hammers and chains.

Dacko himself refused to testify, excusing himself on the grounds that he was president. This was unfortunate, since he knew Bokassa

intimately, and his evidence might have been critical on the controversial charge of cannibalism. It was he, after all, who had informed
the press after Opération Barracuda of his cousin's eating habits.[7]
The cannibalism charge provoked the wildest stories of all. One of
Bokassa's cooks informed the court that his master had been wont
to dine on the testicles of his enemies. He liked them "cooked to a
turn" – they were his special treat. Another claimed that the emperor
had eaten the vagina and breasts of a young virgin in order to retain
his youthful vigour.[8] The most detailed account came from an aging
military man by the name of Philippe Linguissa. Partly paralysed
and either drunk or confused, Linguissa had to be helped to the
witness stand, where he addressed the judge in Sango. Later, a
French translation was provided to the press. Here is the English
version of what he said:

In 1977 a soldier appeared at the military canteen where I worked and gave
me the following orders: "Take a casserole dish full of salt, of spices and
onions, and bring some wine." I got into a waiting car and we drove to
Berengo, eighty kilometres from Bangui. At the palace I was put in a huge
kitchen. It was in Bokassa's wooden house. The emperor arrived. "So,
grandad, you are in the army?" I showed him my military papers and he
said, "So you must obey." He went to open the refrigerator and took out a
man's body. It had no head, no hands, no feet. "You are going to prepare this
like a *méchoui*." I screamed. I said that I had cooked chicken and mutton, but
never man. Without speaking, he pulled out his revolver. I told him to kill
me. "No, I want to eat at 8 PM."

I put myself to work as I would prepare a chicken, stuffing it with rice
and onions and sewing the skin with a needle and thread which Bokassa
had given me. I sprinkled it with gin and Pernod and placed the entire body
in a large vat which I slid into an immense oven. When I pulled it out later
to see how it was cooking, the body started to move, sat up, and pointed at
me with one of its arms. It struggled so much that it messed up the entire
kitchen. I begged its forgiveness and pushed it back into the oven.[9]

This testimony, implausible as it was, made headlines around the
world. More than anything else, it illustrated the carnival mood of
the proceedings. The trial was a farce in every sense. Lasting only
four days, it came to an end on 23 December when the judge, after
a two-hour deliberation, handed down a guilty verdict on all charges
and pronounced the death sentence on the accused.

Bokassa was not directly affected by the outcome. Abidjan was a
secure haven from the wrath of his enemies. Nonetheless, he was
dismayed and grieved by what had transpired. He considered the
charge of cannibalism a grave insult to his dignity, and at every

opportunity he vehemently denied that he had partaken of human flesh. His fury at the French press, an enduring phenomenon, now knew no bounds. He blamed it for what he considered one of the most vile campaigns of character assasination in living memory.

From Dacko's point of view, the trial was an enormous success. It allowed him to pose as a champion of justice and a true opponent of the Bokassa tyranny. Furthermore, the public was reminded that several of his rivals, and in particular Patassé, had been loyal servants of the emperor for many years. Dacko had one other card to play before the campaign began in earnest. At dawn on 24 January 1981, those condemned to death for crimes committed in the imperial era were led out to face the firing squad. Thus perished Captain Mokoa, Dr Dédéavodé, and the others. It was a popular move, especially among the friends and relatives of the students who had died in 1979.[10]

The first stage in the electoral process was the adoption of a new republican constitution modelled on that of France. Article 14 guaranteed a multiparty political system. It was put to a plebiscite on 1 February 1981 and was endorsed by a majority of 97.43 per cent of those who cast ballots. Five men in all entered the presidential election campaign: Dacko, Maïdou, Patassé, Goumba, and François Pehoua. Abel Goumba returned to Bangui on 22 February after almost two decades abroad. He was virtually unknown, except among intellectuals. Although he was the only candidate untainted by collaboration with Bokassa, this did not help him much, since purity is no substitute for popularity in politics. Pehoua too had been abroad for many years and his name was also unfamiliar to the voters. A high official in the Banque centrale des Etats d'Afrique de l'Ouest, he had served briefly as Bokassa's finance minister in the 1970s. He was supported by French business interests close to Robert Galley.[11]

This was the first multicandidate election in the country's history. Indeed, it was a rare event in Africa itself. This being said, the campaign was anything but a showpiece of democracy in action. It was marred by strikes, violent demonstrations, intimidation, and massive fraud. Worse still, some candidates made blatant appeals to ethnic loyalties. Dacko tried to rise above such petty factionalism (his M'Baka being a minority in any case) and pose as the champion of national reconciliation, the inheritor of Boganda. In his role as president he had numerous advantages, and he never hesitated to use them. He could dispense jobs and money, and he did. French soldiers handed out free salt, meat, and oil in the provinces, noting that these were gifts from Dacko's government. As well, the president was reputed to have received financial assistance from nearby Zaïre, Cameroun, and Gabon on condition that he abandon this dangerous experiment in multiparty elections once victory was secured.[12]

Large crowds turned out to exercise the franchise on 15 March 1981. After the ballots had been counted, it was announced that Dacko had won 50.23 per cent, just enough to be elected without a second ballot as provided for in the constitution. Patassé was in second place with 38.11 per cent, while the others trailed badly, Pehoua garnering a mere 5.33 per cent, Maïdou 3.23 per cent, and Goumba 1.42 per cent.[13] Dacko's regime was now legitimate before the world, and in a way so was Opération Barracuda, but this made no difference to its ability to govern. Although repression had disappeared with the fall of Bokassa's empire, disorder had taken its place. Ethnic, political, and social strife had engulfed the country since the restoration of the republic, and Dacko had proved unable to deal with it effectively. After the election, he seemed just as incapable of bringing matters under control. His policies wavered and zigzagged with no direction or consistency. He imposed a state of emergency and then repealed it; he banned opposition parties and later lifted the ban; and he remained evasive on the promised elections for the National Assembly.

The new socialist government in France watched the unfolding drama with a growing conviction that the "parachuted president" was out of his depth. Many in Centrafrique held the same opinion. The population yearned for law and order, and even those in high places were tiring of their president's ineptitude. A strong leader was the answer, and some were openly nostalgic for Bokassa's early days in power. The former emperor was aware of all of this, and through his supporters in Centrafrique he tried to promote himself as the only solution to the prevailing anarchy. With his old enemy gone from the Elysée, he was convinced that the historic moment had arrived for his triumphal return.

"Nothing further can prevent me returning to preside over the destiny of my country," he told a friend in Abidjan. "Since the fall of Valéry Giscard d'Estaing, I have received a great amount of messages inviting me to take my place once more in Centrafrique." Asked if he wished to remount the imperial throne, he was less specific: "I would try to be a good president, nothing more ... since the presidency for life did not make me happy and the title emperor even less so ... I should have listened to Gadhaffi who advised me to be more modest, but it went to my head."[14]

The thought that Bokassa might return one day and assume power terrified Dacko, and he was always ready to flee if his rival turned up in Bangui. The parachuted president also kept a sharp eye on another danger point – the Central African army. He remembered all too well the army's role in putting an end to his first regime on that night of Saint-Sylvestre. The army had disintegrated with the fall of the empire and afterwards had been reconstituted under the command of General André Kolingba. By 1981 there were nineteen hundred soldiers, eight generals, and a dozen colonels in uniform, and they were an unhappy lot. The soldiers received no real training, and army credits in the state budget were miserable. Dacko treated them with undisguised contempt and relied on the Barracudas for his personal security.

That summer the president was facing a number of crises. Old beyond his fifty-two years, he was suffering from hypertension and frequent fainting spells. He knew he needed medical treatment in France but feared that a prolonged absence would pave the way for a coup. Since Giscard's defeat in May he could no longer rely on the French, a fact that was underscored when the Mitterrand government confined the Barracudas to their barracks.[15] Civil disturbances continued, the army was restless, and Bokassa was only a five-hour flight away, promising the strong leadership that Dacko could never hope to give.

On the evening of 14 July an explosion rocked the Club Cinema in downtown Bangui just as a show was ending. Three people, including a French *coopérant*, were killed and another twenty-seven injured. The attack was the work of Iddi Lala, a deranged one-time supporter of Abel Goumba. The incident shook Dacko profoundly. He declared a state of emergency and called on General Kolingba and his army to restore order. The general was pleased and tasted power for the first time. What happened next was almost inevitable.

Early in the morning of 1 September several hundred soldiers under Kolingba's command left Camp de Roux and took up their position around the Palais de la Renaissance. As the general entered the palace grounds, Dacko emerged and submitted his resignation as he was bidden to do.[16] Later in the day the former president was a free man and seemed hardly perturbed by his loss of power. Perhaps he was relieved that it was Kolingba rather than Bokassa who had taken it from him.

Apart from having personal ambition, General Kolingba was sincerely interested in ending the factional rivalry and the mounting disorder that was rending the country apart. The persistence of these conditions had been paving the way for Bokassa's return, and Kolingba had acted before that could happen. The French socialist government had no reason to support Dacko, who had been Giscard's choice. The

eight hundred French soldiers in Centrafrique had orders not to interfere, and this suggests tacit approval of the coup.[17]

Kolingba had engineered his takeover with the help of soldiers
from his own Yakoma people, and he brought men of other ethnic
groups on side by agreeing to the formation of a ruling junta, the
Comité militaire de redressement national (CMRN). However, he was
reluctant to share the spoils of office with the junta or anyone else,
and he soon consolidated power in his own hands as president. His
rule was as absolute as any on the continent. Meanwhile, the fact that
Kolingba was a soldier and was clearly adept at draconian measures
gave the citizenry food for thought, and a semblance of order
returned to the streets. But there was no return to the overt and
arbitrary violence of the Bokassa era.[18]

Contacted in Abidjan by a *Jeune Afrique* reporter, Bokassa said that
the coup in Bangui had not surprised him. "Dacko is used to quit-
ting," he quipped, "This is his second time." When asked if he had
done anything to precipitate his rival's downfall, he replied, "Oh yes!
I prayed. I prayed every day … Hail Mary … I Believe in God …
Our Father … so that Dacko would fall. And he fell. Just as Giscard
fell. Now all three of us are down, but since I was the first to fall I
can be the first to get up and laugh."[19]

Bokassa may indeed have laughed, but he was well aware that
Kolingba's coup was a major setback for his plans to return to power.
With a new strongman in control and busily consolidating his position, the prospects for a Bokassa restoration grew dimmer with each
passing day. He appeared to resign himself to this reality, at least for
a while. When a newsman inquired if he still wished to go back to
Centrafrique, the reply lacked the certainty of old: "No. I want to
stay here in the Ivory Coast near my Papa Houphouët. Perhaps the
army will one day recognize that I am a Central African and then I'll
retire in my country. But I don't want power again. I am not – unlike
Dacko – one of those who plot to grab power. That said, if the country calls me, I shall come."[20]

Bokassa had been in Abidjan now for two years and had grown
accustomed to the place. In August 1981 Houphouët-Boigny had
moved him to a house in the Indénié quarter on the rue des Sambas,
and fifteen of his children had come to live with him. Some of the
older ones, including Jean-Charles and Saint-Cyr, had their own
apartments in the Plateau district. Georges, who lived in Europe,
came on frequent visits; the eldest son had made up with his father
after the overthrow.[21] Catherine also came by from time to time from
her new home in Geneva and brought her children to visit their
papa. But she always stayed with her friend Thérèse Houphouët-

Boigny, never at the villa. She had acquired an Ivorian passport, thanks to Thérèse, and now went by her maiden name, Denguiade.

Bokassa himself had no passport, but Houphouët-Boigny had given him an identity card, which listed his occupation as "ex-emperor."[22] During his night-clubbing he had acquired a live-in companion, a young Ivorienne named Suzanne. She gave birth to a daughter, Marie-Suzanne, but shortly afterwards left the household, unable to endure her partner's mercurial moods. By the summer of 1982, Bokassa had no woman living with him, though he continued to be a fixture on the Treichville night scene. Most evenings his metallic grey Toyota Cressida made the rounds of his favourite watering holes, and he usually found someone to share his memories and his bottle of whiskey. He spent his days in solitude, walking his dog or reading newspapers, from which he cut out articles and created files on subjects of interest. In the afternoon he took a long siesta to gather his energy for another night on the town.[23] There was much time to reflect on all that had transpired. With the fall of Giscard and Dacko, men he despised, Bokassa's bitterness lost some of its edge. Revenge no longer obsessed him, and he more readily accepted the circumstances of his exile. He came to see himself as an elder statesman in dignified retirement.

President Kolingba had little to fear from the *émigré*, at least for the moment. His first major challenge came from another, not unexpected, quarter. On 3 March 1982 Ange Patassé, recently returned to Bangui after a few months in France, attempted a coup. His foremost companion-in-arms, General François Bozize, went on the radio at 11 PM and called for a popular uprising against Kolingba, whom he described as a traitor. By a prearranged plan, a small cadre of supporters raised barricades in Gobongo, Fou, and Malimaka. To their disappointment, nobody rallied to the cause and the coup fizzled out. Soldiers loyal to the president were soon on the spot, and the little band of putschists scattered into the night. Patassé, too, made his escape and went into hiding. A few days later he found sanctuary in the French embassy, arriving there on a motorbike and disguised as a woman. On 13 April he was allowed to go into exile in Togo.[24] According to Pierre Marion, head of the secret service at the time, both Mitterrand and Guy Penne (the president's adviser on African affairs) preferred Kolingba to Patassé since the latter was too erratic and unpredictable.[25]

Other potential opponents of the regime – Dacko, Maïdou, Goumba, and the like – were kept under close surveillance, but they were now dispirited and were resigned to their exclusion from the political game. Freedom of the press, which had flourished briefly during Dacko's second coming, was firmly stifled. To find out what was going on in their country, Central Africans had to tune in to Radio France Internationale as they had done in Bokassa's day.[26] As well, it soon became clear that some of the best jobs in government were going to the Yakoma, especially to Kolingba's friends and relatives. The M'Baka, who had had their own way for so long, were no longer given preference. Moreover, the president spent money lavishly on his native region around Kembé, in the south-central part of the country. There was a new university, an airport, plantations, and a paved road. Meanwhile, many of Bokassa's investments around Berengo – the most modern facilities in the country – were neglected.

It is hardly surprising that the M'Baka became disaffected and that many of them openly declared they would welcome Bokassa's return. With the crushing of Patassé in March 1982, the former emperor's name was frequently on the lips of Kolingba's opponents, regardless of ethnic affiliation. In other words, Bokassa became the rallying point for all the discontented. Although it was denied in the French and Central African press, he retained a solid core of support in his homeland. Furthermore, his followers firmly believed that he would come back one day to reclaim his throne.

Those backing Bokassa were encouraged by the often tense relations between Kolingba and Paris. Jean-Pierre Cot, who had been appointed minister of cooperation after the socialist victory, initially played a key role in redefining French policy towards Africa. An idealist who championed human rights, he was openly critical of the authoritarian governments in Bangui and elsewhere. In June 1982 he made an official visit to the Central African Republic, where his advocacy of reducing the size of the public service and returning to civilian rule naturally irritated his hosts; and when Abel Goumba was given a place of honour at a reception for Cot at the French embassy, it was an undisguised rebuke to the Kolingba regime.

Before long, however, Cot's idea that France should help needy people rather than governments ran afoul of powerful interests: entrenched civil servants, metropolitan commercial concerns operating in Africa, and the ruling élites of the former colonies. Cot's forced resignation in December 1982 was a signal for a return to a more conventional policy. At the same time, decisions were increasingly in the hands of Mitterrand and his son Jean-Christophe, who was assistant to the president's "Monsieur Afrique," Guy Penne.[27] The penchant for military intervention in support of friendly regimes, so characteristic of the Giscard presidency, was seen once more. In 1983, when Libyan-backed rebels challenged the Tchadian government of

Hissène Habré, France launched Opération Manta, a massive military offensive on behalf of Habré. As before, the military base at Bouar proved indispensable. In the circumstances, Mitterrand drew closer to Kolingba, viewing the Central African president as a force for stability in the region and a friend of France.

If Bokassa was aware of the rapprochment between Paris and Bangui, he chose to ignore it. The news he was receiving led him to the inescapable conclusion that his people were unhappy with their government and needed their emperor once more. Roger Delpey had a hand in this development. He helped shake the former emperor out of his retirement mood by promising that power was within easy reach. Together they developed a strategy to bring this about. In many ways it was a continuation of their earlier Operation Revenge, which had been disrupted by financial problems, Delpey's arrest, Kolingba's coup, and Mitterrand's apparent support for the new military regime in Bangui. This time Delpey, Jean-Marie Dupont, and other Bokassa supporters in France raised the money themselves. Belgian diamond firms with fond memories of the free-wheeling imperial era were major contributors.

On 1 January 1983 Delpey mailed five thousand postcards to selected addresses in Centrafrique. The cards showed a photograph of Bokassa on one side, his new year's greeting on the other. To bypass the Central African post office, which would have confiscated them if the contents were known, a fake company name and return address appeared on the envelopes. The postcards were passed around surreptitiously by their recipients, causing a tremor of excitement throughout the land. Their emperor had not forgotten them.

Around the same time, Delpey arranged for the publication of a four-page brochure, signed by Bokassa, which praised his military career. One hundred thousand copies of this "Appeal to my former companions-in-arms" were sent to veterans' associations in France and to African soldiers who had once served in the French army. Delpey was also responsible for the printing of a sumptuous eight-page *Déclaration officielle*. This was Bokassa's political manifesto. It began with the usual denunciations of the Mission de constatation and with denials that children had been massacred in 1979: "I let myself be trapped; never would Sadat, Hassan II, or Mobutu have accepted an equivalent inquiry." Giscard and Dacko received their customary share of abuse, the latter being said to have been "born a ripe banana and … never recovered from it." The heart of the *Déclaration*, however, was Bokassa's agenda. He said that he wished to return to Centrafrique as an emperor who reigned but did not rule, and he promised that his new regime would be genuinely democratic, with political pluralism, a national assembly, freedom of information, and labour union rights – liberties never entertained during his years in power.[28]

The manifesto was distributed to the Paris media, and Bokassa, who had been virtually forgotten in France, was suddenly newsworthy again. As the months went by his name kept appearing, largely as a result of Delpey's efforts. Much of the publicity was positive; Delpey saw to that. Pierre Salinger did a long interview with the ex-emperor for the American television channel ABC. Roger Holeindre made a movie about him for French television. It was a major operation in "image management" – an orchestrated campaign to rehabilitate the man who was best known for killing people and eating them for supper. The French media were intrigued by it all. There was much talk of Bokassa's Napoleonic delusions, of his compulsive urge to stage his own return from Elba even if it ended in disaster. It was all idle speculation, of course. Bokassa had no wish for a tragic end. He wanted only what he had always wanted – absolute power.

Every morning at 5 AM, the villa on Abidjan's rue des Sambas stirred to the voice of Radio France Internationale. This was Bokassa's finger on the pulse of the world, his ear to the winds of political change. Would his country call him? Was it time to go? Down in the basement, seamstresses were busily producing safari suits of his own design to be marketed under the trademark "Bokassa I." The old entrepreneur was at work again. He needed the money to feed and educate his large family, he explained. But a rumour circulated that he was really making uniforms for a secret army that would lead him back to power. Houphouët-Boigny became suspicious and shut down the operation.[29]

By August, Bokassa was stating openly that his return was imminent. In the same month, a new underground movement calling itself Forces centrafricaines libres appeared in Bangui. It spread the word that "our leader, Emperor Bokassa," would soon be back.[30]

CHAPTER TWELVE

La vérité et l'honneur

The return from Elba promised to be a complicated affair. Bokassa was under surveillance in his Abidjan residence, and although he had some freedom of movement, he could not simply pack his bags and leave. But he had loyal supporters in France who had already raised millions of francs in the hope of getting history to repeat itself.[1] Among them was Roger Delpey, who was the mastermind behind a scheme designed to land Bokassa in Bangui early in the morning of Sunday, 27 November 1983. The scheme did not call for mercenaries or private armies. Delpey believed that once the former emperor set foot on Central African soil, his people would acclaim him and the Kolingba government would collapse. So convinced was he of this that he decided to invite along an entourage of twenty French journalists to witness the event for themselves. Bokassa concurred with the plan, believing that his mythical stature would be sufficient to vanquish his opponents once he arrived in his homeland. He had no doubt of the *accueil triomphal* that awaited him.

At 9:30 PM on Friday, 25 November, the journalists who were to record for posterity the triumphant return gathered at the Hôtel Ibis, Porte de Bagnolet, in the east end of Paris. They were met by Bernard de Ducla, a retired colonel, who was in charge of the operation. He gave them little information at first, apart from telling them that if they were questioned they were simply to say that they were a group of tourists on their way to Africa. He further instructed them to remain in their rooms until 4:00 AM, when the plan would be set in motion.

When the journalists gathered in the hotel lobby early the following morning, they met other members of the expedition. There were seven bodyguards – tough-looking young men dressed in blazers and grey trousers – and an international lawyer, seventy-three-year-old Raymond de Geouffre de la Pradelle. He had represented Bokassa in several lawsuits and was to defend him if things went awry when they landed in Bangui. Then there was Vladimir Arapoff, a friend of Delpey, who was carrying Bokassa's marshal's uniform in his baggage. Of Russian ancestry, Arapoff was a choreographer with the Ballet du Casino de Paris. He had met Delpey while serving time in the Santé Prison for allegedly prostituting his dancers and staging pornographic performances.

It was still dark as a bus took the group to Le Bourget airport, just northeast of Paris, where a private airplane – a Caravelle with Arabic writing on the side – was standing by. But they could not go on board immediately; for over an hour they had to wait in the bus, parked by one of the hangers. During this time, an officer of the air and frontier police made an appearance, but when they told him they were tourists bound for Benin, he seemed to believe them and departed.

At 6:50 AM they boarded the plane and met the captain and crew, which included two attractive young hostesses. They took off without delay en route to Abidjan. Later in the morning, at 11:30 AM, they made a technical stopover at Tamanrasset, in the desert of southern Algeria. Since they were in transit, the Algerian police caused no problems and dutifully stamped their passports. The plan called for them to spend two and a half hours there so as to time their arrival in Abidjan for just before nightfall.

By 2:00 PM they were in the air again, continuing their southward journey. At this stage, Colonel de Ducla explained the details of "Operation Elba," as it might be called. Until then, the journalists had not been certain of what was in store. Now, de Ducla told them that Delpey had gone to Abidjan twenty-four hours earlier and would accompany Bokassa as he slipped away from his villa to rendezvous with the Caravelle. Both men would be dressed as pilots and would make their way to the airport in a van. If the timing was right, the aircraft would already be on the ground and they would come aboard by the rear door. The journalists were instructed to remain seated, to make no noise, and to take no photographs when this happened. The window shutters on the plane were to remain closed.

Once Bokassa and Delpey were on the airplane, it would take off for Libreville, Gabon. When it arrived there, Bokassa would stay on board so as to avoid complications with the local authorities. The plane was fitted with a bed, and one of the hostesses – whichever one he chose – would keep him company for the night. The rest of the passengers and crew had reservations in a hotel. On the following morning, Sunday the twenty-seventh, the Caravelle would leave once more, this time in the direction of N'Djaména, Tchad. During the flight the pilot would feign technical problems and request permission to make an emergency landing in Bangui. As this was was taking place, two helicopters, which were standing by in Libreville, would fly in and shower the Central African capital with a million leaflets. Half of the leaflets featured the Centrafrique flag; the other half bore Bokassa's photograph. On the reverse side all one million carried the message "Long live the Central African Republic! BOKASSA is at the airport. He awaits you, come and find him!"[2]

The organizers of the venture reasoned that once this happened, a crowd of at least five thousand would converge on the airport to welcome back *le patron*. From there he would be carried in triumph to the Palais de la Renaissance – and to power. Kolingba and his cronies, it was believed, would flee across the river to Zaïre. The entire plan was based on a number of assumptions that were by no means beyond dispute: the popularity of Bokassa; the unpopularity of Kolingba; and the incompetence of the existing security forces. It was understood that ever since the socialists had come to power in Paris, French troops stationed in Africa were under orders not to interfere in local political matters, although events in Tchad suggested otherwise. The team of journalists was brought along not only to record the event but as a sort of guarantee. Delpey thought that their presence would discourage any violence by the local soldiery towards Bokassa or his supporters.[3]

It was 5:40 PM when the Caravelle touched down in Abidjan. A few minutes later it came to a halt at the end of a runway near some hangers that overlooked the airport road. It was along this road that Bokassa and Delpey were to come in their van. All was set; everything was on schedule. The captain now left the plane – this was according to plan. A nervous wait ensued. Nobody could see outside because of the shuttered windows. Within ten minutes the captain returned and informed the passengers that their history-making odyssey was over and they would have to disembark. As they made their way down the steps, they could see that the plane was surrounded by commandos armed to the teeth. Obviously, something had gone wrong. They were searched for weapons – they had none – and then escorted under heavy guard to the VIP lounge. In an adjacent office uniformed men were waiting to interrogate them. Here they met a dejected Delpey, who explained how his masterplan had come undone.[4]

Rumours about Bokassa's imminent return had been circulating in Paris for weeks. Evidently, the journalists who had been invited

along had not been as discreet as could have been hoped. By the time
the Caravelle left Le Bourget on its abortive mission, the DST knew
in some detail what was going on. The *barbouzes* passed word to the
higher echelons of power and action was duly taken to checkmate
Operation Elba. A key figure in these machinations was Guy Penne,
the small man with thick grey hair who was Mitterrand's adviser on
African affairs.[5] Early in the morning of Saturday, 26 November,
Penne had telephoned Presidents Kolingba and Houphouët-Boigny
with the news that a planeload of armed mercenaries was on its way
to Abidjan to pick up Bokassa and take him on to Bangui. A state of
alert was immediately called in both African capitals, and soldiers
surrounded the airports in preparation for the invaders' arrival. At
9:30 AM Houphouët-Boigny telephoned Bokassa to let him know he
had stopped the operation. Bokassa was dismayed. He and Delpey
visited the Ivorian president later in the day but failed to convince
him to let matters proceed. Houphouët-Boigny was adamant, pointing out that Kolingba had already been warned and had his men on
military alert. The dejected ex-emperor was taken back to his villa,
where he was kept under heavy guard. Delpey was taken to the
airport to await the arrival of the "armed mercenaries."

At 9:00 PM that evening, after Delpey had recounted his tale of
woe to Colonel de Ducla and his travelling companions, they were
escorted aboard the Caravelle and sent back to France. When they
arrived at Le Bourget at 6:30 AM on Sunday, they were thoroughly
searched by the air and frontier police. The great adventure was over.
It had cost its investors between five and six million francs.[6]

That same day, Sunday, 27 November, a journalist for the Paris
daily *Libération* reached Bokassa by telephone and received an earful
of the man's bitterness and frustration. Bokassa railed against the
circumstances of his exile, which he likened to imprisonment, and
appealed to be allowed to leave the Ivory Coast: "I truly hope to be
able to leave here. I need fresh air. I am traumatized. I've been here
for four years and it's always the same thing. I see the sun rise and
the sun set. Who could accept such a routine? I am launching an SOS
to sensitize the entire world to my case. Bangui or not, I have to
change countries."

It was evident that he viewed departure from the Ivory Coast as a
stepping stone to his return to Centrafrique: "In Bangui the people
call me. The population wants me. As long as the people want it, I
will accept being at their head. It is said that the voice of the people
is the voice of God." Asked about Kolingba, he said, "He is not my
enemy. It is I who who promoted him. I found him as a sergeant and
I made him a four-star general ... I am the founder of the army. But

we are all Central Africans. The thing that I want most is to return and remain quietly in my country. I can even do farming or ranching." Nor did he baulk at the prospect of being put on trial: "I want to return to my country even if I must be judged. I've never had an instant to justify myself. One speaks of the rights of man – well I am one as well. To deny me justice for years is inhuman. I am a slave. Why didn't they do that to Sharon after Sabra and Chatilla?"[7]

Bokassa's wish was granted, at least in part. Houphouët-Boigny had had enough of the former emperor after Operation Elba, and he put pressure on France to relieve him of his unwanted and unwilling guest. Mitterrand agreed, and on 4 December Bokassa was escorted aboard the regular Air Afrique flight to Paris. He was accompanied by his latest Ivorian consort, Augustine Assemat, and the children who had shared his villa on the rue des Sambas. The family arrived at Roissy Airport at 7:17 PM that evening and took up residence in the Château Hardricourt. The Abidjan exile was over.

The Quai d'Orsay issued a curt communiqué stating that Bokassa's stay in France was purely temporary. The government was seeking another country to take him in. As before, there were no takers. Mitterrand solved the problem by letting his troublesome guest stay indefinitely at Hardricourt, where a close eye could be kept on him. From the start, a heavy contingent of plain-clothes police manned the gates of the château.[8] They were not there to protect its notorious occupant but to impose a wall of silence around him. The fallen emperor had become a prisoner in his own manor. He could not leave, and all his visitors were carefully screened. Even his son Georges had to show an identity card before being admitted.[9]

Roger Delpey, who lived a short distance away, came by frequently. He gave advice and Bokassa listened, and he helped look after the children, many of whom were still of elementary school age – Jean-Parfait, Jean-Christian, Jean-Bertrand, Jean-Yves, Marie-Jeanne, Marie-Eléanore, Marie-France, Marie-Suzanne, Anne de Berengo, and so on. As the months went by, Bokassa grew increasingly irritated at the *cordon sanitaire* imposed around his residence. He phoned Guy Penne, making promises of good behaviour and begging him to ease the security blockade. The government relented but kept a couple of men on the spot lest trouble arose.

It was important to keep up appearances at the château. Visitors noticed that the interior walls were freshly painted and were adorned with huge portraits of the former Empress Catherine, Jean-Bedel Junior (the dauphin) in his admiral's outfit, and, of course, Bokassa himself at various stages of his career. A bust of Napoleon held a position of honour in the principal salon next to a poster commemorating Dien Bien Phu with the caption "They sacrificed themselves for freedom." The eighteenth-century furniture and carpets were well maintained, and here and there were mementos of the short-lived imperial age – golden eagles and the like. Even so, the perceptive eye could detect an underlying shabbiness. The spacious grounds with their sweeping lawns and stands of trees lacked the meticulous care of bygone days, and weeds, hitherto untolerated, were flourishing with abandon.

Bokassa himself avoided the unkempt look. He greeted his guests in the main salon in well-tailored suits, silk ties, and lizard-skin shoes. Around his neck hung a gold, diamond-encrusted pendant in the form of an eagle with outstretched wings, the sun rising behind it. It served as a small reminder, as if one were needed, that this was no ordinary member of the ex-dictators' club. Yet he never missed an opportunity to complain of poverty – of the difficulty of getting by on his military pension with all his expenses. Only the generosity of his friends enabled him to live with some dignity in his château-prison, he said. He was not even allowed to sell his properties, since they were claimed by the Central African government. He was, however, renting one of the châteaux to his friend Roger Holeindre for use by the Cercle national des combattants, a veterans' welfare group associated with Jean-Marie Le Pen's Front national. The rent was a modest 30,000 francs per annum.[10]

Although a portrait of Catherine adorned the château walls, Bokassa had not forgiven her for her betrayal. His financial woes were a constant reminder of her guile. "She is beautiful, but nasty and heartless," were his words in an August 1984 interview. There was a bitter edge to his thoughts on the other wives too: "The seventeen women that I married all abandoned me. Right up to the last of them, a Tunisienne, who hasn't given a sign of life." Bitterness, yes, but no remorse. Bokassa had no regrets about his amorous adventures. Indeed, his conquests were a source of lingering pride: "I did it like everyone. In Formosa, for example, I hustled the most beautiful woman in the country whom I later married. In Bucharest, the most beautiful woman in Romania; in Libreville, the most beautiful woman in Gabon ... and so on. My criterion was beauty." But now he had grown old and was prepared to content himself with the one woman who lived with him in Hardricourt – Augustine Assemat, the attractive Ivorienne he had acquired in Abidjan.[11]

The months ahead were difficult and depressing. As winter set in over northern France, Bokassa feared that the cost of heating his château would be beyond his means. At the beginning of December the water supply was briefly cut off for non-payment of bills, and in

January the telephone service was interrupted for the same reason. By now Augustine was expecting a baby, and this was an additional source of anxiety. The chilly rooms of the château were no place for a pregnant woman, especially one accustomed to a tropical climate.

Bokassa had often thought of writing a book about his momentous life, and he now had the leisure – and incentive – to do so. He believed that if it contained shocking revelations, it would achieve several aims at once: raise money, further humiliate his old nemesis Giscard, and foster support in France for his eventual return to Centrafrique. Late in 1984 a rumour circulated in Paris that the ex-emperor's memoirs were in preparation and that they would contain extracts from the 187 documents which Roger Delpey had allegedly hidden in a Swiss vault. It looked as if the diamond scandal was about to haunt Giscard d'Estaing once again. The former president had not abandoned politics after his defeat in 1981. Elected to the National Assembly for Puy-de-Dôme, he was widely expected to run again for the presidency in 1988. He would not welcome another episode in the diamond affair.

Bokassa needed a ghostwriter and found one in his longtime friend and admirer Roger Holeindre. A short swarthy Corsican (interesting qualifications in themselves), Holeindre was a survivor of several of France's colonial misadventures and was director of veterans' services for the right-wing Front national as well as being a professional journalist. It will be recalled that he had joined in the campaign to clear Bokassa's name in the summer of 1979, and he had been a frequent visitor to Hardricourt from December 1983 onwards. Although he was a contributor to *Paris Match* and *Minute*, he was an indifferent writer and researcher, and this was reflected in the manuscript he produced. Based on a series of twenty interviews with the former emperor, the book was to be called *Ma vérité* (*My Truth*).

Finding a publisher should have been easy, but many of those approached feared a libel suit and refused. At length, Carrère-Lafon, a small but ambitious publishing company specializing in books on show business, offered a contract, believing that the Bokassa manuscript, although risky, could be lucrative.[12] On 8 May 1985 ten thousand copies of *Ma vérité* rolled off the presses. The book was 218 pages long, with 54 photographs, and its shiny black hardcover featured a golden eagle in a circle of stars. But the bookstores never had the chance to stock it. Warned of the unpleasant nature of its contents, Giscard d'Estaing acquired a copy before it went on sale, and on 11 May his lawyer obtained a court injunction blocking publication on account of the book's "odious and grotesque assertions."

"I have been slandered once; it will not be done a second time," said the ex-president with his habitual air of indignation. "I will not allow a fallen sovereign to attack my honour and reputation in order to avenge himself."[13] Two days later the Tribunal de grande instance de Paris not only forbade the sale of *Ma vérité* but ordered all ten thousand copies destroyed. And so it was done. The French public never had the chance to read the truth according to Bokassa or the "odious and grotesque assertions" he had made about his former "dear cousin."

Nevertheless, a few copies did survive.[14] In many ways, the book is a disappointment, and there are good grounds for doubting that it would have become the bestseller that Bokassa and Holeindre were anticipating. It contained none of the elusive 187 documents regarding Bokassa's relations with Giscard. Indeed, all of the assertions made in *Ma vérité*, grotesque and otherwise, were unsupported by a shred of evidence. Readers would have had only Bokassa's word to go on, and in France this did not amount to much.

For much of the book, Bokassa traversed familiar terrain. He described his youth and gave details of his military career, emphasizing his loyalty and devotion to France. He justified the Saint-Sylvestre coup on the grounds that Dacko and Izamo, in collaboration with the Chinese, had been plotting to assassinate him.

Furthermore, he claimed that he had never wanted to stay in government; he had done so only because of popular acclaim. It was the same with his titles "president-for-life," "marshal," and "emperor." The people had given him these honours; they had done so to prevent him from leaving them and going to live permanently in France. He said that for several years the people had been wanting to crown him emperor and he had acceded to their wishes only after consulting Giscard and various African leaders (all of whom had apparently agreed, only Félix Malloum of Tchad expressing any reservations). In defending the cost of his coronation, about which so much fuss had been made in the press, Bokassa asserted that the oft-cited figure of 100 million francs was only a fraction of the cost of a Mirage jet. And he pointed out that many permanent improvements had been made to Bangui in preparation for the event – new roads, a sewer system, housing, lighting, and so forth – all of which greatly benefited the population afterwards.

In places the book bristled with vigorous debate. Bokassa admitted, for instance, to clipping thieves' ears but ridiculed Kurt Waldheim, who had denounced him for it while remaining strangely silent when Arab countries amputated their thieves' hands: "But then they have oil, and we are mere barbarians." He vehemently denied the charges of cannibalism and infanticide that had been levelled against him. Regarding the former, he recited the testimony that Philippe Linguissa had given at his trial, showing how absurd it was, and he dismissed the presiding judge as one "who had never studied a word of law in his life." On the infanticide question he was less convincing: "I am the father of many children. Contrary to what fools and imbeciles dare to write, I never learned to kill children during the Indochinese war. And anyway, it is disgraceful to let people pretend that in Indochina the French army trained its soldiers to kill children." Page by page, Bokassa took aim at the legion of "fools and imbeciles" who had betrayed him. Jacques Duchemin was "the king of bullshitters, an archflatterer who convinced me he could salvage my image if I gave him a diplomatic passport." Duchemin's book, *L'empereur*, was nothing but "shameful lies." Bernard Loubat was no better. His articles in the French press and his book *L'ogre de Berengo* were "complete nonsense." There were harsh words too for David Dacko, Guy Penne, Bernard Tapie, and others who had crossed him over the years. But Giscard, the man directly responsible for all his misfortunes, was his principal target: "Giscard is responsible for the loss of my spouse (my principal wife), for the loss of my material goods, for the loss of my identity papers, for the loss of my secret files and my documents. That is what Giscard did to me. That is what I want my friends, the French, to discover throughout my book. I want all of this to be spoken about."

Bokassa described the early, easygoing days in which his friend-ship with Giscard had blossomed. The French president had come often to Centrafrique to hunt, but also to get away from the glare of media attention. The two leaders spent relaxing times together dis-cussing politics and other matters of common interest. Then Giscard began to take things for granted and at times went straight to his hunting preserve in the east without even informing Bokassa of his presence. He and his friends came and went as they pleased, helping themselves to the best ivory. And they had the audacity to treat the emperor as their gamekeeper – reproaching him on occasion for not keeping poachers off their land.

According to Bokassa, Giscard often sent a helicopter to N'Djaména to pick up Chedeye, the beautiful sister of Hissène Habré, who called herself the Princess of Bardaï.[15] Chedeye was apparently just one of many of the French president's amours. Here is Bokassa's version:

Sometimes he brought girls along. Giscard is a man like any other. He has never been a priest (not that I know priests very well), but more a man like the rest of us. I must say, and the French will understand this, that I have always been discreet in this matter: Giscard was my relative, my friend, and moreover, he was staying with me as my guest. I never sought to learn the names of these women and girls. I only knew one of them personally, a journalist with *Paris-Match*. One day I wanted to proposition her. However, I stopped myself because she was his.

There was her and others, notably a beautiful French movie actress, small in size but big in talent …

Giscard used to come about twice a year to Centrafrique. He would say to me, "My dear cousin, I want a few stones." I would give him some. That lasted for twelve years. In the end he had collected quite a few. Often he would offer some to the girls; they found them pretty.

What Bokassa really wanted to get at was Giscard's role in his downfall. It all began, if we are to believe him, in the summer of 1979 when the Empress Catherine went to Paris, allegedly at the French president's invitation.

I now know that it was during this period that he [Giscard] started to plot my ruin with her [Catherine]. He spoke to her of my downfall, asking her what ought to be done, what would she think of him if he overthrew me. So my wife said to him, "But he must not be killed. I had many children with him. He must not be killed because the children must not become orphans. They are still very young and they all love and respect their father who, besides, raised them well."

According to Bokassa, Catherine told him this when she visited him in Abidjan shortly after his fall. When he asked her why she had gone along with Giscard's plot, she replied, "When you were in power, you made me suffer from jealousy. You had the Romanian, the Chinese, the Yugoslav, the Greek, without counting, now, the Gabonese, the Central Africans, the French, and the Germans – many women." Jealousy, then, had been at the root of his problems, concluded Bokassa, Catherine's jealousy but also Giscard's lust for her. The president had wanted the emperor out of the way so that he could have the empress for himself.

And when Giscard ruined me, she [Catherine] lived with Giscard and conceived a child with him. He had her admitted to the Hartmann Clinic, Paris 16, for an abortion. She went to this clinic twice, the first time to abort Giscard's child, the second to have her ovaries removed. When I give a woman a child, I take my responsibilities. I keep the child and I raise it …

Giscard has done me irreparable harm. He acted in his own interests, destroying my family and ruining me completely. It's nothing less than piracy. One doesn't go to the house of a man considered a friend and relative to take his goods and, just because he is an African, separate him from his principal wife and make of her a mistress and accomplice.

It is not difficult to see why Giscard wanted the book suppressed. He was simply trying to protect his reputation, tarnished though it was. Ever since the beginning of his presidency, the Paris newspapers had noted his tendency to slip out of the Elysée at night for secret rendezvous. The fact that Anne-Aymone and the children remained at the family house at 11 rue de Bénouville while he stayed at the palace only fuelled the speculation. Among the jet-setting types linked to him were photographer Marie-Laure de Decker and the Italian princess Domietta Hercolani. The president's nocturnal activities had almost caused a scandal in September 1974 when his car struck a milk van at five in the morning as he was heading homeward in the company, it was said, of an attractive television announcer.[16] Yet Giscard's alleged relationship with Catherine was pure speculation, and to claim that he launched Opération Barracuda just to make the empress his mistress was obviously nonsense. These were the musings of a distraught mind – of a man consumed by resentment whose judgment had been impaired by one misfortune after another.

The most convincing passages in the book are those in which Bokassa bemoaned his current circumstances: "Life at Hardricourt has been tough. Bills arrive every day and I have no money to pay. How can I live with fifteen children without money … I don't have any more friends, none … Those around me are often flatterers who betrayed me." There was a poignant note, too, to the concluding paragraphs – a hint of resignation to his fate, perhaps:

I wrote this book so that all the world would at last know My Truth. It is at times severe, that was necessary. But I don't want to finish it without saying publicly to Catherine that I forgive her, and that is without any second thoughts, in homage to her beauty which was a ray of sunshine in my life.

If tomorrow I must leave France, it will be to return to my country, Centrafrique. It is there that I want to die and be buried, in the place where my father lies, in a little African tomb which was razed by a bulldozer on Giscard's orders a few weeks after my downfall.[17]

The suppression and destruction of *Ma vérité* was a major blow to Bokassa, but the exercise had not been entirely futile. The controversy surrounding the book stirred up valuable publicity and reminded the public of the fallen emperor and his grievances. Meanwhile, Roger Delpey had been busy writing another book, this one on Central African politics since the collapse of the empire. *Affaires centrafricaines*, as it was called, was one long broadside at the Kolingba regime, which was accused of corruption, tribalism, and human rights violations. Another controversy now ensued as the Central African government sought to have this book banned, but it failed, and Delpey's work went on sale. In the court hearings surrounding the case, the author and his publisher, Jacques Grancher, were represented by an aggressive young Parisian lawyer named Francis Szpiner. (Szpiner was to play a decisive role in the final chapter of the Bokassa story). In writing *Affaires centrafricaines* Delpey had been hoping to undermine French support for Kolingba and thus pave the way for Bokassa's restoration, but the book made little impact. While it contained much that was true, the author's fanciful conspiratorial theories lent it an air of the surreal. And Delpey's reputation as a Bokassa partisan weakened its credibility.

A discouraging summer was followed by a winter of despair for the imperial family in exile. In November Bokassa invited the press to Hardricourt and there, in the poorly heated principal salon, he accused the French government of holding him a political prisoner without the wherewithal to support his numerous offspring. The cold months were times of anxiety, with mounting bills and an income that was too small to pay them. Even in Abidjan, for all its inconveniences, life had never been so trying. For a man who had grown accustomed to luxury and excess, the new hardship was difficult to take. He complained loudly and often, but to no avail.[18] The occasional newspaper accounts of his plight aroused not a morsel of public sympathy.

New Year's Day, 1986 – the feast of Saint-Sylvestre – marked twenty years since the coup that had carried Colonel Bokassa to power. There were no celebrations of the anniversary in the cool halls of Hardricourt. It was a time for reflection on what had been, on what might have been. There was little to hope for, much to regret. Campaigns to polish up the former emperor's image and discredit Kolingba had foundered on the rocks of scepticism and indifference. France had turned its back on the man who had once gripped its imagination.

In February Bokassa sought international support for his return to Centrafrique. He appealed to the United Nations, to Pope John Paul II, and to Amnesty International to help liberate him from his "imprisonment on French territory." He was ignored. But in March there came a glimmer of hope. A French Jaguar jet fighter crashed in the west end of Bangui killing twenty-two civilians. Anti-French riots followed, and Kolingba had difficulty restoring order. Bokassa regarded the incident as a presage of good fortune and declared himself "the only one capable of putting the Central African Republic back on track and of maintaining the French presence there." He wrote to President Mitterrand with the news that his people now wanted him more than ever. There was no reply.

On 15 June the Paris court of appeal awarded Bokassa ownership of a Corvette airplane which had been claimed by the government of the Central African Republic. If he could sell it – it was valued at six million francs – he would be well off. But his newly found source of potential wealth did not deter him from his abiding obsession – the return to power in his homeland. Indeed, the prospect of having some money only encouraged him to plot and scheme once more.

Security around Hardricourt had relaxed considerably by 1986. Bokassa was free to come and go more or less as he pleased, merely reporting to the police at the gate as he went on his way. As the months went by, the police had far more serious problems on their hands. The French remember 1986 as a year of unprecedented outrages. In March an attack on the Paris–Lyon TGV (rapid train) left ten people injured. In the same month, a bomb at Galerie Point Show on the Champs-Elysées resulted in two dead and twenty-eight injured. Then, between 4 and 17 September, a wave of explosions rocked Paris, leaving in its wake eleven dead and one hundred and sixty injured. Every policeman and secret agent in the country was needed to track down the perpetrators, and security at Hardricourt was abandoned completely.

As Bokassa watched these events unfold, it occurred to him that he could probably leave France unnoticed. Once across the border, there would be nothing to prevent him from boarding a flight to Bangui. He tried out this idea on some of his friends during the summer. Roger Delpey strongly advised against such a move, pointing out that the presidential guard around Kolingba had been greatly strengthened since the attempted return of November 1983.[19] There were others, however, who were encouraging – even eager to help.

Three men appeared in Bokassa's entourage around this time who played a key role in the formulation of his plans: the Paris lawyer Jean-Marie Viala and two former army officers, Commandant Hervé Carlier and Captain Olivier Le Bouet du Portal. All three were connected with the extreme right. They befriended Bokassa, spent a lot of time in his company, and promised to help organize his return to Bangui. They found a Canadian buyer for his Corvette aircraft, thus providing him with some ready money, and arranged for the purchase of air tickets and the printing of fake identity papers for him and his family.

Bokassa's current wife, Augustine Assemat, was only vaguely aware that something was afoot. On the evening of Tuesday, 21 October, Bokassa called her aside to show her a bundle of airline tickets.

They would be leaving for Bangui the next day, he told her. There was barely time for her to pack and get ready. Augustine and the children had Ivorian passports, while Bokassa had a Central African one made out in the name of Christian Solé, a former international footballer who had been chief of protocol at the Central African embassy in Paris during the imperial heyday.

At dawn the next morning Carlier and du Portal arrived at the château, each driving a car. Bokassa and Augustine were already up, and they now awakened four of the youngest children, who were to come with them. A fifth child, Marie-Jeanne, was in residence at Collège Henri-IV at nearby Meulan, and du Portal went to collect her. Before long the two cars were packed with people and suitcases (one of which contained the marshal's uniform), and with Carlier and du Portal in the drivers' seats, Bokassa, Augustine, and the five children set off on the historic journey. No police barred their way at the château gates. Even so, they took secondary roads on their way north lest their absence be noted and the main highways watched. Shortly before reaching the Belgian frontier, the little convoy joined the autoroute, and by early afternoon they had passed out of French territory. In Brussels they boarded a Sabena flight for Rome, arriving in the Italian capital at 10:00 PM. Carlier accompanied them on the flight, but left them in Rome. And all the while, nobody recognized Bokassa in his heavy coat, with his hat pulled down over his head. From Rome, they took the midnight Air Afrique flight to Brazzaville, which had a stopover at Bangui.

Bokassa and his family travelled tourist class. He hoped to remain incognito, at least until arrival. He was calm throughout, often lost in thought. It was not long before he was recognized by some of his fellow travellers, and word of his presence spread quickly through the aircraft. Two Congolese civil servants, travelling first class, came back and greeted him. A member of the cabin crew informed the pilot of his distinguished passenger, but nothing was said or done. The pilot assumed that Bokassa's journey home had the approval of the Central African and French governments.

At 5:00 AM on Thursday, 23 October 1986, the aircraft was over Bangui. A dense fog shrouded the city and the pilot was forced into a holding pattern for forty-five minutes before coming in to land. At 5:45 AM, with dawn just breaking, they were on the runway. A few minutes later Bokassa was descending the steps to make contact once more, after his long and painful absence, with the soil of Centrafrique. It had been seven years and one month since his departure.

Nobody recognized the returning exile at first, and he and his family passed through security and passport control to a large hall, where they were to collect their luggage. Then the cries went up: "It's Bokassa!" ... "The boss is back!" A crowd quickly gathered, and some began to chant anti-Kolingba slogans and "To the presidency!" A number of soldiers and policemen, on duty at the airport, dropped their weapons and fled in terror. "The boss" surveyed this pleasing scene and smiled graciously. Had not his instincts been right all along?[20]

CHAPTER THIRTEEN

Accounting for
His Stewardship

By 1986, Colonel Jean-Claude Mantion was a familiar figure on the streets of Bangui. Forty-four years old, tall and lean, he usually appeared in a pale, open-neck safari suit with a walkie-talkie slung under his arm. This French officer had been sent to Centrafrique after the fall of the empire as part of his country's program of military *coopération*. In time, he had created and trained a 450-man contingent of presidential guards, whom he now commanded. In their red berets and camouflage fatigues, with snarling panther badge on the arm, the guards kept watch over the Palais de la Renaissance and, in effect, kept Kolingba in power.[1] To many observers, Mantion was the real ruler of the Central African Republic. He was known as "le premier flic," "the Bwana of Bangui," and "the president of President Kolingba."[2]

At 6:30 AM on 23 October the telephone rang in Mantion's headquarters at Camp de Roux. The caller was a French *coopérant* who happened to be at the airport. He had startling news: Bokassa was back and was being mobbed by enthusiastic devotees. The colonel quickly assembled a squadron of his men, and in less than twenty minutes they were at the airport entrance. Meanwhile, Bokassa was still in the terminal building, chatting to admirers and to the airport commissioner, who had appeared on the scene and was clearly apprehensive. Suddenly, Mantion and his men burst into the building. The crowd grew ominously silent and began to back away. The colonel approached and informed Bokassa that he was under arrest. Bokassa protested, questioning the Frenchman's authority and asserting his own, but there could be no arguing with the arsenal of cold steel trained in his direction. The soldiers seized him, led him outside, and quickly bundled him into a blue Peugeot to be taken to Camp de Roux.[3]

What had Bokassa expected? He had believed that his supporters would immediately rally round, prevent his arrest, and organize demonstrations in his favour. Kolingba and his cronies, he had convinced himself, would flee the country and power would be his once more. But it had not happened that way. He learned to his great cost that the loyalty of his former subjects was fickle at best. The crowd was a spectator at historical events – it willingly cast its lot with a winner but not with a loser.

At the airport, a tearful Augustine was interrogated in the commissioner's office but was unable to throw much light on her partner's motivation in coming home. When the Air Afrique jetliner was due to depart on the second leg of its southward journey, she and the children were ushered on board. In Brazzaville, where they arrived at 1 PM, the authorities gave them something to eat but would not let them leave the airport. Later, at midnight, when the plane left for Europe, they were again on board. There was another stopover in Bangui on the return flight. All the passengers were allowed to disembark, except for Augustine and the children. They sat there in a state of unrelieved anxiety, wondering what had befallen *le père*, until a French soldier entered the cabin and assured them that there was nothing to worry about; Bokassa was being well looked after. When they landed back to France, they settled in once more to life in Hardricourt.[4]

President Kolingba, who was preparing for a constitutional referendum at the time, suspected French collusion in Bokassa's unexpected return. In Paris, however, the government washed its hands of the affair. "The whole government was surprised by this unexpected departure," an official communiqué noted curtly, and Michel Aurillac, the new minister of cooperation, added that the Central African government was free – indeed obliged – to put the former emperor on trial. Early in the afternoon of 23 October, Kolingba announced on the radio that Bokassa was in detention and would face "the full application of the law." There was a disturbingly ambiguous tone to these words. Bokassa had been under sentence of death since December 1980. Would this sentence now be carried out? Under the country's laws, however, a person convicted in absentia was entitled to another trial if later apprehended, and it was rumoured that this is what the government had in mind.

In France, Bokassa's friends and family rallied round and established a defence committee to save him from the firing squad.[5] Roger Delpey called Francis Szpiner, the lawyer who had represented him in the controversy over his book *Affaires centrafricaines*, and asked him to get involved. Szpiner agreed, flew to Bangui, and discussed with Bokassa the strategies for his defence. He found the former emperor still in a state of shock -- and full of remorse at the folly of his decision to return to his homeland. When Szpiner arrived back in France, he phoned Catherine at her Geneva villa to bring news of her husband's condition. She seemed irritated at the intrusion and made it clear that it was of no concern to her. Later, when Delpey invited her to contribute to the defence fund, she refused.[6] Although she still insisted that she was empress, the man who had given her the title and the wherewithal to live in comfort had been blocked out from her life.

Before leaving France, Bokassa had written a letter to President Mitterrand in which he discussed the reasons for his departure: "I return freely to a free country, and if it happens that I am asked to serve my country, I will place myself immediately at her service, with my only aim her greatness and my only desire to serve my people, but also all men, a philosophy common to those of French culture. If it happens that my country, le Centrafrique, calls me, it will be always on the side of France, just as France will be, it is my great hope, always on the side of my country."[7] The letter (a copy of which was released to the French press by Bokassa's lawyer, Jean-Marie Viala) contained enough ambiguity to be useful regardless of how the return to Bangui worked out. If the ex-emperor was swept back to power, his words would serve to assure France of his friendship; if things went wrong, as they did, there was nothing in the letter that could be used against him.

Interrogated in his cell for several days after his apprehension, Bokassa denied that he had come back in order to seize power. He said that he had returned to clear his name before his people and to wash away the dishonour heaped on him by those who had engineered his overthrow. He wished most of all to face his accusers on the question of his alleged cannibalism, a calumny which troubled him deeply. His interrogators were sceptical, but Bokassa had a clever reply to their doubts: "My cousin, Dacko, who was coming to overthrow me, arrived in a Transall of the French army. I came back on a regular Air Afrique flight."[8]

In France his supporters backed up his claims. Jean-Marie Viala said that Bokassa could not face another winter in the north of France. The grey skies and cold weather had driven him back. Like an old African elephant, he had wanted to go home to die. Meanwhile, President Kolingba had decided to make the best of a difficult situation: he would put Bokassa on trial. A public trial would at once exorcize the ghost of the man who still cast a spell on the country and would also serve as a major public relations coup for his faltering regime. Addressing a large crowd at Boganda Stadium on 31 October, the president announced that Bokassa, whom he claimed had returned to plunge the country into chaos, would be brought before the justice system.

The prisoner was now given a list of all the lawyers practising in the Central African Republic, and he chose three to act on his behalf: Lambert Zokoézo, Nicolas Tiangaye, and Mireille Gotilogoé.[9] He was also allowed to have Francis Szpiner as part of his defence team. Although Szpiner was only thirty-three years old, he had already acquired a formidable reputation in French legal circles, and he had a thriving practice in Saint-Germain-des-Prés. Ever since his appointment to the Paris bar in 1975, he had specialized in difficult cases. These had included his defence of those accused of murdering Ezzadine Kalak, the PLO representative in France; Captain Paul Baril on charges of espionage; and members of the Irish National Liberation Army – "les Irlandais de Vincennes." Unlike Delpey and Holeindre, he was not connected to the political extreme right but favoured Chirac and the Gaullists. He took on the Bokassa case, then, not for ideological reasons or even for the money, but intrinsically out of intellectual interest. It was another controversial lawsuit to add to his collection.[10] Just before the trial opened, a second French lawyer was assigned to the defence. François Gibault – tall, grey-haired, discreet, and diplomatic, in contrast to the short and ebullient Szpiner – claimed that Bokassa had chosen him because he had once served as a French army officer; but other sources suggest that he was working secretly for the French government to ensure that the trial did not become a forum for revelations embarrassing to Paris.[11]

Bokassa had returned at an inopportune moment. President Kolingba was in the middle of a campaign to have a new constitution adopted, and a referendum on the proposal had been scheduled for 21 November. Kolingba decided to press ahead with these plans and leave the trial until later. The constitution was designed to give the regime a semblance of legitimacy. It allowed for the creation of one political party, the Rassemblement démocratique centrafricain, which was supposed to guard against ethnic factionalism. A national assembly would eventually be elected, but real power would remain in the president's hands.

Bokassa was still popular among the M'Baka, and during his referendum campaign Kolingba cancelled a scheduled speech in M'Baïki fearing riots or demands for the ex-emperor's release. Nonetheless, all went well on 21 November. There were 508,976 ballots cast in favour of the constitution and 52,290 against. The president now had a mandate to rule for six more years, as well as the moral

authority to deal with his potentially dangerous rival.[12] He announced
that Bokassa's trial would open on 26 November in the very sports
stadium that had hosted the imperial coronation just nine years earlier. It was to be a public affair with thousands in attendance, and
the president clearly intended that the people would relive the horrors of the previous regime through the testimony of the witnesses.
The annoying nostalgia for the days of Papa Bok would thus be
stifled, he hoped. And if justice was seen to be done, the trial would
do much for the country's image abroad, which was badly in need
of rehabilitation.

Meanwhile, the Ministry of Justice was busily preparing the case
against the former tyrant. It decided to use the same list of accusations that had proved so successful in the trial of December 1980.
There were fourteen charges:

1 Murders and complicity in murders
2 Poisoning and complicity in poisoning
3 Beatings and injuries to children, leading to death
4 Concealing the cadavers of prisoners
5 Concealing the cadavers of children
6 Cannibalism
7 Arbitrary arrests
8 Arbitrary imprisonments
9 Violence and assaults
10 Misappropriation of the coronation jewels from the state
11 Misappropriation of diamonds from the state
12 Misappropriation of public funds
13 Distortion of the laws of trade in gold and diamonds
14 Threatening internal and external state security and collusion
   with a foreign power.[13]

While the prosecution was marshalling the facts and lining up witnesses in support of its case, Bokassa was consulting his legal team
at Camp de Roux. He was under constant watch by a contingent of
presidential guards, who even tasted his food before serving it lest
it be poisoned. Dressed now in simple military fatigues, plastic sandals on his feet, Bokassa seemed bewildered by it all. But the lawyers
were encouraging, and with their words of hope his spirits gradually
lifted.

On Monday, 17 November, he was taken from the camp for the
first time since his arrest. Accompanied by his three Central African
lawyers, he was brought before the court of appeal for the selection
of the six jurors who would decide his fate. He appeared to be calm,

even relaxed, and he said not a word throughout the hearings. Taking notes intently, he occasionally cast a glance around the room, and some felt that he was eyeing them menacingly. A glimmer of the old fear surfaced briefly.

As the trial date approached, Kolingba had second thoughts about holding the hearings in the sports stadium. Colonel Mantion and other French advisers were against the idea, arguing that the security problems would be enormous. The president relented, and the day before the trial was due to begin he announced that it would be held in the Palais de Justice, an old colonial courthouse in the heart of Bangui. Only a carefully screened audience of three hundred would be admitted to the building, but the proceedings would be broadcast live over the radio so that the entire nation could listen.

Hundreds of journalists descended on Bangui for the occasion. While the government was pleased with this – and with the favourable publicity it hoped would accrue from its handling of "the trial of the century" – some officials were clearly irritated that so much interest was shown in Bokassa and his escapades while the recent constitutional referendum had been virtually ignored. The ex-emperor was "a pure product of French military training," explained an exasperated information minister, M. de Silva Nzengue, to a group of eager journalists.[14]

Early on the morning of Wednesday, 26 November, the stage was set for Bokassa to account for his stewardship. But before matters could be set in motion, the defence lawyers objected to the selection of Edouard Franck as the presiding judge of the criminal court. Franck had been involved in the December 1980 trial in absentia, and until 18 November he had served as Kolingba's legal adviser. The defence tried to disqualify him on these grounds, and a three-hour delay was required while the Supreme Court dealt with the objection.

By noon a decision had been reached and the *dramatis personae* of the legal battle were converging on the Palais de Justice. The courtroom was already packed with its three hundred spectators, including a large contingent of photographers and television cameramen. Then Bokassa appeared. Most Central Africans had not seen their emperor since September 1979, and he had aged visibly – the hair and beard were grey, the face had lost its youthful sheen. But he looked vigorous and determined nonetheless. He was dressed as impeccably as ever, in a dark grey suit, white shirt, and striped silk tie. The privilege of looking his best had not been denied him. A heavy contingent of presidential guards surrounded his person, and one could almost believe that the good old days had miraculously returned and that the men in the camouflage fatigues were his loyal imperial soldiers.

The photographers rushed forward flashing their cameras. Bokassa paused – and posed. Then, turning towards one of the television cameras, he announced, "An excellent impression. I wish to thank everyone at Antenne 2 and in particular the president of the French Republic, the prime minister, M. Jacques Chirac, and M. Jacques Foccart, all our French friends, all the police, especially Admiral Philippe de Gaulle and all the family of General de Gaulle. Tell them that their valiant soldier Bokassa, Jean-Bedel, of the Free French Forces and one of the bravest African fighters has answered to the justice of his country."[15]

At 12:22 PM Judge Franck entered the courtroom dressed in the scarlet and black robes and colourful gold-braided pillbox hat of his office. He was accompanied by two similarly attired *assesseurs,* or assistant judges. Then came the public prosecutor, Gabriel Faustin Mbodou, a large man with a reputation for intimidating plaintiffs, lawyers, and witnesses alike. The court fell silent as the judges positioned themselves behind the bench. Bokassa sat just six paces away, flanked by the presidential guards, in front of his lawyers' table. He was respectful rather than defiant – sheepish, perhaps – like a schoolboy caught in an act of mischief. Judge Franck opened the proceedings by reading the decision of the Supreme Court to quash the defence's objections to his hearing the case. He then slapped a fine of 100,000 CFA francs on Bokassa as if in punishment for the challenge to his integrity.

After the six jurors had been sworn in, the prosecutor, Mbodou, approached the accused and asked him if he were Jean-Bedel Bokassa, second-class soldier.

"Ah no, not that!" was the shocked reply. Bokassa could not abide losing his military rank and protested vigorously. He cited the example of Marshal Pétain, who although condemned to death at the end of the Second World War, was allowed to keep his title. But Mbodou, sensing that he had touched a sensitive nerve, pressed on and produced a decree signed by President Kolingba in 1984 which stripped the former emperor of his marshal's title.

Szpiner now sprang up: "That measure is contrary to the spirit of justice and the law. It is inadmissible ... it bears on the innocence of the accused. It suggests a prejudgment. Where is the presumption of innocence in these circumstances?"

Bokassa, gesturing to the crowd, then announced, "I already feel condemned. Is there any further need to continue with this trial?"

Although the proceedings were only a few minutes old, they were already producing lively drama. Aware that matters were getting out of hand, Gibault appealed for reason to prevail, whereupon Franck proposed a compromise that appeared to satisfy both sides: "You will be the accused, Jean-Bedel Bokassa."

With the delicate question of the accused's identity decided, the hearings moved on to the next stage, the swearing in of witnesses. It was then time to read the list of fourteen charges levelled against Bokassa, and Mbodou did so in an unorthodox, long-winded speech, which lasted more than thirty minutes. The beatings, the clipping of ears – all the old atrocities were there. The prosecutor concluded by noting that Bokassa was "sadistic, egotistical, and sexually obsessed."

Bokassa replied with a dignity and sense of authority that recalled his days of power. Rising to his full height, he addressed the court in a voice that even now commanded respect. He began with words of praise for Kolingba, Mitterrand, and Chirac, but quickly turned on the man whom he still blamed for all his woes: "In 1979 Valéry Giscard d'Estaing, then president of France, diverted the French army from its duties, organizing a *coup d'état* which violated the national sovereignty of my country. To justify this act contrary to international law, he orchestrated a campaign of disinformation and manipulation. I was described as a cannibal, a murderer, a thief, a traitor to my country. During my exile I always demanded a fair trial so that the truth could be known." He went on to defend his regime, citing his accomplishments in serving the nation and noting how he had returned voluntarily to be with his people. He renounced all personal ambition and concluded on a poignant note: "My only wish is that General Kolingba will bring to the nation unity and progress and will ensure its independence. As for me, I only want to live in peace, surrounded by my family and cleared of the infamy of these accusations."[16]

It was a powerful speech. On the sidewalk outside the Palais de Justice a large crowd was listening intently to the live radio broadcast of the proceedings. There were shouts of approval at Bokassa's more nationalistic outbursts and even the occasional cry of "Vive l'empereur!" The prosecution was far from happy with the way things were going and, during a ten-minute recess that followed Bokassa's speech, asked that the trial be adjourned until 15 December. Mbodou explained that he needed more time to prepare the case, to gather evidence. The defence lawyers readily agreed, and a little later, in discussing the delay with newsmen, François Gibault observed that the ex-emperor's return had taken the government by surprise. "Their dossier on him is empty – dry as a desert."

Hundreds of journalists had descended on Bangui for the trial, far more than had arrived for the imperial coronation. Many were clearly disappointed at the serious tone of the proceedings and left the city when the adjournment was announced. Only a modest number returned when the trial was resumed three weeks later.

Security was tight around the Palais de Justice on the morning of 15 December. At 9:00 AM Bokassa arrived, dressed as before in an immaculate suit, one wrist hand-cuffed to a presidential guard. He was in a confident mood, his head held high. As he took his place at the dock, he looked for all the world like an old soldier fighting his last battle – his Waterloo perhaps. The proceedings opened with some heated exchanges between defence and prosecution when Bokassa's lawyers challenged the admissibility of the more bizarre charges against their client – cannibalism and the mass murder of schoolchildren. The prosecution refused to give way, however, and their position was upheld.

Now the trial began in earnest as the first of the fourteen indictments – murder and complicity in murder – was presented by Public Prosecutor Mbodou. He began with the case of Lt-Col. Alexandre Banza, who had been eliminated following his abortive coup of 1969. Bokassa rose to answer the charge. Standing at a microphone facing Judge Franck, he once again stressed the voluntary nature of his return and his desire to clear his name and that of his country "so that abroad it can never be said again that Central Africans are killers, cannibals, robbers, and bandits." It was a good opening line and drew murmurs of approval from the audience. Then, turning to the case of Banza, Bokassa explained, "I learned that he had enticed soldiers to arrest me at Berengo. So I had him arrested. He was judged and executed by the justice system."

So far so good, but the prosecutor then pressed Bokassa on the death of Banza's family. Several witnesses spoke of the Banza relatives who had died in Ngaragba. When friends went to find them, they had disappeared. "I did not know that all that was happening at the prison," was all Bokassa had to say. Mbodou reminded him that he had been minister of justice at the time and should have known what was going on.

As the hours passed in the stifling heat of the courtroom, the former emperor became increasingly ill at ease. Although he never lost his fighting spirit, he was clearly shaken and surprised by the number of witnesses who were ready to point the finger of accusation at him. Meanwhile, all around the capital, commercial life ground to a halt as the populace sat spellbound listening to the live broadcast of their former emperor accounting for his misdeeds.

Moreover, Central Africans were hearing something that was almost as novel to them – a public trial following due procedure in the French judicial tradition. The vigilance of Szpiner and Gibault was the best guarantee that this was no parody of justice, and there were additional guarantees in the presence of Jean-Gabriel Senghor of the International League of Human Rights and Biram Sassoum Sy of Amnesty International. The two representatives of the human rights organizations took in every word and made occasional notes but refused to comment even when prompted by Colonel Mantion with, "It's unique in Africa, a trial of such fairness."[17]

By the end of the first day, the general contours of Bokassa's defence strategy were beginning to appear. First, he denied that any crimes had taken place. Then, if faced with overwhelming evidence, he was ready to accept a general responsibility in his role as head of state, but he placed the direct responsibility on his subordinates, whom he accused of excessive zeal. And he tried to pin much of the blame on David Dacko, whom he still despised.

On the following day the prosecution brought up the case of Auguste M'Bongo, minister of public works at the time of his arrest in 1973. He had died in prison several months later, allegedly from starvation and mistreatment. One of the witnesses was Celestine, the deceased's widow. Speaking in Sango, she launched into a long emotional account of her efforts to find and save her husband. Finally, drained by the sorrow of her recollections, she collapsed in a flood of tears, but not before accusing Bokassa of lusting after her and killing her husband when she refused him.

Bokassa was standing just a few steps away, hands clasped before him. When questioned by the prosecutor, he sought refuge in memory loss, stating that he could recall M'Bongo's arrest but nothing more. Other witnesses were then questioned, and their stories served to jog his memory as the day wore on. One said that M'Bongo had had a mistress, an attractive airline waitress, whom Bokassa had wanted for himself – hence the motivation in eliminating his rival. Another claimed that M'Bongo had built a new villa, which he had named La Tanière du Lion – the Lion's Den – a dangerous pretence at power. Now Bokassa remembered why he had ordered the arrest: M'Bongo had rented one of his houses to the East German ambassador and was implicated in a conspiracy with the communist state. Whether this was true or false was not the issue. The prosecution wanted to know if Bokassa had instructed his jailors to starve the prisoner to death.[18]

The M'Bongo case dragged on for a week as witnesses attempted to shed light on the goings-on in the dictator's prisons. Many recounted chilling tales but often lapsed into confusion and contradiction under questioning by the defence. Those who volunteered their testimony were finding that this was no kangaroo court; it was clearly not a repeat of the show trial of December 1980. Moreover, testifying could be dangerous, as Edmond Wogou, Bokassa's nephew and a police captain in 1973, found out. Wogou was the one who had arrested M'Bongo and had supervised his treatment during part of the imprisonment. As he told his story, it dawned upon him that he could be implicated in the atrocity and he began to change a number of details that he had given earlier. The defence lawyers were relentless in their assault on his credibility, and it soon became obvious that his only aim was to save his own skin as he attempted to extricate himself from the web of contradictions he had spun. These efforts brought contemptuous boos and whistles from the audience – a sure sign that he had won few friends during his privileged days as police captain. Prosecutor Mbodou, frustrated at his witness's disastrous showing, demanded his arrest for perjury and for complicity in M'Bongo's death.[19]

By Friday the nineteenth, the defence was ahead on points. All week, Szpiner and Gibault had maintained their campaign of attrition, wearing down witnesses with their relentless questions. They were greatly helped by Mbodou's plodding ineptness. The prosecutor often seemed unsure of himself and relied heavily on advisers in the audience, who were constantly passing him pieces of paper; and he tended to extrapolate freely from witnesses' statements, forming hasty conclusions which by no means followed logically. More than once he showed his frustration by yelling at the defence lawyers to stay quiet. Szpiner was having none of this, however, and shouted back that he would not tolerate threats or intimidation.

In the end, it was impossible to say whether or not Bokassa had ordered M'Bongo's death by starvation. If he had indeed done so, others were implicated as well. The prosecution was forced to admit that many of its key witnesses were compromised by their close association with the former regime. This question of the enlarged circle of responsibility would continue to bedevil the trial in the months ahead.

It was a good beginning for the defence, but Bokassa was feeling the strain. He had been on his feet every day for hours on end, speaking incessantly. Given to long-windedness, he often embarked on long digressions from the matter at hand, taking every opportunity to remind his listeners of his voluntary return and his desire to clear his name. These performances had taken their toll, and now he was hoarse and visibly weary. But the old soldier went battling on.

It was his last chance, his last audience, and he was out to make the best of it.

On Friday morning his lawyers asked that he be allowed to answer questions sitting down, since he was feeling weak and a little tense. They also asked that the trial be adjourned between 23 December and 3 January because of their client's "extreme fatigue" from days of verbal sparring with hostile witnesses. The first request was granted. The second, which was considered over the weekend, was rejected on Monday, 22 December, on the grounds that little progress had been made to date. The court would take 24 and 25 December off for Christmas, that was all. Szpiner, annoyed at the decision, remarked that the lack of progress was mainly due to the prosecution's practice of calling the same witnesses and repeatedly asking them the same questions. But Mbodou was quick to defend his tactics, noting that only step by laborious step would the court come to know the personality of the accused – the "orchestral director of all that took place in Ngaragba." To which Gibault retorted, "A conductor cannot be held responsible for all the wrong notes of his orchestra."[20]

A day later, Szpiner and Gibault flew to Paris to spend Christmas with their families, leaving the defence in the hands of the Central African lawyers. Meanwhile, Bangui remained at an economic standstill, with everyone glued to the radio during the live broadcasts from the courtroom. With so little work being done, the expatriate employer class was in despair and made its displeasure known in the corridors of power, whereupon the government moved the hearings to the afternoon, when commercial activity normally ceased in any case.

For the rest of December 1986 and most of the month of January 1987, the trial continued to deal with the first of the fourteen indictments – "murders and complicity in murders." One witness was Pauline Lingoupou, sister of General Martin Lingoupou, the gendarmerie chief who had been eliminated when he fell under suspicion in 1974. She told the court that Bokassa had killed her mother, the four-breasted "monkey-woman," fearing her prowess in sorcery. Bokassa, of course, stuck to his standard defence strategy: he declared that he knew nothing of the woman's supposed magic powers and had no reason to put her to death. "I never saw the breasts of Lingoupou's mother. I do not know why she was arrested." The debate surrounding the number of Madame Lingoupou's breasts (some claimed it was three, not four) perplexed the French lawyers until they realized that killing a sorceress was not a serious crime in Centrafrique. Certainly, the Central African defence lawyers had no difficulty in arguing that if the woman had been so endowed, Bokassa would have been justified in jailing her in order to protect himself from her evil spells.[21]

Day after day the courtroom audience sat entranced as the litany of gruesome episodes unfolded. Yet in spite of careful rehearsal and prompting by the prosecution, many of the witnesses were far from convincing. The defence lawyers harried them throughout, showing contradictions in their testimony, demanding a precision of detail which they could not supply, and taking them to task for their acquiescence or active participation in the imperial regime's brutality. Often, when faced with acknowledging either moral cowardice or collaboration, witnesses retracted their statements. Even those who withstood the barrage of legal rhetoric and stuck to their stories found that there was still a problem: nobody could establish beyond reasonable doubt that Bokassa had given the orders to kill.

Bokassa did accept responsibility for the numerous arrests and detentions, justifying them on the grounds of conspiracies and threats to state security. He was also prepared to admit that due process of law had often been ignored in such cases, but he argued that this injustice was mitigated by the frequent general pardons he had issued. On most of the murders and disappearances, he professed complete innocence and claimed to have learned of them only after he was in exile in Abidjan. Dacko and Maïdou, he said, were to blame for the crimes of which he was accused. They had carried them out in collaboration with the French in order to destabilize his regime.

Bokassa had other equally implausible lines of defence: "I am a Christian ... I was in Bethlehem, Lourdes, Rome ... Pope Paul VI himself gave me the title 'Apostle of Peace.' I could not therefore have done evil to my people. Moreover, every time that I wanted to free someone, they told me he was dead. How can you then suspect me of such crimes?" Bokassa's daily protestations of innocence – that he did not know what was going on in his prisons – were slowly trying the patience of Prosecutor Mbodou, who finally exploded in rage and addressed the jury with, "Ladies and Gentlemen, we find ourselves before someone utterly irresponsible who directed this country for fourteen years!"[22]

When senior officials of the former imperial government came to testify, they naturally gave a different story from Bokassa's. They were out to exonerate themselves and put the blame on the man at the top. Henri Maïdou professed to have always been opposed to Bokassa's excesses but said he had been unable to organize a coup because the network of spies was everywhere and nobody could be trusted. David Dacko put in a typically pathetic performance. "There was no way to control Bokassa. He became almost crazy," he told the judge. "I used to go on my knees before him to stop him doing evil."

When the aging Joseph Potolot (the one imperial official who had remained faithful to Bokassa) took the stand, nobody knew what to expect. Potolot ridiculed the emperor's former collaborators who were now pretending that they had resisted all along. Casting an accusatory eye around the courtroom, he asked pointedly and to much uncomfortable shuffling, "Where are they today, all those who flattered Bokassa during his reign?" Nor did he hesitate to attack the human rights record of the Kolingba regime and by implication question its moral authority to try the fallen emperor. He revealed that he had been arrested arbitrarily in 1984 and detained without trial for thirteen months on the orders of Christophe Grelombe, the minister of the interior. "Things must change in the Central African society of today," he warned.[23]

In mid-January demonstrations took place outside the Palais de Justice to mark the anniversary of the disturbances of January 1979. The large crowd gathered there waved banners proclaiming "Death to Bokassa, the cannibal, the Nazi torturer!" ... "Down with the comic-opera Emperor!" The protest was too well orchestrated to be spontaneous, and the defence lawyers interpreted it as an attempt at intimidation and a sign of the government's frustration at the way the case was going.[24] Inside the building, Gibault rose to protest both the demonstrations and the increasing attacks on the defence team by the state-controlled media. He and Szpiner had been branded "legal mercenaries" for taking on the Bokassa case.

In spite of the prosecution's many setbacks, Mboudou was confident when dealing with the death of Edmond Broudy. The case was noteworthy in that it involved the murder of a Frenchman, allegedly by Bokassa's own hand. Broudy, who worked for a coffee company and had had problems with his workers in April 1979, had been arrested and taken to Berengo. The soldiers who had escorted him to the palace appeared before the court and gave an account of the incident. Broudy had apparently been an arrogant, swaggering type of person and had insulted the emperor in the course of their conversation, whereupon Bokassa had burst into a rage and beaten the Frenchman to death with his cane. Realizing too late that he had gone too far – and hoping to avoid problems with the French ambassador – he had urged the soldiers to take responsibility, assuring them not only of acquittal but of promotion. All this seemed very damning, but the defence was quick to point out that the case rested entirely on the testimony of soldiers, who were themselves implicated in Broudy's death. Were they lying just to avoid conviction? Who was one to believe? The truth was as elusive as ever.

The charge of "murders and complicity in murders" occupied twenty-four court sittings, and on 27 January Judge Franck asked the prosecution and defence to move at a livelier pace so that he could get through the remaining thirteen charges more expeditiously. The second charge – "poisoning and complicity in poisoning" – referred specifically to the death of the fake Martine's baby. Dr Bruno Dédéavodé, the true Martine's husband, had been convicted of this deed back in 1980, and the prosecutor's task was to show that the doctor had acted on Bokassa's orders. But his only proof was Dédéavodé's own statement which, in any case, had been rejected during his trial and had failed to save him from the executioner's bullet. The defence lawyers lost no time in attacking this one. Szpiner challenged Mbodou to produce a source other than the dead man's word and asked sarcastically if the emperor's telephone was being tapped the day he instructed Dédéavodé to administer the poison. The prosecution's case was anything but airtight.

By late February the court was considering the repression of January and April 1979. The prosecution had been hoping to show that Bokassa had given the order to kill, but officers of the former imperial guard denied having received such an order, and it was impossible to prove otherwise. They also denied that they had been instructed to raze the *kodros* where the rebellion had been centred. And although friends and relatives of those slain on the streets of Bangui or behind Ngaragba's walls told the court of their lost loved ones, once again the deaths could not be linked directly to His Imperial Majesty. Interestingly, while several students had testified to the Mission de constatation and at the trial in absentia that Bokassa had participated personally in the massacres of April 1979, none did so at his trial.

For his part, Bokassa stuck to his defence strategy. He blamed the deaths directly on the excessive zeal of his officers but ascribed a more general responsibility to Dacko, Maïdou, and the French, whom he accused of fomenting the disturbances in order to bring down his regime. He held the same line when responding to the charge of concealing cadavers. This charge focused on the secret burial of those who had died in April 1979 while imprisoned in Ngaragba. Bokassa denied that he had tried to cover up the massacre in this way and said that the action had been taken on the initiative of the prison director and of Henri Maïdou in order that he, the emperor, would not learn of the deaths.

Early in March the trial turned to the charge that everyone had been eagerly awaiting: cannibalism. Attendance at the Palais de Justice had dropped off noticeably during the previous weeks, but now the courtroom was packed again; European journalists had come flocking back to Bangui on the trail of the lurid and bizarre. Ironically, cannibalism is not a serious crime in the Central African Republic, and conviction on this count alone would not have brought a death sentence. But Bokassa, sensitive to European views, considered it a particularly odious stigma and wanted to clear his name of this charge above all others.

Many of the same witnesses who had testified to His Majesty's peculiar eating habits back in 1980 now took the stand again. One woman recalled how she had found her brother's corpse in the imperial freezer, while others regaled the court with tales of cannibalistic feasts attended by thirty people or more, including the unwitting Robert Galley. These witnesses quickly found out that this trial was very different from the previous one. Under sharp questioning from Szpiner and his companions, their stories began to fall apart, and they were forced to admit that they could not remember important details of the alleged incidents – for instance, whether the event had occurred at Kolongo or Berengo.

Then it was learned that the Villa Kolongo had been ransacked by a mob just before the arrival of the French troops in September 1979. Had the mob placed the cadavers in the freezer before the soldiers arrived, just to discredit Bokassa, as the defence claimed? Or had the French troops themselves brought the cadavers along? This was another hypothesis of the defence team. Even David Dacko, who until then had been categorical on the question of cannibalism, was prepared to concede serious doubts. He confessed that he had not seen the cadavers himself but had been convinced of their presence by photographs taken by the French.

The only "solid" witness whom the prosecution could produce was Philippe Linguissa, Bokassa's former cook, whose testimony had captivated the world back in December 1980. Now, bent with the ravages of age, he wept as he told a hushed court how his work in the emperor's kitchen had left him semi-paralysed and impotent. He claimed that Bokassa had left France because "he could no longer eat human flesh and that is the reason he returned to Bangui so he could do it again." Although Linguissa admitted that his mind was faltering and that he could not remember all the details, he managed to instruct the court on the finer points of his craft.

"I shaved his hairy thorax, emptied the entrails, stuffed the body with rice, then proceeded to cook it in the usual manner. When it was well cooked I flambéd it with gin and whiskey." Asked how many people had enjoyed the meal, he recalled that Bokassa alone had done so.

The accused, who had been relatively calm throughout the hearing as his lawyers demolished the credibility of witnesses, was visibly infuriated by Linguissa's story. He denied ever having met the man let alone making use of his culinary skills. "I have never been and never will be a cannibal," he told the court in loud and emphatic tones.

Linguissa's appearance served more as comic relief than anything else, and the defence had little difficulty discrediting him.[25] Even *Ele songo*, a local newspaper that was far from sympathetic to Bokassa, readily admitted that the cannibalism charge was the weakest presented by the prosecution to date.

The trial was by now almost three months old, and the daily hearings were taking their toll on the beleaguered defendant. Bokassa's right foot was swollen with gout, and he hobbled into the court every day wearing a carpet slipper on the infected limb. He was also receiving medication for blood pressure. He seemed but a shadow of his former self. The old fighting spirit was ebbing away. Meanwhile, although the defence's cross-examinations were as devastating as ever, the prosecution was slowly gaining ground simply because of the volume of witnesses and the grisly tales they had to tell. There were just too many disappearances and incidents of arbitrary justice to be explained away with legal cleverness, and it became increasingly difficult to deny that Emperor Bokassa had presided over a regime in which terror had been official policy and basic human rights had been systematically denied.

Charges seven, eight, and nine, relating to arbitrary arrest, imprisonment, and violence, were combined by the prosecution in order to speed things along. There were civil suits connected with these charges in which victims of the empire's rough justice demanded compensation for their suffering. At one point, Bokassa tried to ridicule their claims, urging the court in mocking tones not to execute him lest he be unable to reimburse them. Even so, when three former students appeared and accused him of beating them for refusing to recognize the empire, he admitted that it had happened, but only because he had been angry at the time.

The next series of charges, in which Bokassa was accused of embezzling state funds and helping himself to his country's diamonds, dragged on through April and well into May. The prosecution claimed that Bokassa had pocketed the sum of 13 billion CFA francs during his years in power. During that period state companies involved in coffee, cotton, diamonds, and the like had provided the government with a good portion of its operating revenues, while foreign aid had made up the rest. It was from these sources that Bokassa had allegedly enriched himself.

Since accounting procedures had been makeshift or nonexistent under the imperial regime and since no accurate records had been kept when money changed hands, even when the transfer was legitimate, the prosecution had a serious problem: it could not produce a shred of documentary evidence to show what Bokassa had stolen.[26] Mbodou tried to rely on the personal testimony of directors and former directors of state agencies to make his case, but they were none too convincing, and they only made matters worse by presenting contradictory and confusing sets of figures. The prosecutor himself was perplexed by it all and was constantly lost in adding and subtracting to keep the case consistent. Questions were also asked about the billions of CFA francs which the South African government had poured into Bangui over the years for various development projects, many of which had never been built. As usual, Bokassa tried to pass the blame on to his ministers and civil servants, some of whom were still holding high office in the Kolingba government. He also pointed out that South African aid had ended as soon as he had been overthrown.

In spite of the absence of documentary proof and the cleverness of the defence team, the courtroom dialogue showed that Bokassa's empire had been a cesspool of financial mismanagement, devoid of any measure for curbing profiteering. It was impossible to distinguish between public and private money, and the whole system had been riddled with "secret funds" and "special funds" whose purposes were suspiciously mysterious. Bokassa's French châteaux were proof enough that he had done well during his years in power. He told the court that he had purchased these properties with the profits of his legitimate business ventures. The prosecution did not believe him, but in the absence of proof it could not pursue the matter.

The defence lawyers easily refuted the related charge of stealing the coronation jewels. They pointed out that Bokassa had had no reason to take the crown and other paraphernalia with him on his fateful journey to Libya. Besides, he had been thoroughly searched during his Evreux sojourn and none of the missing items had been found. When Szpiner brought up the pillaging of the imperial residences by the Barracudas and suggested that the "ballet of helicopters" between Berengo and Bangui in September 1979 was the most likely explanation for the jewels' disappearance, the prosecution grew noticeably uncomfortable and abandoned its line of argument.[27]

The prosecution also had second thoughts about the final charge – threatening the internal and external security of the state. Fearing embarrassing revelations concerning the Kolingba regime's relations with France and Libya, it quietly dropped the charge.

On 22 May 1987, the questioning and debating came to an end. After five months, eighty-four hearings, and the testimony of one hundred witnesses, many of whom had appeared over and over again, both defence and prosecution were on the verge of exhaustion. What had begun as "the trial of the century" and a historic rendez-vous with justice had degenerated into a tedious exercise in legal disputation. Certainly, there had been moments of high drama along the way, but passions had calmed as the months of verbal duelling took their toll. Public interest also had waned, and by the end of the hearings the Palais de Justice was almost empty of spectators. Above all, Bokassa had been demoralized by the whole affair. The old defiance was gone and he now sat humbly before his judges. Few could recognize in this old man the marshal-cum-emperor who had imposed his fickle will on a terrified populace for the best part of fourteen years.

The trial had been conducted according to the canons of French courtroom procedure, with the exception of some irregularities that were probably unavoidable in the circumstances. For a start, Judge Franck was strongly biased in favour of the prosecution, and it was said that he never made a decision without consulting President Kolingba. Moreover, he raised no objections when Prosecutor Mbodou intimidated witnesses or threatened the defence lawyers with expulsion – tactics that would not have been tolerated in France. Then there was the fact that the witnesses themselves were a problem. Ten of them were arrested during the trial on one pretext or another, and as word spread that testifying could lead to prosecution, many who might have had important evidence to present simply stayed away.[28] Countless other witnesses saw the courtroom as a platform from which to indulge their prejudices and acquire a fleeting moment of fame. Some spoke at great length, glorifying themselves or airing bitter feuds between families, ethnic groups, or political factions. It was at times difficult to tell that the trial of a former dictator was underway.

On 1 June Prosecutor Mbodou began his *réquisitoire*. It would take him two days to sum up his case and make his final arguments to the jury. Foreign journalists had returned to Bangui for the conclusion of the trial, and the Palais de Justice was crowded once again. With a large audience and full media coverage, Mbodou's opening remarks had a distinctly political tone. He spoke of how the trial represented the triumph of the democratic over the arbitrary and how the presence of international journalists, writers, and human rights groups testified to the government's commitment to the principles of justice. He went on to say that the trial had forced them all to relive a dark period of their history and that the passing of time had not healed the wounds inflicted by the man who had abused power with such abandon. The crimes of that age were engraved permanently on the minds of Central Africans and should not go unpunished. The importance of the trial was to prevent such crimes in future.

Realizing that his case was weak on concrete evidence, Mboudou spent much of his time reminding the jurors of the Bokassa era, of the fear and corruption, and said it was impossible that the emperor had not known what was going on. He reminded the jurors that in the days of the republic, Bokassa had retained for himself an impressive array of government portfolios, that he had had confidence in no one and had not liked to delegate responsibility, especially on such important matters as the arrest of a minister or his execution in jail.

Turning specifically to the collection of charges that involved the misappropriation of funds and property, Mbodou stressed that Bokassa had never made a distinction between his personal fortune and public funds, between his role as a businessman and that of head of state. He spoke of the accused's commercial activities, which had flourished without payment of taxes and often with the benefit of the state's resources; he spoke of gifts to the state from abroad, the aircraft and automobiles that had become the personal property of its ruler, and of the millions in foreign aid that had never been accounted for. Concluding his remarks, Mbodou asked for the maximum penalty on charges eleven and twelve, the misappropriation of diamonds and state funds.

The next afternoon Mbodou dealt with the crimes against persons, the most serious of which were murder and complicity in murder. Elaborating on each one in turn, he outlined the reasons for Bokassa's murderous ways: fear of those who threatened his absolute power; fear that the families of those eliminated might avenge their loved ones; his peculiar conception of justice, in which personal whim replaced due procedure; his exaggerated sense of self-importance, which led him to see insults where none were intended; his procuring bodies for cannibalistic rites; and his simple, uncontrollable rage. Mbodou concluded by asking for the death penalty for direct or indirect involvement in all the major murder cases cited throughout the trial, conceding no extenuating circumstances. He mentioned specifically the cases of Auguste M'Bongo, Edmond Broudy, the Lingoupou family, the fake Martine and her baby, and the young people who had perished in January and April 1979. He was ambivalent on the question of cannibalism, letting the court decide that for itself, but as a final blow he demanded the confiscation of all Bokassa's property.

The next day the defence lawyers had the floor for their summing up, or *plaidoirie*. Each of them in turn demanded an acquittal on all principal charges on the grounds that the prosecution had failed to bring forward concrete evidence against their client. They acknowledged Bokassa's "general responsibility" for the wrongdoing during his regime but insisted, as they had done all along, that it was his subordinates who had committed the atrocities without either his knowledge or his consent. The courtroom was then emptied, and Bokassa was led away to Camp de Roux, where he had a week of nervous waiting while the jury went about its deliberations.

On Friday, 12 June, the Palais de Justice was packed again as Judge Franck pronounced the verdict. Bokassa was found guilty of complicity in at least twenty murders, including those of Martin Lingoupou, Edmond Broudy, and Auguste M'Bongo. There were many others, the court surmised, but these were the only deaths that could be pinned on Bokassa with any certainty. He was also found guilty of complicity in the arrest and detention of schoolchildren, some of them under fifteen years of age, and of torture leading to their death. And he was found guilty of embezzling a sum of 3,143,473,000 CFA francs from the state (about $10 million).

Bokassa was acquitted of several murders that had been attributed to him during the marathon trial, including that of the fake Martine's baby. The court admitted that it had no proof that he had given the order to administer the fatal poison. The verdict was also not guilty on the charges of misappropriating the crown jewels and, much to Bokassa's relief, cannibalism. The court conceded that Philippe Linguissa's testimony was uncorroborated and that the man was "mentally deranged." The charge of threatening state security was said to be beyond the court's competence, which was another way of saying that it was dropped.

Then came the sentence: death by firing squad, which Judge Franck said would be carried out in Ngaragba Prison. Bokassa was standing at attention as the fate he had so often pronounced on others was now visited on himself. He retained his composure. A knowing smile crossed his face. He had expected nothing less. He then turned and embraced his lawyers, who announced that they would launch an immediate appeal. As the condemned man was taken away, he was calm, almost confident, and affirmed to journalists that right was on his side. He knew that Kolingba had commuted all death sentences since coming to power and believed that he too would benefit from a presidential pardon.[29]

Bokassa's supporters had been planning to stage riots and demonstrations if the verdict went against him, but now, buoyed by his self-assurance, they remained calm. The government was relieved to see no trouble on the streets, especially with so many journalists around for the final hearings. Meanwhile, the defence lawyers had much to do. They immediately appealed the death sentence on the grounds that the criminal court had not been competent to hear the case. They based their argument on article 38 of the November 1986 constitution, which guaranteed the president of the republic immunity from prosecution for crimes committed during his term of office, save for high treason. In the event of treason, the case could only be heard by the people's congress. Kolingba had put this clause in the constitution lest he find himself one day in Bokassa's shoes and answerable for his actions. The defence assumed that the protection applied to all presidents, including their client.[30]

Months went by as the appeal was heard. In his prison quarters at Camp de Roux, Bokassa kept up his spirits. Clad now in sandals and khaki fatigues, he awaited the court's decision. In truth, his fate rested not so much with the court as with Kolingba. Ever since the former emperor's unexpected return to Bangui the president had been under pressure from hardliners in his entourage to pull the trigger and get it over with. Had he followed their advice, there would have been no trial at all. Now, with the long judicial process over except for the appeal, the hardliners were even more insistent that he act. Meanwhile, discreet messages were arriving from many African leaders asking that Bokassa's life be spared.[31]

Kolingba bided his time, allowing the passions aroused by the trial to dissipate. Then, on 14 November, five months after the verdict, the Supreme Court rejected Bokassa's appeal. In doing so, it accepted the prosecution's contention that article 38 provided no protection. In a strict interpretation of the law, the constitutional provision applied only to presidents, not to emperors. Although the judges conceded that Bokassa had once been president, they held that he had not been so in a legal sense, for he had seized power in a coup and had never received the people's approval in an election.[32] This was a curious argument considering President Kolingba's own career, but that made little difference. The only matter of importance now was that all avenues of judicial procedure were closed and that the death sentence hung over the prisoner at Camp de Roux.

Bokassa himself never believed that the execution would be carried out, and he was proved right. On 29 February 1988, President Kolingba commuted the sentence to life imprisonment with hard labour. That very day, defence lawyer Lambert Zokoézo visited the ex-emperor in his cell and told him the good news.[33] It was a sensible decision. It saved the country unwanted ethnic strife and open resentment against the Yakoma and their privileges; and it helped the country's international image in the sensitive area of human rights.

There was now speculation that Bokassa might be sent into exile once again, but few countries would have welcomed him – certainly not France or the Ivory Coast. A rumour went about that he was to be taken for safekeeping to Birao in the distant north, where he was unlikely to become the focus of political unrest. But in the end the government decided to keep its prisoner where he was, at Camp de Roux.

Epilogue

By his own admission, Bokassa was well treated during his imprisonment at Camp de Roux. Although conditions were spartan, they were a far cry from the squalid horrors of Ngaragba. His cell was in the middle of a heavily guarded complex where political prisoners considered dangerous by the Kolingba regime were kept under close watch. It was an ordinary, prisonlike room measuring five by three metres. At one end, on a raised concrete platform, was a mattress that served as his bed. Adjacent to the cell was a courtyard of five by ten metres in which he was allowed to walk for an hour a couple of times a day. Confined to these simple surroundings, he wore simple prison clothes – sandals, shirt, and shorts, and sometimes a djellaba. He received three plain meals a day and complained of their monotony. He also complained of the terrible heat and inadequate ventilation.

The former emperor rarely received visitors. His jailors saw to that. A niece and a Central African ex-wife named Chantal were allowed to see him on Saturdays and usually did. The rest of his large family, most of whom lived in Europe, were also permitted to visit, but few of them made the long journey to Bangui. His lawyer, François Gibault, was allowed to meet him for an hour a day when he was in the Central African capital. Apart from these tenuous contacts with his past and the outside world, Bokassa was completely isolated. True enough, he could talk to his guards. The French and Central African soldiers who kept watch over him found their illustrious prisoner a welcome diversion from their dreary duty details at Camp de Roux. He often regaled them with tales of his exploits, and they listened in fascination. Sometimes Colonel Mantion dropped in to check on him, and they exchanged stories of military life.

Bokassa was allowed books and the occasional newspaper but had no access to a radio. Yet he managed to keep abreast of world events, always a great passion of his, through the conversations with his jailors. His books were mainly religious – the Bible, which he read every day, being the most important. Indeed, Bokassa became quite religious, almost mystical, and considered himself an apostle of Christ. Even so, he still bore grudges. He raved sporadically against Catherine and Giscard for their betrayal, and any mention of Dacko or Maïdou was sure to make him mad. He said he was ready to face a firing squad at any moment on condition that those two were at his side.[1] Meanwhile, he wrote letters and was permitted to receive them, subject to the censorship of his jailors. Augustine wrote regularly, complaining of her financial difficulties in maintaining the château and of her problems with the children. Most of those under her care were teenagers now and in the absence of their father's restraining hand were often in trouble with the police. The loss of his last woman was one of Bokassa's great regrets, and he became jealous at any suggestion of another man in her life. Anyone who visited her, even his son Georges, was suspected of trying to seduce her.[2]

It might have ended thus but for political developments, which were as unexpected as they were welcome. The Bokassa trial had aroused public awareness in Centrafrique to the notions of human and civil rights, and had encouraged demands for a restoration of democracy. By 1990 the usually fragmented opposition had joined in an alliance known as the Comité de co-ordination pour la convocation d'une conférence nationale (CCCCN). One if its leading spokespeople was Nicolas Tiangaye, one of Bokassa's defence lawyers. The CCCCN organized rallies and distributed pamphlets, thereby prompting arrests and detentions by the government.

Events outside the country were also acting as a pressure for change. François Mitterrand, after his second electoral victory in 1988, sensed the rising democratic tide, not only in the Central African Republic but in the Côte d'Ivoire, Gabon, Togo, and elsewhere. Spurred on by the fall of the Berlin Wall, he began to demand political reform as the price of continued assistance. His speech to the Franco-African summit at La Baule in June 1990 made this clear. Another motivating factor may have been Nelson Mandela's release from prison in South Africa, which was also powerfully symbolic of an unmistakable trend.[3]

The Kolingba regime, dependent as ever on annual French subsidies of more than two billion CFA francs, and facing growing unrest at home exacerbated by virtual economic collapse, succumbed to the pressure. In April 1991 the government agreed that the next elections would be open to candidates and parties of all persuasions. This did in fact come about, though not until 25 October 1992. Then, poor organization of the elections led to angry demonstrations, and Kolingba cancelled the process hours before the polls were due to close. Having survived in power because of divisions among the opposition, he was trying to avoid a real test of the people's will. But it could not be postponed forever. Students and workers clashed with security forces in Bangui on 26 April 1993,[4] and the agitation persisted. Then, on 6 June, the French withdrew Colonel Mantion from Centrafrique. Paris, too, was keeping up the pressure.

New elections for the presidency and National Assembly were scheduled for 22 August, and this time everything was in order. Eight candidates sought the presidency, including such well-known figures as David Dacko, Abel Goumba, and Ange Patassé. Early returns gave Patassé a comfortable lead, while Dacko and Goumba were in a tight race for second place. Kolingba, with only 11 per cent of the vote, had no chance of being one of the two candidates in the run-off vote set for 12 September. Thus, on 28 August, in a desperate attempt to avoid the inevitable, the president suspended the count. But the next day, when France cut off the flow of aid, he was forced to back down, acknowledge defeat, and allow the electoral process to continue. He still had one last card to play – a spiteful one that he hoped would spoil the victory of his opponents.

On the morning of 1 September, Radio-Bangui announced that in celebration of the twelfth anniversary of his coming to power, President Kolingba was going to free all prisoners in the state, including Bokassa.[5] He probably thought that the former emperor would now become the focus of media attention or that his supporters, jubilant at his release, would disrupt the second round of the election. On receiving his freedom, Bokassa was taken to the Palais de la Renaissance, where he was given one of six luxury suites that were usually reserved for dignitaries from abroad. He was allowed to receive visitors, and they arrived in droves – some out of curiosity, some to pay homage to one who might still have a political future. For a brief while, it even seemed as if the emperor was back on his throne, dispensing favours to his subjects. For his part, Bokassa only hinted vaguely that if his country called him, he would be willing to serve. Otherwise, he would be content to lead a simple life of agriculture and prayer while looking after his family.

Meanwhile, Patassé defeated Goumba in the second round of the presidential election – a contest that went off without mishap. On 25 September, Bokassa wrote to the new head of state demanding the restoration of everything confiscated from him after his overthrow. There was no reply. Undeterred, he made a few dramatic appearances on the streets of Bangui dressed in his marshal's uniform, which had been returned to him on his release. Patassé endured the aggravation for about a month. Then, on 4 November, he ordered that Bokassa be removed from the palace and sent to live in the Villa Nasser under what amounted to house arrest.

The villa, near the cathedral, had once been the Empress Catherine's urban residence. Later it was occupied by the Barracudas. During the years Bokassa lived there, it was run down, the gardens overgrown, the swimming pool empty. Most of the rooms were deserted except for those in one corner where Bokassa resided. The admirers who had greeted him as he emerged from prison had disappeared. They had abandoned him when they realized he was broke. A few relatives dropped in to see him regularly, bringing food, refreshments, and companionship, but otherwise he was isolated and alone, his final days filled with sadness. He felt marginalized and forgotten and not a little resentful that Patassé, whose career he had nurtured, had relegated him and his achievements to obscurity. Even his use of the imperial letterhead and the signature "Bokassa Ier" brought a swift reprimand from the government.[6] The dream of empire, conceived dimly on the night of Saint-Sylvestre many decades ago, had faded into oblivion in this delapidated villa that was once a symbol of its fragile splendour. Within three years its author had gone too. On 3 November 1996, Jean-Bedel Bokassa died of a heart attack in a Bangui medical clinic, where he was being treated for a variety of ailments.[7]

Conclusion

Colonial rule imposed arbitrary and alien forms of government on Africa. At independence, the new states found themselves with political structures divorced from traditional notions of authority and legitimacy. These structures were not only alien in origin; they had put down fragile roots. The cautious devolution of power in the final years of European control had been too short-lived and superficial to have a permanent impact. Ideologies such as socialism and liberal democracy had never taken hold and could not form the basis of post-independence political culture. The authoritarianism of the colonial system was the only legacy of significance.[1]

In a number of instances, European rule was sufficiently short-lived or nondestructive to allow the survival of indigenous political structures. Ethiopia, where Emperor Haile Selassie re-established himself after six years of Italian occupation, is the best example. The legitimacy of Selassie's feudal monarchy was derived from an ancient lineage and was perpetuated through elaborate rituals. In Weberian terms, it was a traditionalist patrimonial state held together by the patriarchal authority of the ruler and the loyalty of the citizenry to his person.

Most postcolonial African leaders could not lay claim to an authentic traditional legitimacy as justification for their autocratic rule. Some sought, nonetheless, to appropriate it. Kwame Nkrumah, for instance, adopted the *kente* cloth and royal stool and staff in order to legitimize his authority; and Sékou Touré, in spite of his professed socialism, often boasted that he was a grandson of Samori Touré, founder of the Mande Empire. The regimes in Ghana and Guinea are thus best described as neopatrimonial, since their authority rested more on charismatic revolutionary leadership and patronage than on genuine appeals to tradition.[2]

The glorification of ancient kingdoms reflected the paradoxical crisis of identity that confronted newly independent Africa. There was a desire to modernize while at the same time seeking out an authentic identity that harkened back to historical antecedents.[3] The Central African Republic/Empire, insofar as it is possible to categorize it, bore many of the characteristics of neopatrimonialism. Bokassa was as concerned with the legitimacy of his regime as any of his contemporary strongmen were of theirs, but unlike Nkrumah and Touré (and we could add Houphouët-Boigny, Kenyatta, Senghor, and others), he had not led his people to independence and therefore lacked revolutionary credentials. As a usurper, his claim to power was always suspect. That he went to extremes in appropriating symbols and rituals to make his regime respectable can be understood in the circumstances. His choice of French rather than African models was eccentric, to say the least, and betrayed a certain vanity or even megalomania, but the purpose of the appropriation was the same as that in other personal regimes: the search for legitimacy.

Bokassa's attempt to create a hereditary monarchy was practical in another sense as well. If events unfolded favourably, the wealth and power he had accumulated would remain in his family for generations. In his dynastic ambitions, he was not unique among his contemporaries. In regimes as different as Haiti's Papa Doc Duvalier and North Korea's Kim Il Sung, to cite some non-African examples, the rulers chose their sons as their successors.

The centralization and personalization of power are key features of African neopatrimonial regimes. Whether military or one-party civilian, the executive is supreme while the legislative and the judicial arms of government, if they exist at all, serve it meekly. Personal rule is linked to the notion of charismatic leadership, which implies an emotional bond between ruler and ruled.[4] The ruler, either by natural charisma or by a carefully orchestrated personality cult, becomes the human embodiment of the state and in turn treats its resources as personal possessions. In such a system, institutions with clear rules and procedures do not govern political life; rather, it is the personal relations binding ruler, supporters, clients, and rivals that do so.[5] The ruler, needing supporters, cultivates allegiance by dispensing patronage, usually in the form of jobs. Patron-client relations spread out from the centre, creating a network of obligations that connects its participants to the ruler. No moral code regulates the distribution of jobs and services; there is no ethic of public allocation. Everything depends on personal relations.[6]

Throughout his republican and imperial phases, Bokassa's power was supreme. One of his first acts was to suspend the constitution and rule by decree. He also abolished the National Assembly and never recreated it, in spite of his promises to do so. Consequently, there was no legislative branch of government throughout his regime. This meant that there were no institutional avenues through which even the mildest criticism of the government could be voiced. Although the judiciary continued to exist, it was never independent of the marshal/emperor's will. With most offences, whether criminal or political, due process was the exception rather than the rule. In some of the more noteworthy plots against the ruler – those of Banza and Obrou, for instance – military tribunals conducted the hearings and their decisions were never in doubt.

Bokassa shared his executive power only minimally with his cabinet. Initially, he held so many portfolios that the cabinet concept was almost meaningless. After 1975, when he appointed a prime minister, there was still little real delegation of authority, since nobody dared to make a decision of any significance without consulting him. And with the creation of the empire, his imperial cabinet at Berengo ensured that the prime minister never grew too independent.

Bokassa's absolute power was reinforced by his style of heroic leadership. The institutions named in his honour, the unstinting praise in the media, the bronze statues at the capital's major intersections, the medals, uniforms, increasingly grandiose titles, and general flamboyant self-assertion all lent his authority a surreal legitimacy. He was the father of the nation – Papa Bok – the personification of the state. Bokassa's rule was also personal in that he treated the resources of the state as his own possessions. The state became a source of wealth and patronage. Even the lowliest official was tied into a network of obligation that led all the way to the top. Appointments, promotions, and dismissals were often unrelated to criteria such as merit or credentials. The arbitrary inclination of the ruler or of his immediate subordinates was what mattered. Second-Lieutenant François Bozize's promotion to general on a Bokassa whim is a case in point, and Bozize remained a faithful client of his patron ever after.

When there is this form of political monopoly with no recognized avenues of opposition, factional rivalry often appears within the ruling oligarchy, and it has to be curbed lest it lead to plots, coups, or civil war. Shrewd personal rulers purge potential rivals before they become too powerful, sending them into exile, to jail, or ordering their execution.[7] Bokassa's incarceration of Dacko and his supporters and his elimination of Banza, M'Bongo, and Lingoupou were purges in this sense. His constant cabinet shuffles were less drastic measures to the same end.[8]

Purging one's opponents has an importance beyond the countering of imminent threats. In Bokassa's case, it fostered the image of a powerful and ruthless leader whom it was virtually impossible to defy. This encouraged acquiescence and even a pragmatic loyalty, since followers rally round the survivors in politics rather than the weak-willed and ephemeral – and Bokassa was, above all else, a survivor. His image as a strongman was also enhanced by his wealth, which in an African context is not always viewed in a negative light. Powerful men who acquire wealth and circulate it in society are honoured. Houphouët-Boigny, for instance, once ridiculed a political opponent for owning nothing, not even a bicycle. Countless other examples could be given. Bokassa's money, then, was more than just the product of avarice; it was an expected accoutrement of power.[9]

The symbiosis between the worlds of politics and business in Centrafrique is not surprising, since it was built on practices that were well established during the days of the colonial concessionary companies. Politics and profiteering had always gone hand in hand. Independence gave the indigenous élites access to the apparatus of state, which in turn allowed them to regulate the economy. Through nationalization, the appropriation of foreign aid, and other mechanisms, the local state bourgeoisie was able to accumulate capital for its own expansion.[10] This was done either in collaboration or in competition with the expatriate corporate sector. The creation of ONCPA and the subsequent confiscations of oil company installations and French-owned media outlets in the early 1970s were attempts by the Central African élite to bring a greater share of the country's economy under their control. This paralleled similar moves elsewhere, as a nationalistic mood swept the continent. In November 1973, for example, Mobutu announced a program to "recover" foreign-owned property in Zaïre which resulted in the immediate enrichment of the president and his cronies.[11]

In spite of the politics of ethnicity and occasional plots against the president/emperor, the Central African élite was a reasonably cohesive group of people who were increasingly bound together by common experiences and interests. Small in number and characterized by their French education, they knew each other well. Their similar backgrounds, whether in university or in military school, and their socialization into the rituals of the modern sector gave them a unity and sense of purpose that transcended other elements in their origins. The various upheavals and purges over the years may be explained as part of the struggle for class formation rather than as proof of insurmountable cleavages. The continuity is much more remarkable than the change. When Bokassa was overthrown in 1979, his successors in government – Dacko, Maïdou, Ayandho, Bozize, and others – were all men who had once served under him. And in the presidential election of 1993, the major candidates were all familiar names from the days of empire and before – Dacko, Goumba, Patassé.

It would be wrong to view Bokassa and his entourage simply as a "comprador élite" in the sense used by dependency theorists. This mechanistic model, borrowed from Latin American examples and applied to the African context by Samir Amin and others, suggests that the new privileged classes that emerged at independence were completely dependent on external aid and showed no economic dynamism of their own.[12] In Centrafrique the reliance on France for budgetary supplements, investment capital, and technical assistance was real enough, but it was never a question of slavish dependence. Bokassa's confiscations and appropriations did result in indigenous capital accumulation, some of which was reinvested in productive activities, and he did seek alternatives to French aid. Admittedly, these initiatives failed to disrupt significantly the domination of the former colonial power, but that may have been because of the extent of the domination rather than the subservience of the Central African élite.

Dependency, of course, works both ways. In spite of official denials, France's economic stability is tied to its trading relations with Africa. It is dependent on its former colonies for supplies of uranium, phosphate, bauxite, manganese, copper, chromium, and other raw materials that are vital to its aeronautics, nuclear energy, and weapons industries. Its military presence throughout its *chasse gardée africaine* keeps friendly governments in power and guarantees it privileged access to these resources. Moreover, France needs its role in Africa as its principal claim to world-power status.[13] It might be better to say that France and the African countries it dominates are interdependent, and that ruling élites on all sides of the equation serve mutual interests, even if the equation is far from evenly balanced.

Bokassa was certainly vulnerable, but he was never a willing tool of the French, as he showed on numerous occasions. Towards the end, when Giscard pressured him to resign, he refused. Subsequently, when French aid was cut off he made a deal with Libya, which in all likelihood would have kept him in power. (It was not unlike Sékou Touré's approach to the Soviets after his break with Paris in 1958.) These were not the actions of a "comprador" leader, and it took a full-scale invasion by France's élite troops to get rid of him.

France has intervened militarily in sub-Saharan Africa dozens of times since granting its colonies independence, but never with such single-minded audacity as in Opération Barracuda. It was the publicity surrounding Bokassa's excesses that made it politically impossible for Paris to continue supporting him; and when the loss of this support drove him into the arms of Gadhaffi, Paris felt compelled to act rather than lose its influence in Centrafrique. This was followed by more bad publicity to discredit the fallen emperor and thus justify his overthrow.

The role played by the French media was critical in all of this and there can be no arguing that they exposed some serious abuses of power. At the same time, their coverage of Bokassa invariably took on a prurient, negative tone that was not always warranted. It was as if France, disappointed at its loss of empire, consoled itself with the thought that Africans were unable to rule themselves. Bokassa continued to furnish evidence for this illusion with his excesses of greed, extravagance, and brutality.

There were excesses, as we have seen. But have they been exaggerated? How do they compare with those of his contemporaries? Does Bokassa deserve his place in the pantheon of the continent's worst tyrants? The emperor's actual wealth has proved impossible to estimate with any accuracy, as the prosecution discovered during his 1986–87 trial. At the time, he was found guilty of embezzling over three billion CFA francs – roughly $10 million. His properties in France were valued at around $5 million shortly after his overthrow. These are comparatively modest sums when one considers that Mobutu's foreign bank accounts are said to hold around $4 billion.[14] This is not to suggest that Bokassa was less venal than his neighbour to the south. The difference is more likely to be the result of the relative wealth of Centrafrique and Zaïre, as well as Mobutu's political longevity. Nonetheless, these figures put matters in better perspective, since Bokassa's wealth has often been exaggerated.

The exaggeration can be attributed to the Central African ruler's tendency to ostentation, which was typified by his imperial coronation. The event cost an estimated $22 million and was roundly condemned as extravagant self-glorification. This is a fair criticism in the sense that the money could have been devoted to worthier causes, especially in such a poor country, but when compared with other examples of vainglorious waste on the continent it was truly on a small scale. Consider, for instance, Houphouët-Boigny's basilica at Yamoussoukro – a pharaohlike monument to his immortality – which cost an estimated $300 million.[15] Then there is Omar Bongo, who spent around $1 billion in 1977 hosting the Organization of African Unity summit in Libreville, most of the money going to a futuristic palace for himself.[16]

Similarly, on the question of brutality and repression, Bokassa's regime was no worse than those of some of his contemporaries. It was certainly a lot better than the regimes of the notorious pair with whom he is often categorized – Idi Amin and Macias Nguema. In Amin's Uganda, an estimated 250,000 people lost their lives in eight years of terror.[17] In Nguema's Equatorial Guinea, a figure of 50,000 dead in eleven years is usually given.[18] For Bokassa's Centrafrique, the number of dead and disappeared is calculated at around 500 over the best part of fourteen years. Several other examples of African rulers far more brutal than Bokassa can, unfortunately, be cited. Two will suffice. In post-imperial Ethiopia, thousands were killed in purges of the previous regime, but the repression avoided the condemnation it deserved by being dressed up in the language of "revolutionary justice."[19] In Burundi in 1972, between 100,000 and 150,000 Hutus were systematically slaughtered in an officially sanctioned genocidal campaign.[20] Yet in general works on African politics, the names of Presidents Mengistu Haile-Mariam and Michel Micombero are not often mentioned in reference to brutal repression, whereas Bokassa's name invariably is.

It might also be said that the Central African Republic/Empire never experienced the destructive civil wars that ravaged so many African countries in the postcolonial era – Angola, Ethiopia, Liberia, Nigeria, Somalia, Sudan, and Tchad. Nor did it experience the ethnic massacres that broke out with depressing regularity not only in Burundi but also in Rwanda. In spite of its temperamental ruler and the absence of human rights, Centrafrique may have been one of the safer places to live on the continent.

Linking Bokassa's name with Idi Amin and Macias Nguema is doubly unjust since the latter two were quite deranged and completely destroyed the economy of their respective countries. The emperor, for his part, could point to a long list of positive achievements that tended towards modernization – airport, schools, university, television station, and his own farms and factories. To be sure, there was mismanagement, waste, and profiteering by the state bourgeoisie and the foreign corporations, but Central Africans remember the first decade of Bokassa's rule as the most prosperous and stable in their history. There is some truth to this, and it explains the lingering nostalgia for the emperor in the years after his overthrow.

Similarly, although much has been made of Bokassa's wives, it is often overlooked that he was one of the most progressive of his

African contemporaries on the question of women's advancement. One of his first decrees was a ban on female circumcision, a practice that was defended, it should be noted, by Jomo Kenyatta and others. Bokassa was also the first African head of state to appoint a female prime minister, and few others have done so since.

Why, then, is the Bokassa name the incarnation of evil? Why is his place in the triumvirate of tyranny (along with Idi Amin and Macias Nguema) so firmly established? The answer lies in the newsworthiness of his activities and alleged activities, especially those that fed into the Western stereotype of the madcap African ruler. Bokassa was a media event, not only because of his women and his coronation, but because of his reported cannibalism, his throwing his enemies to lions and crocodiles, and his beating schoolchildren to death. It was these much-publicized manifestations of his cruelty that fostered his enduring odious reputation. Let us examine these allegations once more.

The question of cannibalism is a difficult one since it involves one of the persistent negative images of Africa in developed countries. Whether the practice exists or not is hardly the point. What matters is what is believed about it. In Centrafrique the idea persists that those who eat human flesh take on the spiritual strength of the deceased, live long lives, and acquire extraordinary powers. Bokassa was happy to see stories of his cannibalism circulating while he was in power. It suited him to have people believe that human flesh had given him omnipotence, sexual vigour, clairvoyance, and the gift of many lives. It cultivated an atmosphere of fear, it discouraged those who sought to replace him, and with people disappearing without a trace, it was easy to think that their bodies were being taken for dark practices. But once Bokassa was out of power, the stories of his peculiar eating habits no longer served his interests. In fact, they did the opposite. They discredited him thoroughly and thwarted all efforts at a political comeback. Small wonder that he now vigorously denied them.

In all likelihood, there was nothing to the stories in the first place beyond a ruse to intimidate the population. At the 1986–87 trial no credible witness came forward to testify to Bokassa's cannibalism, and the court cleared him of the charge. The wild reports in the press following Opération Barracuda – cadavers in the freezer and so forth – were most probably the result of a deliberate smear campaign by the SDECE and its *agent provocateur* Jacques Duchemin. In order to justify their blatant invasion of the empire, the French had to destroy the reputation of its ruler. Alexandre de Marenches, head of the secret service at the time, admitted several years later that his men had sought evidence of cannibalism in vain: "The most improbable stories have been told about him [Bokassa]. We even looked in the refrigerator of the presidential palace to see if it contained human flesh, but there was not any."[21]

Much the same can be said about those who allegedly died in the jaws of lions or crocodiles. After his fall, Bokassa explained that he had kept the creatures at the Villa Kolongo as part of a zoo for the Romanian. This is the most believable explanation. Even so, he was heard at times to threaten people with the pond or the cage, and so the stories began to make the rounds. The lions and crocodiles became part of the terror apparatus, part of Central African folklore, but there is no evidence that anyone was ever fed to them. At the Villa Kolongo today, guides still spin tales of midnight trials and of victims dispatched to a grisly fate. It is well to be sceptical of such claims, as with many things one hears in Bangui.

If there were wild and exaggerated stories spread about his cruelty after his fall, Bokassa had only himself to blame. After all, it was he who had made remarks about voodoo, cannibalism, and crocodiles in order to frighten and shock people. He planted fear and reaped the consequences. Moreover, he was certainly not blameless. His responsibility for the repression of 1979 and for death of dozens, if not hundreds, of students is not in question. But his personal participation in the killings is another matter. The Mission de constatation considered his participation to be "almost certain," but no witnesses were found during the lengthy trial of 1986–87 to corroborate it. The image of Bokassa beating schoolchildren to death and gouging out their eyes endures because of the reports circulated by French journalist Bernard Loubat, which have been repeated uncritically by Jeff Harman, Alex Shoumatoff, and others.

The student demonstrations and their bloody dispersal in 1979 would probably have gone unnoticed had Bokassa been an unknown president of an unimportant state. Incidents of this sort happen frequently enough in Africa without international repercussions.[22] Such was Bokassa's reputation, however, that the repression attracted unusual attention and set off a course of events that led to his fall.

Nevertheless, the emperor's reputation was at least partially deserved, and it would be fair to say that 1966–79 was a dark age of uncertainty and arbitrary violence for the Central African people. Sadly, Bokassa was not the only African ruler to behave in this way, and he was by no means the worst. It might be well to conclude by giving him the last word on the subject, since he was tormented by a sense of unjust victimization throughout his years of exile and imprisonment: "Seul Bokassa a tué? Les autres n'ont pas tué? Non vraiment, il faut être juste ... On m'a présenté comme un monstre en inventant cette histoire de cannibalisme parce que l'on voulait ma peau. C'est cela la vérité."[23]

Notes

PREFACE

1 Soyinka, *Opera Wonyosi*, 2.
2 This is the title given to the essay on Bokassa in Shoumatoff, *African Madness*.
3 Decalo, *Psychoses of Power*, 15.
4 Wiseman, *Political Leaders in Black Africa*, 33.
5 Decalo's *Psychoses of Power* is, of course, the best example of this but there are numerous others: Patrick Chabal's "Introduction: Thinking about Politics in Africa," in his *Political Domination in Africa*, 2; Chaliand, *The Struggle for Africa*, 8; Hodder-Williams, *An Introduction to the Politics of Tropical Africa*, 114; Jackson and Rosberg, *Personal Rule in Black Africa*, 240–4.
6 Stone, "The Revival of Narrative," 22.
7 Jackson and Rosberg, *Personal Rule in Black Africa*, 3.
8 Chabal, "Introduction: Thinking about Politics in Africa," 3–4.
9 Stone, "The Revival of Narrative," 4.
10 Bayart, *L'Etat en Afrique*; Coquery-Vidrovitch, *Afrique noire*.

CHAPTER ONE

1 Gide, *Voyage au Congo*, 99–100.
2 O'Ballance, *The Story of the French Foreign Legion*, 42–60, 98–104, 115–31.
3 Hargraves, "British and French Imperialism in West Africa, 1885–1898," 261–82.
4 Thompson and Adloff, *The Emerging States of French Equatorial Africa*, 6–9.
5 Echenberg, *Colonial Conscripts*, 88; Foltz, "Africa in Great-Power Strategy," in Foltz and Bienen, *Arms and the African*, 7.

6 The name was derived from the Oubangui River, a major tributary of the Congo, which formed the territory's southern boundary. The Chari was another river, and it flowed in a northwesterly direction to empty into Lake Tchad. Gide described the Chari as "cet étrange fleuve qui tourne le dos à la mer" (*Voyage au Congo*, 119).

7 No reliable census was carried out during the period of French rule. Enumeration was associated in the popular mind with taxation and the hated policy of forced labour, and hence was resisted. In December 1962 the population was given as 1,279,642, but President Dacko's census of 1965 produced a total of 2,088,000. The latter figure is believed to be exaggerated by at least a half million (Kalck, *The Central African Republic*, 9).

8 Ibid., 11–26, 46–56.

9 The Brazzaville–Pointe Noire railway was the one major investment in transportation systems, and it was built by a whole army of forced labourers (Sautter, "Le chemin de fer Congo-Océan, 1921–34").

10 For a detailed analysis of the concessionary companies and their "regime," see Coquery-Vidrovitch, *Le Congo français au temps des grandes compagnies concessionaires, 1898–1930*.

11 "To produce the largest possible quantity … of colonial products at the lowest possible price" (Marseille, *Empire colonial et capitalisme français*, 218–28).

12 The fullest account of this war is given in Nzabakomada, *L'Afrique centrale insurgée*. For a shorter, English narrative, see O'Toole, "The 1928–1931 Gbaya Insurrection in Ubangi-Shari."

13 Kalck, *The Central African Republic*, 75.

14 The date of Bokassa's birth is actually unknown since circumstances at the time did not require his parents to register the arrival of their son. Many years later, in 1962, a local tribunal of three dignitaries declared 22 February to be the official date. This suited Bokassa because, once in power, he was able to turn his birthday into a national celebration (Baccard, *Les martyrs de Bokassa*, 16).

15 The details of Bokassa's early life and military career are found in his suppressed autobiography, *Ma vérité*.

16 De Lusignan, *French-Speaking Africa*, 7–8.

17 Delpey, *La manipulation*, 166–7.

18 Bokassa, *Ma vérité*, 18. Translations from books written in French and interviews conducted in French have all been done by the author.

19 Echenberg, *Colonial Conscripts*, 105–23.

20 W.B. Cohen, *Rulers of Empire*, 166–7.

21 Mortimer, *France and the Africans*, 75–6.

22 De Lusignan, *French-Speaking Africa*, 11–12. He gives the figure of 80,000 dead in Madagascar.

23 Kalck, *The Central African Republic*, 75–8.
24 M'Bokolo, "French Colonial Policy in Equatorial Africa in the 1940s and 1950s," 199–200.
25 Mortimer, *France and the Africans*, 267–83.
26 W.B. Cohen, *Rulers of Empire*, 185–6.
27 Mortimer, *France and the Africans*, 267–83.
28 De Lusignan, *French-Speaking Africa*, 13–19.
29 A useful summary of these developments is found in Kalck, "Panorama de l'histoire centrafricaine."
30 Thompson and Adloff, *Emerging States*, 395–6.
31 Péan, *Bokassa Ier*, 55–6. See also "L'enquête sur la mort de M. Boganda," *L'Express*, 7 May 1959, 12.
32 Decalo, *Psychoses of Power*, 140–2.
33 De Lusignan, *French-Speaking Africa*, 29–37; Mortimer, *France and the Africans*, 362–9.
34 Kalck, *The Central African Republic*, 119.
35 Collier, *Regimes in Tropical Africa*, 29–34.

CHAPTER TWO

1 There is a fascinating biography of Foccart by French investigative journalist Pierre Péan, *L'homme de l'ombre*. Purchasers of the book will be surprised to find a little note inserted between its pages by Foccart protesting against the invasion of his privacy. He was allowed to do this in a legal judgment handed down on 16 November 1990.
2 For a glimpse of this world, see Faligot and Krop, *La Piscine*.
3 Kalck, *The Central African Republic*, 130.
4 O'Toole, *The Central African Republic*, 46.
5 Médard, "The Underdeveloped State in Tropical Africa: Political Clientelism or Neo-patrimonialism?" 183.
6 Clapham, "Clientelism and the State," in his *Private Patronage and Public Power*, 14.
7 Collier, *Regimes in Tropical Africa*, 119–21.
8 Welch, "The Roots and Implications of Military Intervention," in his *Soldier and State in Africa*, 18–21.
9 In the 1959–60 academic year, only 40 per cent of school-aged children were receiving elementary instruction. The country had one *lycée* in Bangui staffed by nineteen European teachers, twelve of whom were university graduates. There was virtually no technical education of any sort. See Maïdou et al., *Philosophie de l'Opération Bokassa*, 2:154–60.
10 The bureaucratic explosion occurred in most post-independence African states as the demand for work in the civil service and parastatal agencies grew. In Senegal, for example, state employment grew from

10,000 at independence to 61,000 in 1973 (Williams, *Political Corruption in Africa*, 44).

11 Zoctizoum, *Histoire de la Centrafrique*, 2:23–4.

12 Serre, "Six ans de gouvernement Dacko." Dacko's homily was certainly preferable to that of his neighbour, President Mobutu of Congo/Zaïre, who once advised government party workers, "If you steal, do not steal too much at one time. You may be arrested. Steal cleverly, little by little" (Manning, *Francophone Sub-Saharan Africa*, 198).

13 Interview, Theodore Ngoulé (former Dacko minister), Paris, April 1990.

14 Andreski, *The African Predicament*, 92; Williams, *Political Corruption in Africa*, 45–6.

15 Clayton, "Foreign Intervention in Africa," 205–6.

16 Bokassa, *Ma vérité*, 21.

17 Péan, *Bokassa Ier*, 15.

18 Interview, David Dacko, Bangui, March 1990. Dacko's precautionary measures were similar to those of Ghana's Kwame Nkrumah, who had his own presidential guard to counter threats from the regular forces (Bretton, *The Rise and Fall of Kwame Nkrumah*, 204n7).

19 Bokassa, *Ma vérité*, 24.

20 Ibid., 25.

21 Péan, *Bokassa Ier*, 15.

22 Baccard, *Les martyrs de Bokassa*, 22.

23 Several sources (Decalo, Péan, for example) claim that Izamo, Adama-Tamboux, and other Dacko "loyalists" were hatching their own plots against the president at year's end. The evidence for this is rather thin. It seems to have originated with Bokassa's oft-repeated claim that he seized power to pre-empt an Izamo coup.

24 Bokassa, *Ma vérité*, 26–7.

25 Several detailed and sometimes contradictory accounts of the coup are available, including Bokassa's own self-serving version. Particularly valuable are those of Baccard, *Les martyrs de Bokassa*, 15–32, and Bigo, *Pouvoir et obéissance en Centrafrique*, 48–53. My reconstruction is based on these accounts, supplemented by interviews with Dacko and others in Bangui.

26 Quoted in Loubat, *L'ogre de Berengo*, 13.

27 Later, Bokassa denied all knowledge of Izamo's death, claiming that the police chief had in fact escaped from detention and disappeared (Delpey, *La manipulation*, 171–4).

28 Interview, David Dacko, Bangui, March 1990.

29 Kalck, *The Central African Republic*, 158. It is worth observing that at this time Tombalbaye was facing a growing rebellion in the northern part of Tchad.

30 Baccard, *Les martyrs de Bokassa*, 37–8.

31 Decalo, *Coups and Army Rule in Africa*, 3–21. The literature on this topic is vast and does not warrant review here. Several good essays, including one by Decalo, are found in Baynham, *Military Power and Politics in Black Africa*.

CHAPTER THREE

1 These photographs are in the Agence France-Presse collection in Paris.
2 Bigo, *Pouvoir et obéissance*, 9.
3 See "Acte constitutionnel no. 2 du 8 janvier 1966 fixant l'organisation provisoire de pouvoirs de la République," in Maïdou et al., *Philosophie de l'Opération Bokassa*, 2:236–8. The Revolutionary Council soon became known simply as the Council of Ministers.
4 "Bokassa and the Chinese," *West Africa*, 15 January 1966, 77; "Dacko and Bokassa," *West Africa*, 12 February 1966, 186. Denunciations of corruption and embezzlement following regime changes seem to be a standard practice in Africa. Not only do they justify the coup but they attempt to root out rival factions in control of public institutions. It is often a prelude to embezzlement by the new power brokers (Bayart, *The State in Africa*, 226–7).
5 For an update on the practice, see "Circoncision féminine: La tradition à quel prix?" *Afrique magazine*, October 1990, 84–8.
6 These groups have now disappeared, but Bangui retains a lively musical scene, especially in the nightclubs around Kilomètre 5.
7 Kalck, *The Central African Republic*, 159–64.
8 Soffer, *Le diamant noir*, 205.
9 Decalo, *Psychoses of Power*, 149.
10 For a firsthand account of life in Ngaragba, see Gallo, *N'Garagba, maison des morts*. An excellent analysis is also found in Bigo, "Ngaragba, l'impossible prison." In addition, I interviewed survivors of the prison in Bangui.
11 Interview, David Dacko, Bangui, March 1990.
12 Kalck, *The Central African Republic*, 167–8.
13 Many of the details of Banza's downfall and the elimination of his family came out in Bokassa's trial in 1986–87. The account found in Baccard, *Les martyrs de Bokassa*, 69–89, is also instructive.
14 Interviews with several informants, Bangui, February 1990.
15 Bokassa, *Philosophie de l'Opération Bokassa*, 1:87–8.
16 Bigo, *Pouvoir et obéissance*, 54–5.
17 Bokassa, *Philosophie de l'Opération Bokassa*, 1:103.
18 "La république de Bokassa," *Jeune Afrique*, 19 August 1972, 16–17.
19 Péan, *Bokassa Ier*, 79–80. In fact, Bokassa's rather flippant characterization of the U.N. secretary general was not far off the mark. In 1986,

during Waldheim's successful campaign for the presidency of Austria, it was revealed that he had deported Balkan Jews to Nazi death camps during the Second World War.

20 Bigo, *Pouvoir et obéissance*, 112.

21 The details of M'Bongo's death were discussed in detail many years later at Bokassa's trial.

22 The Lingoupou case also was the subject of much discussion at Bokassa's trial.

23 Interviews, Bangui, February 1990.

24 Ibid.

CHAPTER FOUR

1 "Un châtelain nommé Bokassa," *Jeune Afrique*, 15–22 August 1984, 36–40.

2 Bokassa, *Ma vérité*, 153.

3 Delpey, *La manipulation*, 193–4.

4 Interview, Jacques Duchemin, Paris, April 1990.

5 Péan, *Bokassa Ier*, 25, 28.

6 Ibid., 36; "Le Président Bokassa maréchal," *L'année politique africaine*, 1974, 18–20.

7 "Bokassades," *Jeune Afrique*, 3 October 1979, 38–9.

8 Interviewed in Werner Herzog documentary film, *Echos d'un sombre empire*, 1991.

9 Interview, Georges Bokassa, Paris, April 1990.

10 Bokassa, *Ma vérité*, 54.

11 Péan, *Bokassa Ier*, 26–7; "Le Président Bokassa maréchal," *L'année politique africaine*, 1974, 18–20.

12 "Bokassades," *Jeune Afrique*, 3 October 1979, 38–9.

13 Interview, Georges Bokassa, Paris, April 1990.

14 Baccard, *Les martyrs de Bokassa*, 129.

15 Shoumatoff, *African Madness*, 105.

16 "Etre ambassadeur à Bangui," *Le Monde*, 21 September 1979, 1, 4.

17 Interview, Martine Bokassa, Nancy, May 1990.

18 This episode is recounted by Thierry-Jacques Gallo, one of those arrested, in his *N'Garagba, maison des morts*, 15–27.

19 Considering the victory of the communist forces in the Vietnam War in 1975, it is doubly unlikely that she would have returned to Saigon, now Ho Chi Minh City.

20 The story of the two Martines is well known and has become part of Central African folklore. Bokassa's version is found in Delpey, *La manipulation*, 196–203. The most complete account is in Baccard, *Les martyrs de Bokassa*, 184–215.

21 The Shah, for instance, was a generous patron of Madame Claude's call-girl service in Paris (Shawcross, *The Shah's Last Ride*, 96).

22 Médard, "The Underdeveloped State in Tropical Africa," 172.

CHAPTER FIVE

1 Zoctizoum, *Histoire de la Centrafrique*, 252–79.

2 Declaring his support for Houphouët-Boigny's controversial dialogue with Pretoria, Bokassa sent a delegation to South Africa in February 1975. This resulted in a loan of 4 million rand for the construction of a hotel complex in Bangui ("Mme. Domicien premier ministre," *L'année politique africaine*, 1975, 16–19).

3 For a brief overview of Bokassa's foreign policy, see Cornevin, "La politique étrangère du gouvernement de Bangui."

4 "Diary," *West Africa*, 1 March 1969, 244.

5 Péan, *Bokassa Ier*, 46.

6 Jarry, *The Ubu Plays*.

7 Giscard, *Le pouvoir et la vie*, 292–3.

8 Interview, former French government official, Paris, October 1989.

9 Bigo, *Pouvoir et obéissance*, 121; Zoctizoum, *Histoire de la Centrafrique*, 35–9.

10 Bokassa, *Philosophie de l'Opération Bokassa*, 1:121. Although Bokassa's name was on the cover as author, the book was written by a committee of his ministers headed by Henri Maïdou. The second volume, which appeared in 1976, credited Maïdou and the others with the authorship.

11 Interestingly enough, these figures were given in Maïdou et al., *Philosophie de l'Opération Bokassa*, 2:96–8.

12 Bigo, *Pouvoir et obéissance*, 117; Péan, *Bokassa Ier*, 75; "Le Président Bokassa maréchal," *L'année politique africaine*, 1974, 18–20.

13 Ardagh, *France in the 1980s*, 620; Bruno, *La saga des Giscard*, 15–18; Frears, *France in the Giscard Presidency*, 39.

14 Giscard, *Le pouvoir et la vie*, 295–7.

15 Delpey, *La manipulation*, 216–23. During the 1970s the safari-tourism business was controlled almost exclusively by French concerns. One notable operation was Safaris Jean d'Orgeix, which had an exclusive hunting concession to a 17,500 km² area around Birao. See d'Orgeix's memoirs, *J'étais un Africain blanc*.

16 Bruno, *La saga des Giscard*, 225–9; "Un patrimoine étroitement lié aux sociétés opérant outre-mer," *Le Monde*, 11 October 1979, 9.

17 Giscard, *Le pouvoir et la vie*, 299–302.

18 The Bangui summit was, in fact, the second in the series. The first had been hosted by President Pompidou in Paris in November 1973. They

have been held annually ever since, alternating between France and African countries (Martin, "The Historical, Economic, and Political Bases of France's African Policy," 202).

19 "Communiqué sur la visite du Président Giscard d'Estaing en République centrafricaine," 8 March 1975, *La politique étrangère de la France: Textes et documents*, 1er semestre 1975, 108–9.

20 *Paris Match*, 22 March 1975, did a special on the summit and on Bokassa and his family. In typical *Match* fashion, it featured memorable photographs of the children and wives, including Gabriella, "la Roumaine."

21 For a detailed analysis of France's reliance on nuclear energy, see Samy Cohen, *La monarchie nucléaire*.

22 Péan, *Bokassa Ier*, 127–32; Zoctizoum, *Histoire de la Centrafrique*, 216–18.

23 Bruno, *La saga des Giscard*, 239–49; "Treize Giscard à table," *Canard enchaîné*, 9 May 1979, 4.

24 Kalck, *The Central African Republic*, 159–60.

25 Interview, former official of the Taillerie nationale de diamant, Bangui, March 1990.

26 Péan, *Bokassa Ier*, 91–5.

27 Diamond Distributors Inc. had been operating in the country since 1947 and was not ready to give up so easily. Its director, Albert Jolis, grimly tolerated occasional confiscations and kept coming back for more. Later, he would get a revenge of sorts on Bokassa (see chapter 6).

28 Delpey, *La manipulation*, 216–17.

29 Zoctizoum, *Histoire de la Centrafrique*, 220–30.

30 Prioul, "Industrie et commerce en RCA," 413.

31 Zoctizoum, *Histoire de la Centrafrique*, 278–9.

32 Many details of Bokassa's wealth and business activies came out at his trial. I visited the properties in question when I was in Bangui. Pacifique 2 was occupied at the time by Rassemblement démocratique centrafricain, President Kolingba's political party.

33 Bigo, *Pouvoir et obéissance*, 122.

34 Delpey, *La manipulation*, 206. Bokassa still owns most of these châteaux, and I was invited to visit some of them in 1990.

35 Maïdou et al., *Philosophie de l'Opération Bokassa*, 2:140.

36 Péan, *Bokassa Ier*, 96.

37 There are several dozen renditions of Gadhaffi's name from Arabic into Roman script. The version that I have chosen has no special claim to orthodoxy.

38 Baccard, *Les martyrs de Bokassa*, 219–23.

39 "S.M. Bokassa Ier," *L'année politique africaine*, 1976, 16–20.

40 Kennedy, *African Capitalism*, 73–5.

CHAPTER SIX

1 Lamb, *The Africans*, 201–3.
2 Péan, *Bokassa Ier*, 100.
3 Mobutu's quest for authenticity led him to change his country's name from the Congo to Zaïre and to ban Christmas and European attire. He also dropped his given names, Joseph Desiré, to become Mobutu Sese Seko Kuku Ngbendu Waza Banga.
4 Interview, former French government official, Paris, May 1990.
5 Interview, former imperial cabinet minister, Bangui, February 1990.
6 "Bokassa Ier ou la folie des grandeurs," *Jeune Afrique*, 17 December 1976, 17–21.
7 Interview, David Dacko, Bangui, March 1990.
8 Interview, Georges Bokassa, Paris, April 1990. Georges was part of the Central African delegation to China.
9 "Premières pages d'une chronique impériale," *Jeune Afrique*, 24 December 1976, 30. In statements to the media Bokassa encouraged the notion that he might retire (for example, "Cartes sur table," Antenne 2 television show, broadcast 23 November 1977, featuring an interview with Bokassa).
10 Péan, *Bokassa Ier*, 162.
11 Interview, Georges Bokassa, Paris, April 1990.
12 Baccard, *Les martyrs de Bokassa*, 238–47. Additional information was supplied by David Dacko, Georges Bokassa, and others.
13 Interview, Georges Bokassa, Paris, April 1990.
14 "Papa Bok: Self-Styled Emperor of Central Africa ... and the Amazing Story of His Casual Brutality to a British Journalist," *Sunday Times*, 21 August 1977, 17A.
15 "Cartes sur table," Antenne 2 television show, 23 November 1977.
16 Péan, *Bokassa Ier*, 167–70.
17 Bokassa, *Ma vérité*, 173–6.
18 "Préparatifs pour un sacre," *Jeune Afrique*, 12 August 1977, 16–19.
19 Stunning colour photographs of the clothes are featured in "Bokassa reçoit Paris Match," *Paris Match*, 11 November 1977, 54–9.
20 Epstein, *The Rise and Fall of Diamonds*, 240–2.
21 Interview, Georges Bokassa, Paris, April 1990.
22 Lamb, *The Africans*, 51.
23 In fact, the sabre dated from the Second Empire of Napoléon III and was bought in a store specializing in military antiques on the rue de Miromesnil in Paris. The "joke" was Journiac's idea (Giscard, *Le pouvoir et la vie*, 304).
24 "L'heure empereur," *Jeune Afrique*, 16 December 1977, 81.

25 Two useful descriptions of the coronation ceremony are Crabb, "The Coronation of Emperor Bokassa," and Harmon, "His Former Majesty, Bokassa." Bokassa's own version is found in *Ma vérité*, 43–53. Roger Delpey allowed me to examine various memorabilia from the event in his private collection, including official invitations and the program of events. The Institut national de l'audiovisuel in Paris has excellent film footage of the ceremony and related events.

26 Giscard, *Le pouvoir et la vie*, 305.

27 Shawcross, *The Shah's Last Ride*, 38–44.

CHAPTER SEVEN

•

1 The residential quarters of Berengo are now abandoned and in ruins. Some of the farms and factories are being used to train young people by the Service civique nationale pour la promotion des jeunes. The entire complex is open to visitors, and I went there in February 1990 during my stay in the Central African Republic.

2 "L'empire de Bokassa ébranlé," *Jeune Afrique*, 31 January 1979, 18–19.

3 Péan, *Bokassa Ier*, 21.

4 Bokassa, *Ma vérité*, 53.

5 I have a piece of this letterhead in my personal collection of imperial memorabilia.

6 Interview, Ange Patassé, Paris, October 1989.

7 Bigo, *Pouvoir et obéissance*, 135–7.

8 "Efficiency in the Empire," *New African*, September 1978, 53–4.

9 "Bokassa's Bankrupt Empire," *New African*, March 1979, 19–21.

10 "Bokassa à l'éprouve du protocole," *Jeune Afrique*, 17 May 1978, 31; "Ce cher collègue," *Jeune Afrique*, 7 June 1978, 31.

11 "The Emperor's Wet Clothes," *Times*, 20 June 1978, 7.

12 Giscard, *Le pouvoir et la vie*, 309–10.

13 Moose, "French Military Policy in Africa," 70–6.

14 Interview, Georges Bokassa, Paris, April 1990.

CHAPTER EIGHT

1 Kodro, "Où en sont les droits de l'homme et de la femme en Centrafrique?"

2 Interview, former imperial cabinet minister, Bangui, February 1990.

3 "Un profond malaise," *Le Monde*, 24 January 1978, 8.

4 Men and women who work for various government departments participated in these events and described them to me.

5 Several erroneous accounts of the events circulated afterwards, largely based on poorly researched newspaper stories. See, for example,

Decalo, *Psychoses of Power*, 162, where he claims that the repression was the work of 300 Zaïrean troops called in by Bokassa when his imperial guards proved unequal to the task.

6 "Dieu, l'argent et moi, votre papa," *Jeune Afrique*, 14 March 1979, 71–2.

7 Interviews, former students, Bangui, February 1990.

8 My reconstruction of these disturbances is based on the common elements in a number of conflicting accounts and interpretations, supplemented by my own interviews in Bangui. See, for instance, Bigo, *Pouvoir et obéissance*, 192–201; Delpey, *La manipulation*, 25–37; and "Les cent jours qui ont ébranlé l'empire," *Jeune Afrique*, 20 June 1979, 15–17.

9 Gallo, *N'Garagba, maison des morts*, 123–9.

10 Baccard, *Les martyrs de Bokassa*, 297–307.

11 Loubat, *L'ogre de Berengo*, 159–65. It is hard to take Loubat's claim seriously, since his book is filled with incidents which are difficult to believe and which I found impossible to verify.

12 I am taking into account here the fact that no witness came forward during the 1986–87 trial to testify to Bokassa's personally killing students in 1979. Reasonable doubt does exist, but it has not prevented writers from condemning the emperor unequivocally. According to Decalo, "hundreds of children were undescriminately [sic] bayoneted. Several hundred more were arrested only to be tortured and killed in prison – some by Bokassa himself" *(Psychoses of Power*, 163).

13 "Le dernier combat de Bokassa Ier," *Jeune Afrique*, 23 May 1979, 18–19.

14 Independent of political, economic, and religious influences, Amnesty International opposes torture and the death penalty, and campaigns for the release of prisoners of conscience. Its annual report is a chilling indictment of human rights abuses around the world. The scourge of tyrants everywhere, it was given long-overdue recognition in 1977 when it was awarded the Nobel Peace Prize.

15 "L'alibi de Kigali," *Jeune Afrique*, 6 June 1979, 17.

16 Interview, former French government official, Paris, October 1989; Giscard, *Le pouvoir et la vie*, 313–15.

17 "Réponses de M. Jean François-Poncet, ministre des Affaires étrangères, à des questions d'actualité," *La politique étrangère de la France: Textes et documents*, 2ème trimestre, 1979, 107.

18 "Sylvestre Bangui: Pourquoi maintenant?" *Jeune Afrique*, 6 June 1979, 16.

19 In Bokassa's own account of the Kigali summit (*Ma vérité*, 61–71), he claimed that the investigation was his idea. This is completely at odds with all other accounts.

20 "Bokassa accusé," *Paris Match*, 1 June 1979, 60–1.

21 OCAM was the acronym for Organisation commune africaine et malgache, which sought to create a common trading market between francophone states in Africa. Its headquarters were in Bangui.

22 "Une victoire des droits de l'homme," *Jeune Afrique*, 3 October 1979, 42–7. The article consists of a lengthy interview with Youssoupha N'Diaye.

23 Interview, Jacques Duchemin, Paris, April 1990. When I asked him about his role in the SDECE, he remained curiously evasive but did not deny it. Today he describes himself as a consultant. For a glimpse of Duchemin's activies in Katanga in the early 1960s, see Péan, *L'homme de l'ombre*, 299–302.

24 "Le 'sauveur' de Bokassa," *Jeune Afrique*, 12 September 1979, 47–52.

25 The book was a minor success and served to whet French appetites for lurid accounts of Bokassa's excesses. Duchemin told me that Bob Guccione, publisher of *Penthouse* magazine, was so impressed that he contemplated basing a movie on it: "Caligula II."

26 Interview, Roger Delpey, Paris, April 1990.

27 The text was published by Bokassa in the appendices of *Ma vérité*, 181.

28 "M. Jean François-Poncet au Club de la presse," *La politique étrangère de la France: Textes et documents*, 3ème trimestre 1979, 21–2.

29 Galley was a regular visitor to the empire, where he indulged his great passion for collecting butterflies. He also had a family connection of sorts. In 1960 he had married Jeanne Leclerc de Hautecloque, daughter of Maréchal Leclerc, the man who had organized the Free French army in Equatorial Africa in 1940. These connections tended to make him less critical of Bokassa.

30 Interview, David Dacko, Bangui, March 1990.

31 "Bokassa a … des successeurs," *Jeune Afrique*, 27 June 1979, 21–2.

32 "M. René Journiac, successeur discret de M. Foccart," *Le Monde*, 29 September 1979, 3; H. Machin, "The President's Men," 95.

33 "Largage d'un empereur," *Jeune Afrique*, 14 November 1979, 41–4.

34 *Rapport de la Mission de constatation des événements de Bangui*, 3.

35 "Un château en Ile de France," *Jeune Afrique*, 12 September 1979, 51.

CHAPTER NINE

1 "L'opposition dénonce une nouvelle vague de répression," *Le Monde*, 18 September 1979, 14.

2 "Communiqué publié par le ministère de la Coopération," 17 August 1979, *La politique étrangère de la France: Textes et documents*, 3ème trimestre, 1979, 58.

3 Giscard, *Le pouvoir et la vie*, 318–20.

4 Interview, French Ministry of Defence official, Paris, October 1989.

5 Interview, former French government official, Paris, May 1990; "La semaine où tout s'est joué," *Jeune Afrique*, 3 October 1979, 24–9.

6 Interview, David Dacko, Bangui, March 1990.

7 Ockrent, *Dans le secret des princes*, 161–5; "Bangui: Opération Barracuda," *L'Express*, 6 October 1979, 66–8.

8 Giscard, *Le pouvoir et la vie*, 300, 321, 323.

9 This reconstruction is based on Bokassa's own account found in Delpey, *La manipulation*, 111–22, and on the testimony of another participant now resident in the Central African Republic.

10 There may have been a deliberate irony in the choice of name. A French company that makes camouflage for the army is also called Barracuda. It was founded by Jacques Foccart.

11 Ockrent, *Dans le secret des princes*, 161–80; "Sur la chute de Bokassa," *Jeune Afrique*, 14 November 1979, 44–52.

12 Quoted in Loubat, *L'ogre de Berengo*, 13–14.

13 Interview, Georges Bokassa, Paris, April 1990. He told me that he and other members of the family then resident in France were watched carefully by the police in the months ahead.

14 "Déclaration à France-Inter de M. Alain Peyrefitte, Garde des Sceaux, à propos de l'ex-empereur Bokassa," 22 September 1979, *La politique étrangère de la France: Textes et documents*, 3ème trimestre, 1979, 78.

15 "Galley: 'La France est intervenue à la demande des Centrafricains,'" *France-Soir*, 26 September 1979, 4.

16 The reconstruction of the events at Evreux is based on Bokassa's own version as found in *Ma vérité*, 9–14, and in Delpey, *La manipulation*, 122–46. I also interviewed one of the other Central African participants.

CHAPTER TEN

1 "Hold-up du siècle à Bangui," *Canard enchaîné*, 10 January 1980, 1.

2 On 12 October, speaking at a luncheon meeting organized by the Association de la presse étrangère, Jean François-Poncet denied that archives had been taken from Berengo. He also denied it in the National Assembly on 23 November. See *La politique étrangère de la France: Textes et documents*, 4ème trimestre 1979, 34, 115–16.

3 "Bokassa anthropophage?" *France-Soir*, 26 September 1979, 4; "Des cadavres dans les réfrigérateurs de l'empereur," *Le Monde*, 26 September 1979, 3; "Bokassa's Crocodiles Ate His Enemies," *Daily Telegraph*, 2 October 1979, 3D; "Bokassa Ministers Dined on Body of Colleague," *Daily Telegraph*, 3 October 1979, 5A.

4 *Canard enchaîné*, 3 October 1979, 3.

5 Interviews, several informants, Bangui, February 1990.

6 Interview, Theodore Ngoulé, Paris, April 1990.

7 Interview, Georges Bokassa, Paris, April 1990.

8 Bouchet, *L'aventure Tapie*, 97–101; "L'homme qui a roulé Bokassa," *Jeune Afrique*, 9 January 1980, 56–7.

9 Bokassa, *Ma vérité*, 115–17.

10 Bouchet, *L'aventure Tapie*, 101–02.

11 In truth, the legal judgment was but a temporary setback in the mete-
oric rise of "Takeover Tapie." Ever since, he has been expanding his
business empire, and he did launch a political career. Much of what he
turns to, however, including his soccer team, Olympique Marseilles,
becomes embroiled in scandal.

12 A standard argument of Jean François-Poncet was that French aid was
given to the people of Africa, not to governments. He also denied that
aid to Centrafrique had been diverted from its intended purpose (Communiqué, Commission des Affaires étrangères de l'Assemblé nationale,
11 October 1979, *La politique étrangère de la France: Textes et documents*,
4ème trimestre 1979, 27).

13 The *Canard* was founded in 1916 for the amusement of soldiers in the
trenches. In 1959, when de Gaulle was trying to muzzle parliament
and the media, Roger Frezzoz became editor and redirected the newspaper towards investigative journalism.

14 *Canard enchaîné*, 17 October 1979, 1.

15 Giscard, *Le pouvoir et la vie*, 331–4.

16 Bokassa reproduced this document in the appendices of *Ma vérité*
(209). It could, of course, be a fake. Some independent sources in Paris,
however, believe that Catherine did spend time at the clinic in question.

17 Delpey, *La manipulation*, 175–223.

18 The reference was to the American hostages then being held in Teheran.

19 "Une heure avec le Président de la République," 27 November 1979, *La
politique étrangère de la France: Textes et documents*, 4ème trimestre 1979,
124–5.

20 *Canard enchaîné*, 19 December 1979, 1.

21 Interview, Roger Delpey, Paris, April 1990.

22 Giscard, *Le pouvoir et la vie*, 344.

23 The letter appears in the appendices of Delpey, *La manipulation*, 250–3.

24 Delpey, *Prisonnier de Giscard*, 9–19.

25 The State Security Court was established by de Gaulle in 1962 at the
height of the Algerian crisis. Functioning outside of the regular judicial
system, it is responsible for such crimes as treason, espionage, conspiracies, attacks on state security and attacks on the integrity of the
national territory.

26 "Bokassa téléphone au Canard," *Canard enchaîné*, 17 September 1980, 3,
4.

27 Interview, Roger Delpey, Paris, April 1990.

28 "Giscard libère son prisonnier," *Le quotidien de Paris*, 29 November
1980, 1; "Bokassa Innocence Is Claimed in Interviews," *Times*, 9 December 1980, 6A.

29 Interview, Roger Delpey, Paris, April 1990.

30 Giscard, *Le pouvoir et la vie*, 347.

31 Wright, *Continuity and Change in France*, 1–17.
32 "Jeune Afrique fait parler Bokassa," *Jeune Afrique*, 2 September 1981, 14–27. Bokassa made similar remarks in an interview with his old acquaintance Michael Goldsmith ("Bokassa Claims One Million Pound Gifts Helped Defeat Giscard," *Times*, 19 August 1981, 5D).

CHAPTER ELEVEN

1 Interview, Theodore Ngoulé, Paris, April 1990.
2 "Déclaration de M. Stirn, secrétaire d'Etat aux Affaires étrangères, à Radio France Internationale, à propos de Centrafrique," 27 September 1979, *La politique étrangère de la France: Textes et documents*, 3ème trimestre, 1979, 103–4; "Bangui: Les Européens se barricadent," and "Pattassé menace de provoquer des troubles en Centrafrique," *France-Soir*, 28 September 1979, 6.
3 "Et maintenant?" *Jeune Afrique*, 3 October 1979, 40.
4 "Dirty Facts of the Ivory Trade," *Sunday Times*, 22 February 1981, 3A.
5 Bigo, *Pouvoir et obéissance*, 244–54.
6 Interview, Theodore Ngoulé, Paris, April 1990.
7 "Bokassa n'a pas été jugé," *Jeune Afrique*, 7 January 1981, 18–20.
8 "Les méchouis de l'empereur," *Libération*, 25 December 1980, 11.
9 This is a translation from Bokassa's *Ma vérité*, 95–6. Bokassa was quoting an account from an article by Jacques-Marie Bourget published in *VSD*, December 1980. He was showing how ridiculous it was.
10 "Requiem pour six comparses," *Jeune Afrique*, 4 February 1981, 20.
11 "Les héritiers enterrent l'empire," *Jeune Afrique*, 25 March 1981, 18–20.
12 Interview, Theodore Ngoulé, Paris, April 1990.
13 Delpey, *Affaires centrafricaines*, 185–9.
14 "Les rêveries d'un soudard solitaire," *Jeune Afrique*, 24 June 1981, 43.
15 Interview, David Dacko, Bangui, March 1990.
16 Bigo, *Pouvoir et obéissance*, 259–62.
17 Pierre Marion, head of the SDECE at the time, admitted later that French military adviser, Col. Jean-Claude Mantion, played a role in the coup. This suggests a more direct involvement from Paris. See "L'ancien chef des services secrets se met à table," *Jeune Afrique plus*, May–June 1991, 40–55.
18 Interview, former civil servant, Bangui, February 1990.
19 "Bokassa: 'Je vous l'avais bien dit,'" *Jeune Afrique*, 9 September 1981, 28.
20 "Le pouvoir? Non, merci," *Jeune Afrique*, 16 September 1981, 23–5.
21 Interview, Georges Bokassa, Paris, April 1990.
22 Roger Delpey showed this card to me. It is now in his personal archives.
23 "Bokassa: 'L'interdit de Mitterrand,'" *Jeune Afrique*, 23 July 1982, 36–7.

24 In his *Affaires centrafricaines*, Roger Delpey offers an alternative explanation for this episode. According to Delpey, Kolingba was under pressure from France to hold elections, but he was reluctant to do so lest Patassé win. He therefore staged a fake coup in order to get rid of Patassé and to show the French how unstable things were in Centrafrique. My Central African informants consider this theory preposterous.

25 "L'ancien chef des services secrets se met à table," *Jeune Afrique plus*, May–June 1991, 40–55. On 4 April 1982 the SDECE vanished in a major shake-up and reform. It then reappeared as the DGSE (Direction générale de la sécurité extérieure). The role of the new organization was specifically limited to intelligence overseas. In Alexandre de Marenche's time, the SDECE had often operated in France provoking problems with the police and the DST. De Marenches stepped down in May 1981 with Giscard's defeat paving the way for the reform that the socialists had promised.

26 Demafouth, "Landlocked and Uninformed."

27 Bayart, *La politique africaine de François Mitterrand*, 26–48.

28 Roger Delpey has copies of these documents which he kindly showed me.

29 Interview, Georges Bokassa, Paris, April 1990.

30 Interview, Theodore Ngoulé, Paris, April 1990.

CHAPTER TWELVE

1 The actual identity of Bokassa's financial backers can only be surmised. Roger Delpey remains tight-lipped on the subject. According to other informants, the likeliest suspects were businessmen associated with the diamond and ivory trades, elements in the French extreme right, and perhaps even Libya. Jean-Pierre Dupont, an importer of agricultural products from Centrafrique who had done well for himself in Bokassa's day, was a probable contributor.

2 I have one of these leaflets in my collection of imperial memorabilia.

3 Interview, Roger Delpey, Paris, April 1990.

4 "Le rendez-vous manqué de la Caravelle de Bokassa," *Libération*, 29 November 1983, 22. Additional details were supplied by Roger Delpey.

5 A dental surgeon by trade and a personal friend of President Mitterrand, Penne knew virtually nothing about Africa when he was appointed to this key position after the socialist victory in 1981. He remained in office until October 1986, when he resigned over involvement in a scandal connected with the Ministry of Cooperation. See "L'Africain de l'Elysée saute avant le carrefour," *Libération*, 20 October 1986, 2.

6 Bokassa, *Ma vérité*, 108–12. Additional details were supplied by Roger Delpey.

7 "Bokassa: Le retour manqué en Centrafrique," *Libération*, 28 November 1983, 24–5.

8 The agents were members of the Compagnie républicaine de sécurité, one of France's numerous security forces.

9 Interview, Georges Bokassa, Paris, April 1990.

10 "La petite cour de l'empereur," *L'Express*, 7 November 1986, 19.

11 "Un châtelain nommé Bokassa," *Jeune Afrique*, 15–22 August 1984, 36–40.

12 Interview, Christiane Pauvert, Carrère Editions, Paris, September 1989.

13 "Polémique," *Jeune Afrique*, 19 June 1985, 37–8.

14 Bokassa kept two copies for himself, and later they became the possessions of his friend Roger Delpey. Delpey kindly permitted me to photocopy the book when I visited his home west of Paris.

15 I tried to confirm this story on a visit to Tchad but without success. The circumstantial evidence suggests that it is untrue. Hissène Habré was an enemy of the French-backed Malloum regime until August 1978, when he joined a government of national unity. After that time Giscard never went hunting in the Central African Empire.

16 Ardagh, *France in the 1980s*, 358; "Giscard: The Paris Parlour Game," *Time*, 23 December 1974, 25–6.

17 All quotations are from *Ma vérité*. The translations are my own.

18 Interview, Augustine Assemat, Hardricourt, May 1990.

19 Interview, Roger Delpey, Paris, April 1990.

20 Some weeks later, when all had come undone, Bokassa wrote a fourteen-page letter to Roger Delpey describing the circumstances of his return. Delpey allowed me to read this letter. Augustine Assemat also filled in some details.

CHAPTER THIRTEEN

1 "L'énigmatique Colonel Mansion" [*sic*], *Afrique magazine*, October 1991, 55–7.

2 At the time France had *chefs blancs* in several of its other African client states. The role was played by Antoine Caesareo in the Ivory Coast and by Jean Collin in Senegal.

3 Interview, Colonel Jean-Claude Mantion, Bangui, March 1990.

4 Interview, Augustine Assemat, Hardricourt, May 1990.

5 Interview, Georges Bokassa, Paris, April 1990.

6 Interview, Roger Delpey, Paris, April 1990.

7 "L'étrange retour au pays de l'ex-empereur Bokassa," *Libération*, 24 October 1986.

8 "Faut-il exécuter Bokassa?" *Jeune Afrique*, 24 June 1987, 20–1.

9 Gotilogoé withdrew from the defence team before the trial began in earnest.

10 When I asked Szpiner who had paid for his services during the trial, he smiled wryly and replied, "I exercise my right to refuse to answer." He was, however, extremely helpful in discussing other aspects of the hearings.

11 Jean-Baptiste Placca, "Accusé Bokassa, levez-vous!" in Bourgi, *Grands procès*, 20.

12 "Kolingba n'a pas fait oublier Bokassa," *Jeune Afrique*, 3 December 1986.

13 "Le procès Bokassa devant la Cour suprême centrafricaine," *Revue juridique et politique: Indépendance et coopération* 42, no. 1 (1988): 1–28.

14 "Kolingba n'a pas fait oublier Bokassa," *Jeune Afrique*, 3 December 1986.

15 Paris, Institut national de l'audiovisuel, film footage of trial.

16 "Les juges sèchent sur Sa Majesté Bokassa," *Libération*, 28 November 1986.

17 "Dans la vulgarité d'un procès ordinaire," *Jeune Afrique*, 7 January 1987, 38–9.

18 "Bokassa fait son cinéma," *Libération*, 17 December 1986, 18.

19 Interview, Francis Szpiner, Paris, October 1989.

20 "Morts à Ngaragba sans motif connu," *Jeune Afrique*, 21 January 1987, 35–6.

21 Interview, Francis Szpiner, Paris, October 1989.

22 "Bokassa à l'heure du châtiment," *Jeune Afrique*, 17 June 1987, 24–8.

23 "Tristes déballages autour de Bokassa," *Jeune Afrique*, 18 February 1987, 31.

24 Interview, Francis Szpiner, Paris, October 1989.

25 Paris, Institut national de l'audiovisuel, film footage of trial.

26 Interview, Ministry of Justice official, Bangui, February 1990.

27 Interview, Francis Szpiner, Paris, October 1989.

28 They could hardly be blamed when one considers the case of Patrice Zemoniako-Liblakenze, a former mayor of Bangui and an unrepentant Bokassa partisan. When appearing on the witness stand, he gave answers that annoyed the judge and was sentenced to a year in prison for contempt of court.

29 For the concluding part of the trial I have relied on Bigo, *Pouvoir et obéissance*, 294–313, and on interviews, newsreels, and personal observation.

30 Interview, Francis Szpiner, Paris, October 1989.

31 "Faut-il exécuter Bokassa?" *Jeune Afrique*, 24 June 1987, 20–1.

32 "Le procès Bokassa devant la Cour suprême centrafricaine," *Revue juridique et politique: Indépendance et coopération* 42, no. 1 (1988): 1–28.

33 Placca, "Accusé Bokassa, levez-vous!" 31.

EPILOGUE

1 Interview, Colonel Jean-Claude Mantion, Bangui, March 1990.

2 Interview, Augustine Assemat, Hardricourt, May 1990.

3 Bayart, *The State in Africa*, x-xi.
4 "Demain, il sera trop tard," *Jeune Afrique*, 13–19 May 1993, 20–2.
5 "Grâce et peau de banane," *Jeune Afrique*, 9–15 September 1993, 14–16.
6 "Bokassa en son empire fantôme," *Jeune Afrique*, 31 March–6 April 1994, 26–30.
7 "Flamboyant Self-Crowned Emperor Dies," *Irish Times*, 5 November 1996.

CONCLUSION

1 David Goldsworthy, "Armies and Politics in Civilian Regimes," in Baynham, *Military Power and Politics in Black Africa*, 101; Sandbrook, *The Politics of Africa's Economic Stagnation*, 84–5.
2 LeVine, "African Patrimonial Regimes in Comparative Perspective," 659–69.
3 Mazrui, *Violence and Thought*, 217–18.
4 Hodder-Williams, *An Introduction to the Politics of Tropical Africa*, 140–1.
5 Bratton and van de Walle, "Neopatrimonial Regimes and Political Transitions in Africa," 458–9.
6 Clapham, "Clientelism and the State," in his *Private Patronage and Public Power*, 2–7.
7 Jackson and Rosberg, *Personal Rule in Black Africa*, 19–53.
8 President Mobutu employed identical strategies to keep himself in power (Sandbrook, *The Politics of Africa's Economic Stagnation*, 90–1).
9 Bayart, *The State in Africa*, 242.
10 Harsch, "Accumulators and Democrats," 36–7.
11 Lamb, *The Africans*, 45–6.
12 Amin, *Le développement du capitalisme en Côte d'Ivoire*, 279–80.
13 Martin, "The Historical, Economic, and Political Bases of France's African Policy," 196–8; Moose, "French Military Policy in Africa," 59–61.
14 Sandbrook, *The Politics of Africa's Economic Stagnation*, 95.
15 Toungara, "The Apotheosis of Côte d'Ivoire's Nana Houphouët-Boigny," 52–3.
16 Lamb, *The Africans*, 98–9.
17 Decalo, *Psychoses of Power*, 100.
18 Ibid., 58.
19 Jackson and Rosberg, *Personal Rule in Black Africa*, 238.
20 Kay, *Burundi since the Genocide*. France continued to provide assistance to the Burundi government while these massacres were taking place.
21 Ockrent, *Dans le secret des princes*, 165.
22 There are curious parallels between the repression in Centrafrique and that in neighbouring Zaïre in 1979. In Zaïre there were sporadic strikes and student demonstrations throughout the year resulting in dozens of arrests and detention without trial. Many of those arrested were held

in appalling conditions at Ekafera detention camp in which hundreds of prisoners had died from mistreatment over the years. In July an estimated two hundred people were shot by the armed forces in various incidents (*Amnesty International Report*, 1980, 88–92).

23 "Was Bokassa the only one who killed people? Didn't others kill as well? One has to be fair ... By inventing this cannibal story, they have depicted me as a monster because they wanted my skin. That is the truth" ("Je dirai la messe et je cultiverai la terre," *Jeune Afrique*, 16–22 September 1993, 39).

A Note on Sources

In researching this book, I relied on a variety of sources: books, articles, newspaper and magazine reports, documents, video recordings, and interviews conducted mainly in France and in the Central African Republic. There were limitations to all these sources, as I indicate below, but in combination and in checking them against one another, a reasonably accurate picture emerged of the events and episodes that marked the career of Emperor Bokassa.

Books that either touch on the subject or provide the broader context are numerous enough, as the bibliography shows. Those that deal directly with Bokassa, however, are few in number, restricted in scope, and for the most part are available only in French. Kalck's *Central African Republic* (1971) is still the best general history of the country from the colonial period to independence and beyond, but its publication date means that it has little to say on the Bokassa years. Zoctizoum's *Histoire de la Centrafrique* (1984) is more up to date, but the focus is on the economy and and it is presented in strong ideological tones.

For the Bokassa period in particular, three books are of major importance. Bigo's *Pouvoir et obéissance en Centrafrique* (1988) is invaluable. Perceptive, thoroughly researched, and scholarly, it focuses not so much on Bokassa's person as on the complex internal politics of Centrafrique. Baccard's *Les martyrs de Bokassa* (1987) is mostly a tribute to the men and women who fell victim to the imperial prisons and firing squads. Written by a French jurist who served the Kolingba regime for a number of years, its partisanship is suspect in places. I noticed that it was the only book on the Bokassa era for sale at the Papeterie centrale in Bangui. Nonetheless, it contains valuable information and research clues. Péan's *Bokassa Ier* (1977) was written at least in part to capitalize on the publicity surrounding the imperial coronation. While chronologically it does not go beyond the preparations for this event, it provides important insights into the economic ties between France and the empire.

Chierici's *L'imperatore* (1980), Duchemin's *L'empereur* (1981), and Loubat's *L'ogre de Berengo* (1981) also focus on Bokassa but they are largely worthless. I was able to verify few anecdotes in these muckraking pieces of journalism.

For Bokassa's own perspective on things, nothing ranks with his autobiography, *Ma vérité* (1985). The book is a story unto itself. At the instigation of Valéry Giscard d'Estaing, it was suppressed on a French court order before its release to the public, and most copies were destroyed. The former emperor's friend, Roger Delpey, has one of the surviving volumes and he allowed me to photocopy it when I visited his home near Paris. Delpey's *La manipulation* (1981) is mainly a series of interviews conducted with Bokassa before and after his overthrow. It offers further commentary on events as Bokassa saw them.

Decalo's *Psychoses of Power* (1989) contains a forty-three-page essay on the emperor, which is the only item of substance on the man available in English. While Decalo's analytical concepts are interesting, his research is superficial. He is unaware of the most important sources in French, and he repeats stories that are without foundation.

A number of journal articles shed light on Bokassa's coronation and trial and on Ngaragba Prison. These are authoritative sources for the most part. On the other hand, although newspaper and magazine reports were a useful guide to the structure of the story, they tended to be anecdotal, sensational, and overly reliant on hearsay and unsubstantiated rumour. I used them with caution. *Jeune Afrique*, the excellent French weekly, is the exception. Its journalists are scrupulous and thorough and have given Bokassa extensive coverage from the beginning. *L'année politique africaine* is also reliable.

Primary documents for the Bokassa era are a problem. Government records in the Central African Republic are usually in a chaotic state and unavailable to researchers. This confusion became painfully embarrassing to the present regime when, during his 1986–87 trial, it was unable to produce documentary evidence of wrongdoing by Bokassa. It is as well to remember that the emperor's personal archives were carefully removed by French soldiers during Operation Barracuda. The government in Paris refuses all comment on this, and the whereabouts of these papers remains a mystery.

The major French players in the politics of Centrafrique are no more forthcoming in providing key documentation on their roles in these events. For example, in 1981, at the end of his *septennat*, Giscard d'Estaing deposited 3,981 files, measuring 500 metres thick, in the National Archives. The sensitive files cannot be consulted by historians until 2041. The archivist to whom I spoke would not say so directly but hinted that there might be Bokassa material in these files.

Some of the personages I interviewed during the course of my research allowed me to examine documents and correspondence in their private collections, which I greatly appreciated. In addition, since Bokassa's career unfolded in the age of film and television, I was able to make effective research use of these media. Video recordings of his coronation, trial, press conferences, and so forth are all available. The Institut national de l'audio-visuel in Paris has an excellent collection.

This is a piece of contemporary history and many of the major players are still alive. Some of the most important research, therefore, took the form of personal interviews. Finding people was often a challenge; getting them to speak honestly was even more so. Members of the Bokassa family, now mainly resident in France, were willing to be interviewed but tended to be defensive and anxious to project a positive image of *le père*. This is understandable. There has been so much nonsense written about him that they can hardly be blamed for wanting to redress the balance. The former Empress Catherine, however, refused an interview, claiming that she had put her life with Bokassa behind her.

French government officials and politicians were also reticent on the topic. I sensed an almost universal embarrassment at their country's relationship with Bokassa. Some asked for anonymity as an interview condition; others clearly wished to forget the entire imperial connection. Giscard d'Estaing, for instance, would only refer me to the second volume of his memoirs, *Le pouvoir et la vie*, which was in press at the time.

I faced different challenges in the Central African Republic. Here, people were more than willing to discuss the Bokassa years. Indeed, the ex-emperor and his escapades remain a favourite topic of conversation throughout the country. All the same, a certain nervousness surrounds such dialogue, largely because of the unstable political conditions. My interest in the fallen emperor made me the target of some suspicion in official circles. I was refused permission to meet him in prison on the grounds that only his lawyers and immediate family members had visiting privileges. Asking too many questions in Centrafrique can be dangerous, as several confidants warned me. "Listen and look, but do not talk" was the advice of one expatriate Frenchman, although I did not heed it. I was followed a number of times, and more than once a gendarme "volunteered" to accompany me to my destination. On two occasions I was interrogated rather persistently by the gendarmerie about my "connections." The nature of their suspicions can only be surmised, and I thought that I might even experience Ngaragba at first hand.

Because of the continuing political difficulties in the country, I have chosen to leave most of my Central African informants anonymous. These informants include former and present-day government officials as well as individuals who have never held such positions. I thought it important to seek out ordinary Central Africans whose perspectives on the Bokassa era provided a welcome counterbalance to the often strident partisanship of office holders past and present. I usually met such people through a network of personal contacts by prearrangement in bars and cafés in the *kodros*, or popular districts, of Bangui. These encounters were fairly informal, as dictated by the venues. Most of the time I was talking with people who had had some relevant experience – been involved in a demonstration, been in Ngaragba, or witnessed some event, for example. I also spoke with people in a number of centres in Lobaye, including Boubangui, Bokassa's birthplace.

Admittedly, whether in formal interviews or unstructured conversations, whether in France or Centrafrique, I was told many stories that were simply unbelievable. I checked and double-checked as much as possible before committing anything to print. History is never the whole truth, but it should at least be a plausible reconstruction, and this is what I aimed for.

Most of my printed sources and all my interviews were in French. Direct quotations and transcripts of conversation are therefore translations from the original into English. The translations are my own.

Bibliography

Abamby, A.N.Z. "Barthélémy Boganda ou l'Abbé Grégoire de l'Afrique coloniale." *Revue juridique et politique: Indépendance et coopération* 44, no. 1 (1990): 60–5.

Adrien-Rongier, Marie-France. "Les kodro de Bangui: Un espace urbain 'oublié.'" *Cahiers d'études africaines* 21, nos. 1–3 (1981): 93–110.

Africa Contemporary Record. Vols. 1–9. New York and London: Africana Publishing, 1968–79.

Aldrich, Robert, and John Connell, eds. *France in World Politics*. London and New York: Routledge, 1989.

Amin, Samir. *Le développement du capitalisme en Côte d'Ivoire*. Paris: Editions de Minuit, 1967.

Amnesty International Report. London: Amnesty International Publications (various years).

Andreski, Stanislav. *The African Predicament: A Study in the Pathology of Modernization*. London: Michael Joseph, 1968.

Ardagh, John. *France in the 1980s*. New York: Viking Penguin, 1983.

Baccard, André. *Les martyrs de Bokassa*. Paris: Editions du Seuil, 1987.

Bayart, Jean-François. *La politique africaine de François Mitterrand*. Paris: Karthala, 1985.

– *The State in Africa: The Politics of the Belly*. London and New York: Longman, 1993. First published in French as *L'Etat en Afrique: La politique du ventre*, 1989.

Baynham, Simon, ed. *Military Power and Politics in Black Africa*. New York: St Martin's Press, 1986.

Beti, Mongo. "M. Giscard d'Estaing, remboursez!" *Peuples noirs/Peuples africains* 13 (Jan.–Feb. 1980): 35–56.

Bigo, Didier. "Approche pour une théorie du pouvoir personnel, un example priviligié: Le Centrafrique." *Etudes polémoliques* 36 (1985): 67–94.

- "Ngaragba, l'impossible prison." *Revue française de science politique* 39, no. 6 (1989): 867–86.
- *Pouvoir et obéissance en Centrafrique*. Paris: Karthala, 1988.
- "Le procès Bokassa." *Afrique contemporaine*, 144 (1987): 51–4.
Bokassa, Jean-Bedel. *Ma vérité*. Paris: Carrère-Lefon, 1985.
- *Philosophie de l'Opération Bokassa*. 2 vols. Paris: Firmin Didot, 1973.
Bouchet, Christophe. *L'aventure Tapie: Enquête sur un citoyen modèle*. Paris: Seuil, 1992.
Bourgi, Albert, ed. *Grands procès de l'Afrique contemporaine*. Paris: Japress, 1990.
Bratton, Michael, and Nicolas van de Walle. "Neopatrimonial Regimes and Political Transitions in Africa." *World Politics* 46, no. 4 (July 1994): 453–89.
Bretton, Henry L. *The Rise and Fall of Kwame Nkrumah*. New York: Praeger, 1966.
Bruno, Pol. *La saga des Giscard*. Paris: Editions Ramsay, 1980.
Chabal, Patrick, ed. *Political Domination in Africa: Reflections on the Limits of Power*. Cambridge: Cambridge University Press, 1986.
Chaffard, Georges. *Les carnets secrets de la colonisation*. Paris: Calman-Levy, 1967.
Chaliand, Gérard. *The Struggle for Africa: Conflict of the Great Powers*. New York: St Martin's Press, 1982.
Chierici, Maurizio. *L'imperatore*. Milano: Rizzoli Editore, 1980.
Clapham, Christopher, ed. *Private Patronage and Public Power: Political Clientelism in the Modern State*. New York: St Martin's Press, 1982.
Clayton, Anthony. "Foreign Intervention in Africa." In *Military Power and Politics in Black Africa*, ed. Simon Baynham. New York: St Martin's Press, 1986.
Cohen, Samy. *La monarchie nucléaire: Les coulisses de la politique étrangère sous la Ve République*. Paris: Hachette, 1986.
- *Les conseillers du Président – de Charles de Gaulle à Valéry Giscard d'Estaing*. Paris: Presses Universitaires de France, 1980.
Cohen, Samy, and Marie-Claude Smouts, eds. *La politique extérieure de Valéry Giscard d'Estaing*. Paris: Presses de la Fondation nationale des sciences politiques, 1985.
Cohen, William B. *Rulers of Empire: The French Colonial Service in Africa*. Stanford University: Hoover Institution Press, 1971.
Collier, Ruth Berins. *Regimes in Tropical Africa: Changing Forms of Supremecy, 1945–1975*. Berkeley: University of California Press, 1982.
Conchon, Georges. *L'Etat sauvage*. Geneva: Famot, 1980.
Coquery-Vidrovitch, Catherine. *Afrique noire: Permanences et ruptures*. Paris: Payot, 1985.
- *Le Congo français au temps des grandes compagnies concessionnaires, 1898–1930*. Paris: Mouton, 1972.

Coquery-Vidrovitch, Catherine, and Henri Moniot. *L'Afrique noire de 1800 à nos jours*. Paris: Presses Universitaires de France, 1984.

Corbett, Edward M. *The French Presence in Black Africa*. Washington, DC: Black Orpheus Press, 1972.

Cordell, D.D. *Dar al-Kuti and the Last Years of the Trans-Saharan Slave Trade*. Madison: University of Wisconsin Press, 1985.

- "La paix de la misère: The Central African Republic." *Canadian Journal of African Studies*, 18, no. 3 (1984): 615–21.

Cornevin, Robert. "La politique étrangère du gouvernement de Bangui." *Revue française d'études politiques africaines* 117 (Sept. 1975): 1971–80.

Cour suprême (Bangui). "Le procès Bokassa devant la Cour suprême centrafricaine: Rapport du président da la Cour suprême." *Revue juridique et politique: Indépendance et coopération* 42, no. 1 (1988): 1–28.

Crabb, John. "The Coronation of Emperor Bokassa." *Africa Today* 25, no. 3 (July–Sept. 1978): 25–44.

Dampierre, Eric de. *Un royaume Bandia du Haut-Oubangui*. Paris: Plon, 1967.

Decalo, Samuel. "African Personal Dictatorships." *Journal of Modern African Studies*, 23, no. 2 (1985): 209–37.

- *Coups and Army Rule in Africa: Studies in Military Style*. New Haven: Yale University Press, 1976.

- *Psychoses of Power: African Personal Dictatorships*. Boulder and London: Westview Press, 1989.

De l'Empire centrafricain à la République centrafricaine ou de Bokassa Ier à Dacko 2. Poitiers: Collectif Tiers-Monde, 1980.

Delpey, Roger. *Affaires centrafricaines*. Paris: Jacques Grancher, 1985.

- *La manipulation*. Paris: Jacques Grancher, 1981.

- *Prisonnier de Giscard*. Paris: Jacques Grancher, 1982.

De Lusignan, Guy. *French-Speaking Africa since Independence*. New York: Praeger, 1969.

Demafouth, J.J. "Landlocked and Uninformed." *Index on Censorship* 14, no. 5 (1985): 22–3.

Denis, Stéphane. *La chute de la Maison Giscard*. Paris: J.C. Lattès, 1981.

D'Orgeix, Jean. *J'étais un Africain blanc*. Paris: Presses de la Cité, 1980.

Duchemin, Jacques. *L'empereur*. Paris: Editions Albin Michel, 1981.

Echenberg, Myron. *Colonial Conscripts: The Tirailleurs Sénégalais in French West Africa, 1857–1960*. London: James Currey, 1991.

Epstein, Edward J. *The Rise and Fall of Diamonds*. New York: Simon and Schuster, 1982.

Faligot, Roger, and Pascal Krop. *La Piscine: Les services secrets français, 1944–1984*. Paris: Seuil, 1985.

Foltz, William J., and Henry S. Bienen, eds. *Arms and the African: Military Influences on Africa's International Relations*. New Haven: Yale University Press, 1985.

Frears, J.R. *France in the Giscard Presidency.* London: Allen and Unwin, 1981.

Gallo, Thierry-Jacques. *N'Garagba, maison des morts: Un prisonnier sous Bokassa.* Paris: L'Harmattan, 1988.

Gide, André. *Voyage au Congo.* Paris: Gallimard, 1927.

Gifford, Prosser, and W. Roger Louis, eds. *France and Britain in Africa.* New Haven: Yale University Press, 1971.

– *The Transfer of Power in Africa: Decolonization, 1940–1960.* New Haven: Yale University Press, 1982.

Giscard d'Estaing, Valéry. *Le pouvoir et la vie.* Vol. 2, *L'affrontement.* Paris: Compagnie Douze, 1991.

Grellet, Gérard, Monique Mainguet, and Pierre Soumille. *La République centrafricaine.* Paris: Presses Universitaires de France, 1982.

Grey, Robert D. "A Balance Sheet on External Assistance: France in Africa." *Journal of Modern African Studies* 28, no. 1 (1990): 101–14.

Hargraves, John D. "British and French Imperialism in West Africa, 1885–1898." In *France and Britain in Africa*, ed. Prosser Gifford and W. Roger Louis. New Haven: Yale University Press, 1971.

Harmon, Jeff B. "His Former Majesty, Bokassa." *Harper's Magazine,* May 1980, 34–9.

Harsch, Ernest. "Accumulators and Democrats: Challenging State Corruption in Africa." *Journal of Modern African Studies* 31, no. 1 (1993): 31–48.

Hodder-Williams, Richard. *An Introduction to the Politics of Tropical Africa.* London: Allen and Unwin, 1984.

Jackson, Robert H., and Carl G. Rosberg. *Personal Rule in Black Africa: Prince, Autocrat, Prophet, Tyrant.* Berkeley: University of California Press, 1982.

Jarry, Alfred. *The Ubu Plays.* London: Methuen, 1968.

Julien, Charles-André, Catherine Coquery-Vidrovitch, Magaly Morsy, and Yves Person, eds. *Les Africains.* 12 vols. Paris: Jeune Afrique, 1977–78.

Kalck, Pierre. *The Central African Republic: A Failure in Decolonization.* New York: Praeger, 1971.

– *Historical Dictionary of the Central African Republic.* Translated by Thomas O'Toole. Metuchen, NJ, and London: Scarecrow Press, 1980.

– "Panorama de l'histoire centrafricaine." *Revue française d'études politiques africaines* 117 (Sept. 1975): 32–54.

Kay, Reginald. *Burundi since the Genocide.* Minority Rights Group Report no. 20. London: Minority Rights Group, 1987.

Kennedy, Paul. *African Capitalism: The Struggle for Ascendancy.* Cambridge: Cambridge University Press, 1988.

Kodro, Nguinza Akamgbi. "A propos des barricades et des massacres de Bangui." *Peuples noirs/Peuples africains* 11 (Sept.–Oct. 1979): 16–48.

– "Où en sont les droits de l'homme et de la femme en Centrafrique?" *Peuples noirs/Peuples africains* 2 (Mar.–Apr. 1978): 31–82.

Kolingba, André. *Citations.* Paris: Hatier, 1988.

Lachaud, J.P. "Les activités informelles et l'emploi à Bangui: Analyse et stratégie de développement." *Canadian Journal of African Studies* 18, no. 2 (1984): 291–317.

Lamb, David. *The Africans.* New York: Vintage Books, 1987.

La politique étrangère de la France: Textes et documents. Paris: La Documentation française (1975–1980).

LeClercq, C. "La constitution de la République centrafricaine du 21 novembre 1986." *Revue juridique et politique: Indépendance et coopération* 40, nos. 1–2 (1986): 94–8.

– "La constitution de la RCA du 21 novembre 1986 et les statuts du Rassemblement démocratique centrafricain." *Afrique contemporaine* 144 (1987): 49–51.

Lee, J.M. *African Armies and Civil Order.* New York: Praeger, 1969.

LeVine, Victor T. "African Patrimonial Regimes in Comparative Perspective." *Journal of Modern African Studies* 18, no. 4 (1980): 657–73.

Loubat, Bernard. *L'ogre de Berengo.* Paris: Editions Alain Lefeuvre, 1981.

Machin, H. "The President's Men: Advisers and Assistants at the Elysée Palace." In *Continuity and Change in France,* ed. Vincent Wright. London: Allen and Unwin, 1984.

Maïdou, Henri, et al. *Philosophie de l'Opération Bokassa. Vol. 2, Opération Bokassa et développement.* Paris: Presses de Bernard Neyrolles, 1976.

Manning, Patrick. *Francophone Sub-Saharan Africa, 1880–1985.* Cambridge: Cambridge University Press, 1988.

Marseille, Jacques. *Empire colonial et capitalisme français: Histoire d'un divorce.* Paris: Albin Michel, 1984.

Martin, Guy. "The Historical, Economic, and Political Bases of France's African Policy." *Journal of Modern African Studies* 23, no. 2 (1985): 189–208.

Mazrui, Ali A. *Violence and Thought: Essays on Social Tensions in Africa.* London and Harlow: Longmans Green, 1969.

Mbokolo, Elikia. "French Colonial Policy in Equatorial Africa in the 1940s and 1950s." In *The Transfer of Power in Africa,* ed. Prosser Gifford and W. Roger Louis. New Haven: Yale University Press, 1971.

Médard, Jean-François. "The Underdeveloped State in Tropical Africa: Political Clientelism or Neo-patrimonialism?" In *Private Patronage and Public Power,* ed. Christopher Clapham. New York: St Martin's Press, 1982.

Moose, George E. "French Military Policy in Africa." In *Arms and the African,* ed. William J. Foltz and Henry S. Bienen. New Haven: Yale University Press, 1985.

Mortimer, Edward. *France and the Africans, 1944–1960: A Political History.* New York: Walker and Co., 1969.

Mouly, J. "The Young Pioneers Movement in the Central African Republic." *International Labour Review* 93, no. 1 (Jan. 1966): 19–28.

Nzabakomada, Raphaël. *L'Afrique centrale insurgée: La guerre de Kongo-Warra, 1928–31.* Paris: L'Harmattan, 1985.

O'Ballance, Edgar. *The Story of the French Foreign Legion*. London: Faber and Faber, 1961.

Ockrent, Christine. *Dans le secret des princes*. Paris: Stock, 1986.

O'Toole, Thomas E. *The Central African Republic: The Continent's Hidden Heart*. Boulder, Colo.: Westview Press, 1986.

– "Jean-Bedel Bokassa: Neo-Napoleon or Traditional African Ruler?" In *The Cult of Power: Dictators in the Twentieth Century*, ed. Joseph Held. New York: Columbia University Press, 1983.

– "The 1928–1931 Gbaya Insurrection in Ubangui-Shari: Messianic Movement or Village Self-Defense?" *Canadian Journal of African Studies* 18, no. 2 (1984): 329–44.

– "Shantytowns in Bangui, Central African Republic: A Cause for Despair or a Creative Possibility." In *Slum and Squatter Settlements in Sub-Saharan Africa*, ed. R.A. Obudho and Constance C. Mblanga. New York: Praeger, 1988.

Péan, Pierre. *Bokassa Ier*. Paris: Editions Alain Moreau, 1977.

– *L'homme de l'ombre: Eléments d'enquête autour de Jacques Foccart, l'homme le plus mystérieux et le plus puissant de la Ve République*. Paris: Fayard, 1990.

– *Secret d'Etat*. Paris: Fayard, 1986.

Prioul, C. "Les cultures maraîchères à Bangui." *Cahiers d'outre-mer* 86 (1969): 191–202.

– "Industrie et commerce en RCA." *Cahiers d'outre-mer* 88 (1969): 410–23.

Rapport de la Mission de constatation des événements de Bangui. Abidjan: July 1979.

Ronen, Dov, ed. *Democracy and Pluralism in Africa*. Boulder: Lynne Rienner, 1986.

Rotberg, Robert I., and Ali A. Mazrui, eds. *Protest and Power in Black Africa*. New York: Oxford University Press, 1970.

Rothchild, Donald, and Naomi Chazan, eds. *The Precarious Balance: State and Society in Africa*. Boulder and London: Westview Press, 1988.

Samarin, William J. *The Black Man's Burden: African Colonial Labour on the Congo and Ubangi Rivers, 1880–1900*. Boulder, Colo.: Westview Press, 1989.

– "The Colonial Heritage of the Central African Republic: A Linguistic Perspective." *International Journal of African Historical Studies* 22, no. 4 (1990): 697–712.

– "French and Sango in the Central African Republic." *Anthropological Linguistics* 28, no. 3 (1986): 379–87.

– "Religion and Modernization in Africa." *Anthropological Quarterly* 39, no. 4 (Oct. 1966): 288–97.

Sandbrook, Richard. *The Politics of Africa's Economic Stagnation*. Cambridge: Cambridge University Press, 1985.

Sautter, Gilles. "Le chemin de fer Congo-Océan, 1921–1934." *Cahiers d'études africaines* 7, no. 26 (1967): 219–99.

Serre, Jacques. "Six ans de gouvernement Dacko (1960–1966)." *Revue française d'études politiques africaines* 117 (1975): 73–104.

Shawcross, William. *The Shah's Last Ride: The Story of the Exile, Misadventures and Death of the Emperor*. London: Chatto and Windus, 1989.

Shoumatoff, Alex. *African Madness*. New York: Knopf, 1988.

Sklar, Richard L. "The Nature of Class Domination in Africa." *Journal of Modern African Studies* 17, no. 4 (1979): 531–52.

Soffer, Ovadia. *Le diamant noir*. Paris: R. Laffont, 1987.

Soyinka, Wole. *Opera Wonyosi*. Bloomington: Indiana University Press, 1981.

Stevens, Stuart. *Malaria Dreams: An African Adventure*. New York: Atlantic Monthly Press, 1989.

Stone, Lawrence. "The Revival of Narrative: Reflexions on a New Old History." *Past and Present* 85 (Nov. 1979): 3–24.

Suret-Canale, Jean. *French Colonization in Tropical Africa, 1900–1945*. New York: Pica Press, 1971.

Tapie, Bernard. *Gagner*. Paris: Robert Laffont, 1986.

Thompson, Virginia, and Richard Adloff. *The Emerging States of French Equatorial Africa*. Stanford: Stanford University Press, 1960.

Toungara, Jeanne Maddox. "The Apotheosis of Côte d'Ivoire's Nana Houphouët-Boigny." *Journal of Modern African Studies* 28, no. 1 (1990): 23–54.

Vergiat, A.M. *Les rites secrets des primitifs de l'Oubangui*. Paris: Payot, 1936.

Villien, François. "Habitat et habitations dans les quartiers populaires de Bangui." *Cahiers d'outre-mer* 38, no. 151 (1985): 235–62.

Weinstein, Brian. "Félix Eboué and the Chiefs: Perceptions of Power in Early Oubangui-Chari." *Journal of African History* 11, no. 1 (1970): 107–26.

Welch, Claude E., Jr, ed. *Soldier and State in Africa*. Evanston: Northwestern University Press, 1070.

White, Dorothy S. *Black Africa and de Gaulle: From the French Empire to Independence*. University Park and London: Pennsylvania State University Press, 1979.

Williams, Robert. *Political Corruption in Africa*. Aldershot: Gower Publishing, 1987.

Wiseman, John A. *Political Leaders in Black Africa: A Biographical Dictionary of Major Politicians since Independence*. Brookfield, Vt.: Ashgate Pub. Co., 1991.

Wright, Vincent, ed. *Continuity and Change in France*. London: Allen and Unwin, 1984.

Zoctizoum, Yarisse. *Histoire de la Centrafrique*. Paris: L'Harmattan, 1984.

Index

Abidjan, 119, 135, 138–41, 143–5, 149–51, 155, 157, 161, 165–71, 175, 193
Académie française, 134
Adama-Tamboux, Michel, 17, 40
Adolf Hitler, l'affaire, 120
Affaires centrafricaines, 176, 182
Agence France-Presse, 70
Air Centrafrique, 69
Aka pygmies, 26, 30
Alazoula, Louis, 48
Algeria, 3, 4, 116, 119, 167
Aluswisse, 72, 73
Amega, Atsu-Koffi, 116
Amin, Idi, x, 79, 92, 124, 132, 135, 214, 215
Amin, Samir, 212
Amnesty International, 114, 116, 117, 119, 121, 177
Anagnostelli, Andrée, 74
Anagnostellis, Dmitri, 74
Angola, 214
Antenne 2 TV, 144, 145
Antwerp, 74
Arapoff, Vladimir, 167
Argentina, 134
Arslanian, 74
Assemat, Augustine, 170, 171, 178, 179, 182, 205
Association nationale des étudiants centrafricains (ANECA), 106, 110, 111

Aurillac, Michel, 182
Awakaba National Park, 60
Ayandho, Bernard, 152, 155, 212

Baccard, André, 112
Bakongo, 3
Bakouma, 72, 73, 128
Ballet du Casino de Paris, 167
Bambari, 106
Banda, 5, 63
Bandio, Jean-Arthur, 24
Bangui, 5, 59, 68, 69, 79, 93–7, 106, 108, 109, 117, 119, 131, 136, 162, 179, 181, 186, 189, 192
Bangui, Sylvestre, 115, 119, 122, 126, 143, 152, 155
Bangui M'Poko Airport, 60, 109, 121, 153
Banque centrale des Etats d'Afrique de l'Ouest, 158
Banque française du commerce extérieur, 73
Banque nationale de Paris, 69
Banza, Alexandre, 26–31, 34, 41–4, 63, 67, 189
Banza, Beouane, 43
Banza, Goboulo, 43
Barberot, Roger, 16, 20
Bardoux, May, 70

Baril, Paul, 184
Bar-sur-Aube, 102
Baya, 5, 6, 7
Bayard, François, xii
Beijing, 56, 84
Belgian Congo, 3, 4, 25
Belgium, 90
Benghazi, 129, 131
Benin, 4, 30, 167
Berbérati, 16, 106
Berengo, 42–3, 76, 81, 86–8, 99–101, 117, 157, 196, 198, 210
Berlin Conference, 4
Berne, 140
Bertrand, Arthus, 45, 90
Bible, 205
Bigeard, General Marcel, 23
Bimbo, 64
Birao, 43
Blagué, Alphonse, 111
Boda, 3, 16
Boganda, Barthélémy, 7, 12–16, 20, 22, 23, 31, 34, 35, 122, 158
Boganda Stadium, 36
Bokassa, Anne (de Berengo), 56, 57, 170
Bokassa, Charlemagne, 57
Bokassa, Dieu-Béni, 57
Bokassa, Gaboula, 57
Bokassa, Georges, 57, 58, 64, 85, 86, 87, 104, 119, 133, 161, 205

Bokassa, Jean-Bedel:
attempted return of,
166–9; autobiography,
172–6; children, 57–60,
85–7, 104, 161, 162, 170;
consolidation of per-
sonal power, 33, 34, 36,
43, 44; coup d'état, 26–
32; economic policies,
68–70, 72, 73; exile in
France, 170–9; exile in
Ivory Coast, 138–41,
143–7, 149, 151, 161–2,
164–5, 169–70; final
days, 207; foreign pol-
icy, 66, 67; imperial
coronation, 89–98;
imprisonment, 204–6;
military career, 9–11;
and the occult, 49, 50;
overthrow of, 125–7,
130–5; personality, 23,
24, 33, 44–6, 67; plots
against, 41–3, 48, 49,
60–3; popular image of,
ix, 213–16; reforms, 34,
35; relations with de
Gaulle, 66, 67; relations
with Gadhaffi, 79, 80,
85, 127–30; relations
with Giscard d'Estaing,
70–2, 83, 85, 102, 103,
122, 123, 141–51, 174–6;
return from exile, 178–
83; trial of (1986–87),
185–203; wealth, 74–8,
213; wives and mis-
tresses, 51–7, 85–7, 143,
144, 162, 171
Bokassa, Jean-Bedel, Jr
(prince héritier), 57, 87,
94, 95, 97, 170
Bokassa, Jean-Bertrand,
57, 170
Bokassa, Jean-Charles, 57,
58, 161
Bokassa, Jean-Christian,
170
Bokassa, Jean-Claude, 57
Bokassa, Jean-Legrand, 57
Bokassa, Jean-Parfait, 170
Bokassa, Jean-Serge, 57

Bokassa, Jean-Yves, 57,
170
Bokassa, Marguerite, 57
Bokassa, Marie-Anne, 57
Bokassa, Marie-Béatrice,
57
Bokassa, Marie-Claire, 57
Bokassa, Marie-Eléonore,
57, 170
Bokassa, Marie-France,
57, 170
Bokassa, Marie-Jeanne,
57, 170, 179
Bokassa, Marie-Laure, 57
Bokassa, Marie-Suzanne,
162, 170
Bokassa, Martine (fake),
58–61, 63, 69, 154, 195,
201
Bokassa, Martine (real),
59, 60, 63, 139, 195
Bokassa, Nestor, 57, 58
Bokassa, Nicaise, 57, 58,
139
Bokassa, Nicole, 57
Bokassa, Reine, 57
Bokassa, Saint-Cyr, 57,
58, 139, 161
Bokassa, Saint-Jean, 57,
85, 86
Bokassa, Saint-Sylvestre,
57
Bonaparte, Napoléon, 83,
95, 170
Bongo, Omar, 54, 60, 88,
92, 99, 102, 122, 123,
127, 148, 213
Bossangao, 110
Bouar, 54, 103, 110, 128,
164
Bougangui, 7, 26, 38, 43,
134
Bouca, 30, 110
Bourges, Yvon, 126, 141
Boy Rabé, 109, 112
Bozize, François, 44, 109,
152, 162, 210, 212
Brazil, 134
Brazzaville, 4, 6, 8–11, 40,
51, 52, 86, 179, 182
Brazzaville–Pointe Noire
Railway, 78

Bria, 106
Brice, Olivier, 90, 92
Brooks-Randolph, Angie,
116
Broudy, Edmond, 194,
195, 201
Brussels, 101, 179
Brussels Conference, 4
Bucharest, 55, 171
Burkino Faso, 4, 30
Burundi, 214

Cambodia, 105
Cameroun, 4, 54, 91, 145,
159
Camp de Roux, 25, 27,
29, 31, 33, 34, 40, 41,
43, 160, 181, 185, 201–4
Camp Kassaï, 26, 28, 29,
42, 43, 60, 62
Canard enchaîné, 141–3,
145–7, 149, 150
cannibalism, ix, 50, 137,
144, 156–8, 173, 185,
188–9, 196–7, 200–1,
215, 216
Carlier, Hervé, 178, 179
Carole, Martine, 59
Carrère-Lafon, 172
Cathédrale de Notre-
Dame, 92, 95
Catholicism, 80
Ceausescu, Nikolai, 55
Centradiam, 74
Centrafricain Jazz, 35
CentraHydro, 70, 81
Central African Empire:
economy, 107, 108, 124;
establishment of, 84,
85; fall of, 125–31; political repression in, 87,
88, 104, 106–14; politi-
cal structures in, 100,
101
Central African Republic:
Dacko regime (1960–
65), 20–6, (1979–81),
152, 160; economy, 65,
68–70, 72–81; elections
in, 20, 158, 159, 206;
Kolingba regime, 160–
4, 181, 182, 184, 205,

206; political instability in, 31, 32, 159, 160, 162; political repression in, 37–41, 46–9

Cercle national des combattants, 171

Chabal, Patrick, xi

Château Boganda, 113, 117

Château Hardricourt, 78, 124, 132, 171–2, 176–8, 182

Château Mézy, 78

Château Saint-Louis Chavanon, 77

Château Villemorant, 74, 77, 83, 104

Châtou-Croissy, 148

Chiang Kai-shek, 56

China, People's Republic of, 25, 66, 84, 107

Chirac, Jacques, 127, 184, 187, 188

clientelism, xi, 209

Cocody, 138, 139

Collège Henri-IV, 179

Colombey-les-deux-Eglises, 66, 67, 102

Comité de co-ordination pour la convocation d'une conférence nationale (CCCCN), 205

Comité militaire de redressement national (CMRN), 161

Commissariat à l'énergie atomique (CEA), 72–3

Compagnie du Cambodge, 76

Compagnie d'uranium de Bakouma (URBA), 72, 81

Compagnie forestière de la Sangha-Oubangui, 3, 6, 7, 71

Compagnie française des minerais d'uranium (CFMU), 72, 73

Compagnie industrielle oubanguienne des textiles (CIOT), 107

Comptoir national du diamant, 141

Congo, Republic of, 76, 105

Congo River, 4

coopérants, 106, 107, 111, 125, 160

Coquery-Vidrovitch, Catherine, xii

Coronation Cup, 97

Cot, Jean-Pierre, 163

Cottencière, La, 77

Couronne, La, 75

Cousin, Michel, 90

crocodiles, 137, 138, 156, 215, 216

Croix de guerre, 10, 45

Dacko, David, 15–18, 20–7, 29, 31–3, 40–1, 80, 84, 121–2, 127, 130–2, 137, 151–6, 158–64, 183, 190, 196, 206, 212

David, Louis, 95

de Brazza, Pierre Savorgnan, 4

Decalo, Samuel, ix, 31

Dévéavodé, Dr Jean-Bruno, 60, 63, 139, 154, 158, 195

de Decker, Marie-Laure, 176

de Ducla, Bernard, 166, 167, 169

Deferre, Gaston, 13, 14

de Gaulle, Charles, 8, 9, 14, 17, 19, 25, 29, 30, 41, 66–8, 70, 72, 102, 187

de Gaulle, Philippe, 67, 187

de Gaulle, Yvonne, 67

de Geouffre de la Pradelle, Raymond, 146, 167

Delpey, Roger, 120, 132, 143–50, 164–70, 176, 177, 178, 182, 184

de Marenches, Alexandre, 126, 127, 133, 215, 216

Denguiade, Catherine (empress), 52–3, 56, 61, 85–7, 90, 93–7, 117, 124, 132, 138, 143–5, 161–2, 171, 175–6, 183, 207

de Saint-Mart, Pierre, 9

de Schonen, Albert, 59

Diamond Distributors, 75, 81, 91, 92

diamonds, 74, 75, 77, 107, 136, 141–3, 146, 148, 149, 151, 198

Dien Bien Phu, 9, 13, 171

Direction de la sûreté du territoire (DST), 19, 142, 148, 169

Djéma, 70

Domitien, Elizabeth, 83, 84, 156

Douai, 56

Douate, Jean-Paul, 24, 29

Drimba, Gabriella, 55, 56, 86

Duchemin, Jacques, 119, 120, 144, 174, 215

Dupont, Jean-Pierre, 119, 120, 164

Eanes, Ramalho, 142

Eboué, Félix, 9

Echos d'un sombre empire, ix

Ecole de formation des officiers du régime transitoire des territoires d'outre-mer (EFORTOM), 10, 25

Ecole nationale d'administration et de magistrature, 108, 109

Ecole normale supérieure, 108, 111

Ecole Sainte-Jeanne d'Arc, 8

Ecole Saint-Louis, 8

Ele sango, 197

Elysée Palace, 19, 30, 67, 102, 103, 123, 144, 176

Enrici, Monseigneur Domenico, 92

Equatorial Guinea, x, 105, 214

Ethiopia, 82, 208, 214

European Economic Community, 101

Evreux, 133–5, 137, 143, 198

Eyadéma, Gnassingbé, 115, 147, 148

Fauvet, Jacques, 142
female circumcision, 35, 143, 215
First World War, 5, 6
Foccart, Jacques, 19, 73, 187
Fonds d'aide de la coopération (FAC), 76
forced labour, 6
Forces centrafricaines libres, 165
Fort Archambault. See Sarh
Fou, 109, 162
France: colonial policies, 3–7, 11–18; economic ties with Centrafrique, 65, 71–4, 76, 78, 79, 110, 206; military interventions in Africa, 103, 125–7, 130, 131; relations with former colonies, 19, 20, 212
Franceville, 123, 125, 132
Franck, Edouard, 186–9, 195, 199, 201
franc monetary zone, 23
François-Poncet, Jean, 126
Franco-Prussian War, 4
Free French forces, 9
Fréjus, 9, 10, 102
French Community, 15, 17
French Equatorial Africa, 3, 5–7, 9, 13–15, 17, 71
French Foreign Legion, 3, 37
French Union, 12–14
French West Africa, 4, 13, 14
Frolinat, 103
Front de libération des oubanguiens (FLO), 122
Front national, 171, 172
Front patriotique oubanguien (FPO), 122

Gabon, 4, 5, 9, 14, 15, 26, 53, 72, 76, 122, 159, 171, 205

Gadhaffi, Muammar, 79, 80, 103, 125, 127–30, 132, 134–5, 153, 213
Galerie Point Show, 178
Galley, Robert, 93, 96, 121, 137, 141, 158, 196
Gallo, Thierry-Jacques, 112, 118
Geddaï, Adrian, 53, 74
Geddaï, Alda, 53
Geneva, 162, 183
Germany, 5, 9, 89
Ghana, 31, 208
Gibault, François, 184, 188, 190–2, 204
Gide, André, 3, 5
Giscard d'Estaing, Anne-Aymone, 53, 75, 149, 176
Giscard d'Estaing, Edmond, 6, 70, 71
Giscard d'Estaing, François, 73, 75, 93, 141, 145, 147, 149, 150
Giscard d'Estaing, Jacques, 73, 75, 141, 145, 147, 149, 150
Giscard d'Estaing, Olivier, 141
Giscard d'Estaing, Valéry, 67, 70–3, 75, 78–9, 85, 93, 97, 102–4, 110, 115, 121–7 passim, 132, 134–6, 141–51, 159–62, 164, 172–6, 188, 212
Gobongo, 109, 110, 162
godobé, 47, 109
Gold Coast, 14
Goldsmith, Michael, 87, 88, 93, 101
Goldsmith, Roxane, 88
Gonen, Samuel, 99
Gotilogoé, Mireille, 184
Gotoas, Nicholas, 111
Goumba, Abel, 15–17, 20, 122, 126, 155, 158–63, 206–212
Grancher, Jacques, 177
Green, Marguerite, 51, 86
Greenpeace, 19
Grelombe, Christophe, 194
Grimari, 15

Guichard, Jacques, 131
Guinea, Republic of, 4, 15, 17, 208
Guiselin, 90

Habré, Chedeye, 174
Habré, Hissène, 164, 174
Harman, Jeff, 216
Hartmann Clinic, 175
Hassan II, King, 164
Hassen, Clément, 26, 27
Hassen, Marie-Reine, 54, 55
Hercolani, Domietta, 176
Herzog, Werner, ix
Hijazi, Ali, 128, 132
Hirohito, Emperor, 82, 92, 102
Holeindre Roger, 116, 165, 171, 172, 173, 184
Hôtel Ibis, 166
Houphouët-Boigny, Félix, 12, 14, 115, 127, 135, 139, 161–2, 165, 169, 170, 211, 213
Houphouët-Boigny, Thérèse, 161, 162
Hua Kuo-feng, 84
Hunt, Pierre, 142, 143
Hutus, 214

Idris, King, 129
Imalé, Monique, 49, 192
"Imperial March," 89, 94
"Imperial Waltz," 89, 96
Imprimerie centrale d'Afrique, 69
Indénié, 161
indigénat, 11
Indochina, ix, 9, 10, 12, 13, 45, 58, 116, 174
infanticide, 173, 185
Iran, 84, 109
Irish National Liberation Army, 184
Irish Republican Army (IRA), 79
Islam, 46, 47, 79, 80, 84, 85, 127
ivory, 52, 75, 141, 154
Ivory Coast, 4, 12, 135, 161, 169, 203, 205

Izamo, Jean, 24, 26, 27, 29, 173

Jackson, Robert H., ix
Japan, 45, 84
Jarry, Alfred, 66
Jeune Afrique, 114, 120, 146
Johannesburg, 87, 88
John Paul II, Pope, 177
Jolis, Albert, 91, 92
Jourdain, Michelle, 13, 16
Journiac, René, 73, 93, 123, 126, 127, 132, 134, 141, 145
Juan Carlos, King, 92

Kalak, Ezzadine, 184
Karnu, 6, 7
Katouka, Eugène, 128, 135, 138
Kembé, 163
Kennedy, John F., 63
Kettego, Albertine, 137
Kezza, Antoine, 34
Khashoggi, Adnan, 74
Kigali, 114, 116
Kilomètre 5, 47, 79, 109
Kim Il Sung, 102
kodros, 47, 109, 195
Kolingba, André, 160–4, 168, 176, 178, 180–4, 186, 188, 194, 198, 199, 202–6
Kolwezi, 103
Kombo, Julienne, 43
Kondotene, Guillaume, 39
Kone, Tia, 116
Koran, 46, 85
Kouda, Albert, 41
Koumbola Reserve, 70
Koyamba, Alphonse, 128, 152, 156
Kuwait, 110

La Baule, 205
Labouisse, Henry, 140
Lala, Iddi, 160
La Manipulation, 150
Lanvin, House of, 90
le Bouet du Portal, Olivier, 178, 179
Le Bourget, 139, 167, 169

Légion d'honneur, 10, 45
Le Monde, 142, 149
L'empereur, 174
Leopold II, King, 3, 4
LePen, Jean-Marie, 171
Le Roy Ladurie, Emmanuel, x
Liberia, 214
Librairie Hachette, 69, 80
Libreville, 53, 130, 167, 168, 171, 214
Libya, 66, 79, 80, 84, 91, 124, 128–30, 132–4, 143, 198, 199, 212
Li Hsien-nien, 84
Lingoupou, Martin, 48, 49, 156, 192, 201, 210
Lingoupou, Pauline, 192
Linguissa, Philippe, 157, 173, 196, 197, 201
Linus, Hans, 89
lions, 137, 156, 215, 216
Lobaye, 5, 6, 7, 15, 33, 37, 41, 125
L'ogre de Berengo, 174
loi-cadre, 10, 14, 126
Loubat, Bernard, 113, 174, 216
Lycée Boganda, 108, 111
Lycée Bokassa, 108
Lycée Pie XII, 52

Macias Nguema, Francisco, x, 124, 214, 215
Madagascar, 12
Magalé, André, 48
Maïdou, Henri, 101, 107, 110, 117, 121, 127–8, 145–6, 152, 155, 158–9, 162, 212
Malendoma, Timothée, 27, 74
Maleombho, Pierre, 17, 60, 62
Mali, 4
Malimaka, 109, 162
Malloum, Félix, 103, 173
Malraux, André, 17
Mandaba, Jean-Claude, 27, 42, 43
Mande Empire, 208
Mandela, Nelson, 205

Mantion, Jean-Claude, 181, 186, 190, 204, 206
Marcelin, Lamine, 48
Marion, Pierre, 162
Massanquet, Jean-Robert, 137
Mauritius, 56, 57, 92
Ma vérité, 172–6
Mayomokola, Josephat, 109, 112, 124, 154
Mazza, Olympio, 126
M'Ba, Léon, 26
M'Baïki, 7, 8, 48, 184
M'Baka, 5, 7, 15, 17, 23, 37, 38, 48, 49, 52, 57, 99, 115, 126, 127, 143, 153, 155, 158, 184
M'Balanga, Catherine, 49, 64, 139
Mbodou, Gabriel Faustin, 187–9, 191–5, 198–200
M'Bongo, Auguste, 27, 48, 137, 190, 191, 201
M'Bongo, Celestine, 190
Médaille militaire, 10, 45
Mengistu Haile-Mariam, 214
Meng Yieng, 25
Méry, Guy, 126
Meulan, 78, 179
Mexico, 134
Meya, Martin, 60–2
Mgboundoulou, Mindo-gon, 7
Michelin, 71
Micombero, Michel, 214
Miroux, Brigitte, 56, 69
Miskine, 109
Mission de constatation des événements de Bangui, 116–19, 121–4, 146, 164, 195, 216
Mitterrand, François, 70, 125, 126, 141, 151, 160, 162–4, 169, 170, 178, 183, 188, 205
Mitterrand, Jean-Christophe, 163
Mobutu, Sese Seko, 61, 83, 85, 92, 103, 115, 116, 127, 130, 134, 135, 164, 211, 213

Mokinda, 41
Mokoa, Joseph, 38, 112,
    113, 154, 156, 158
Monrovia, 122
Montpellier, 52
Morocco, 4, 26, 84
Motte-Cordonnier-
    Afrique (MOCAF), 76
Motte-Cordonnier
    d'Armentières, 76
Mounoumbaye, Prosper,
    24, 29
Mouvement de libération
    du peuple centrafricain
    (MLPC), 122, 154
Mouvement d'évolution
    démocratique de
    l'Afrique centrale
    (MEDAC), 17, 20
Mouvement d'évolution
    sociale d'Afrique noire
    (MESAN), 13, 20, 21, 25,
    31, 34, 83, 84, 106, 113,
    118, 155
Mouyoundzi, 16
Moyen Congo, 5, 14, 15
Mzafio, Fidèle, 39

Nasser, Gamal Abdal, 68
N'Diaye, Youssoupha,
    116–19
Nditifei, Daniel, 111
N'Djaména, 71, 130, 131,
    168, 174
Ndodé, Albert, 111, 112,
    119
N'Douta, Martine, 86
Ndrès Cemetery, 63
neopatrimonialism, ix, 209
Netherlands, 74
Neuilly, 144
Neung-sur-Beuvron, 77
Neuvy-sur-Barangeon, 77
New York, 140
Ngakola, 33
Ngaragba Prison, 28, 37–
    41, 43, 46–9, 54, 58, 63,
    86, 87, 112–14, 118–19,
    154, 156, 189, 192, 195,
    201
Ngbongo, Edouard, 37, 38
Ngoma, Jean-Jacques, 128
N'guyen-Thi-Hué, 9, 51

Nguyen-Thin-Than,
    Jacqueline, 52, 57
Nicaragua, 105
Nice, 78, 90, 147, 148
Niger, 4, 72, 119
Nigeria, 31, 214
Nixon, Richard, 72
Nkrumah, Kwame, 208,
    209
Normandy, 90
North Korea, 102

Obrou, Fidèle, 60–4, 84,
    96, 99, 112, 154
Office national de com-
    mercialisation des pro-
    duits agricoles
    (ONCPA), 68, 80, 211
Omnisports Stadium, 62,
    79, 84
Opération Barracuda, x,
    130–9, 141, 144, 154,
    159, 176, 213
Opération Bokassa, 68, 69
Operation Elba, 166–9
Opération Manta, 164
Operation Revenge, 146–
    8, 164
Organization of African
    Unity, 87, 122, 214
Orly Airport, 133
Oubangui-Chari, 5, 6, 7,
    9, 11, 12, 14, 15, 21, 37
Oubangui River, 4, 5, 16,
    29, 49, 61, 78, 112

Pacifique apartment
    blocks, 76, 77, 109
Pahlavi, Shah Moham-
    mad Reza, 63, 67, 82,
    92, 97, 102, 105, 124
Palais de Justice, 186,
    188, 189, 194, 196, 199,
    201
Palais de la Renaissance,
    24, 27, 34, 41, 46, 54,
    55, 80, 93, 96, 160, 181,
    206
Palestine Liberation Orga-
    nization (PLO), 79, 184
Paris, 25, 42, 53, 58, 102,
    115, 119, 121, 133, 148,
    166, 168

Patassé, Ange, 34, 48, 79,
    83, 85, 100–1, 119, 122,
    126, 153–6, 158–9, 162,
    206–7, 212
Paul IV, Pope, 92, 193
Payrefitte, Alain, 134, 149
Péchenart, Marc, 103
Pehoua, François, 158, 159
Penne, Guy, 162, 163, 169,
    170
Pétain, Henri Philippe, 8,
    187
Picquet, Robert, 126
Pius VII, Pope, 92
Pompidou, Georges, 30,
    67, 69, 70
Potolot, Joseph, 79, 117,
    118, 128, 194
Prison de la Santé, 149,
    167
Promotion africaine, 10
Puy-de-Dôme, 172

Quai d'Orsay, 66
Quilici, Oriano, 92

Radio-Bangui, 27, 28, 66,
    85, 206
Radio France Inter-
    nationale, 163, 165
Rafai, 70
Ramgoolam, Sir Seewoosa-
    gur, 92
Randall, Jonathan, 87, 88,
    101
Rassemblement démo-
    cratique centrafricain
    (RDC), 184
Rassemblement pour la
    république, 127
Red Cross, 118, 124,
    151
Régiment parachutiste
    d'infanterie de marine
    (RPIMA), 130, 131
Rhodesia, 97
Roissy Airport, 133, 153,
    170
Romania, 55, 66, 68, 171
Rome, 179
Romorantin, 78, 144
Rosberg, Carl G., xi
Rwanda, 214

Sacher, Otto, 28, 37, 38, 118
Sadat, Anwar, 164
Safari Hotel, 56, 70, 88
Saigon, 10, 51, 58
Saint-Louis de Sénégal, 9, 10
Salah Bachir, Bachir, 128
Salinger, Pierre, 165
Samba, Simon, 26, 27, 29, 40
Sango, 13, 36, 57, 95, 157, 190
Sara, 153
Sarh, 30, 52
school uniforms, 107, 108, 110
Schumann, Maurice, 67
Second World War, 5, 7, 10, 11
Selassie, Emperor Haile, 67, 68, 82, 100, 208
Semineca, Fulgence, 116
Senegal, 3, 4, 12
Senghor, Jean-Gabriel, 190
Senghor, Léopold, 12, 115, 127
Service de documentation extérieure et de contre-espionnage (SDECE), 19, 20, 119, 120, 126, 130–2
Shaba, 103, 130, 135
Shoumatoff, Alex, 216
Sibut, 106
Société africaine forestière et agricole (SAFA), 76
Société d'exploitation forestière et industrielle (SEFI), 76
Société financière française et coloniale (SFFC), 71
Société financière pour la France et les pays d'outre-mer (SOFFO), 71
Sokpawo, Lucienne, 49
Soldats de la boue, 120
Solé, Christian, 179
Sologne, 77, 78, 104
Somalia, 214
sorcery, 49, 50, 192

south Africa, 66, 72, 87, 97, 198, 205
Soviet Union, 45, 66, 68
Soyinka, Wole, ix
Stanley, Henry Morton, 4
state bourgeoisie, 21, 65, 211
State Security Court, 149, 150
Stone, Lawrence, x, xi
Sudan 4, 25, 214
Swaziland, 82
Switzerland, 140
Sy, Biram Sassoum, 190
Szpiner, Francis, 177, 182–4, 190–2, 194–5, 198

Taiwan, 55, 66
Tamanrasset, 167
Tamraz, René, 74
Tapie, Bernard, 139–41, 144, 145
Tarbes, 131
Tchad, 4, 9, 14, 15, 30, 52, 71, 103, 119, 153, 168
Tere, 33
Tiangaye, Nicolas, 184, 205
Tito, Joseph Broz, 68
Togo, 4, 30, 162, 205
Tombalbaye, François, 30, 119
Touré, Samori, 208
Touré, Sékou, 15, 17, 208, 209, 212
Treichville, 151, 162
Treiki, Ali, 130, 131
Tribunal de grande instance de Paris, 173
Tripoli, 128–30, 132, 134, 153
Tshombe, Moïse, 119
Tunisia, 4, 26

Uru Roi, 66
Uganda, 105, 214
Union des femmes centrafricaines, 35
Union pour la Démocratie française (UDF), 142
United Nations, 15, 47, 146, 177

United States, 74, 86, 88, 101
Université Bokassa, 92, 106, 108, 111, 112
uranium, 72, 73, 128, 145, 212
Uranium de Centrafrique (URCA), 73, 81

Van Erpe, Astrid Elizabeth, 52
Van Erpe, Gilberte, 75
Viala, Jean-Marie, 178, 183
Vibro-Succès, 35
Vietnam, 14, 58, 59
Villa Kolongo, 55, 58, 76, 86, 136, 137, 156, 196, 216
Villa Nasser, 63, 207
Viol, André, 102

Wahl, Jacques, 142
Waldheim, Kurt, 47, 173
War of the Hoehandles, 6
Weber, Max, xi
Wengue, Gaston, 137
West Germany, 101
Wogou, Edmond, 191
World Health Organization, 122

Yakoma, 161, 163, 203
Yamoussoukro, 213
Yangongo, Barthélémy, 119
Yokowo, Marie, 7, 57
Yomboda, Paulin, 46
Young, Andrew, 88
Yugoslavia, 66

Zaïre, 30, 61, 103, 113, 114, 118, 134, 135, 159, 168, 211, 213
Zande, 42
Zémio, 70
Zokoézo, Lambert, 184, 203
Zolberg, Aristide, xi
Zongo, 112, 118
Zurich, 72